PREVENTING THE DISPUTE BEFORE IT BEGINS

Proven Mechanisms for Fostering Better Business Relationships

Kate Vitasek, James P. Groton, Ellen Waldman, and Allen Waxman

AMERICANBARASSOCIATION
Business Law Section

Cover design by Catherine Zaccarine.

Printed in the United States of America.

28 27 26 25 24 5 4 3 2 1

ISBN: 978-1-63905-555-5

Dedication

We would like to dedicate this book to all of the individuals and organizations that have the courage to embrace a dispute prevention mindset.

Praise for *Preventing the Dispute Before It Begins: Proven Mechanisms for Fostering Better Business Relationships*

Praise from Business Representatives

The dispute prevention mechanisms detailed in this book are not just nice theories. I've seen, literally, billions of dollars of construction being completed without any litigation, and with all disputes being resolved during the projects.

Howard Carsman
Construction Claims Manager (retired)
Intel Corp

Preventing the Dispute Before It Begins contains essential tools to keep business relationships on track and free from value killing disputes. The book details a practical continuum all businesses can follow. Dispute prevention commences in the pre-contract relationship development phase, before misalignment and unresolved problems spiral into destructive and counterproductive activity. Whether you are involved in contracting or managing business-to-business relationships, this book is an invaluable resource for companies to avoid and manage the waste associated with disputes.

Bill Dodero
Senior Vice President & General Counsel
Bayer USA

ISS is one of the world's largest facility services companies with several thousand customers. It has been a privilege to help lead ISS's efforts in piloting and adopting many of the dispute prevention mechanisms shared in *Preventing the Dispute Before It Begins*. I have to admit—I was a skeptic at first. For example, when I first heard about the Vested sourcing business model and using a neutral as a Deal Facilitator, I questioned the value. But the more we apply the mechanisms taught in the book—the more we create better alignment with our clients which ultimately reduces—and even eliminates disputes. Case in point: we now have six Vested agreements and these are some of the best relationships we have in the world. If you are a skeptic—consider picking one or two of the concepts from this book and try piloting them. I trust you will begin to see the benefits like ISS has.

Jens Holmberg
Legal Director and General Counsel
ISS Sweden

I lead a team of global lawyers at one of the world's largest energy companies in providing strategic legal advice to our businesses. In this role, I am a firm believer in the need for our teams that enter into business relationships with other companies to be thoughtful up front in how we can prevent disputes from occurring. I found this book to be the first clear resource I have come across in reviewing the variety of mechanisms that can be deployed to prevent disputes in business-to-business relationships. It is easy to read and understand. We will all benefit from using its guidance in focusing our energies on growing our business relationships rather than wasting those energies on unnecessary conflict.

Laura Robertson
Vice-President and Deputy General Counsel
Conoco-Phillips
Chairperson of the Board of Directors, CPR

Praise from the Academic Community

Preventing the Dispute Before It Begins is immensely valuable not only for contract professionals—but for all who reflect seriously on problem prevention and resolution. The authors perceive the complexity of problems and conflicts. If well understood and approached with systemic tools, conflict can enable creativity, value, and relational growth. But if neglected or approached adversarially, conflicts can escalate destructively. This book masterfully offers a variety of practical dispute management measures through case studies, brilliant visualizations, and its sophisticated understanding of contracting and business relationships.

Thomas D. Barton
Emeritus Professor
California Western School of Law, San Diego

This book brings to the fore a lesson all lawyers who seek to create value for their clients and draft contracts that will be implemented with maximum ease would do well to learn: namely, that a contract begins long before negotiation over its terms begins. Indeed, lawyers who fail to internalize this lesson are likely to be put out of business by AI or by more skilled lawyers who are able to draw on their unique skill set to contribute to the pre-contract phase of business relationships.

Lisa Bernstein
Wilson-Dickenson Professor of Law
University of Chicago Law School

An excellent read! The authors continue their groundbreaking work in conflict prevention, expanding the dispute management continuum and providing a tested, thoughtful approach for significantly reducing conflict in complex contracting relationships.

Rachel Goedken
Director, Werner Institute for Negotiation & Conflict Resolution
Creighton University School of Law

The authors do a great job, in plain, simple language, of detailing tactics to reduce and avoid disputes. A must-read for those seeking less friction in contract negotiations and management.

Helena Haapio
Contract Strategist, Lexpert Ltd
Professor of Practice, University of Lapland

The world of contracts is changing in exciting ways with new ideas about how parties can foster productive relationships that go well beyond sticking to the letter of an agreement. *Preventing the Dispute Before It Begins* provides a terrific "tour d'horizon" of the latest developments. As well as being invaluable to practitioners it will be of great interest to academics who want to understand how much contracts can achieve.

Oliver Hart
Nobel Laureate in Economic Sciences
Lewis P. and Linda L. Geyser University Professor, Department of Economics
Harvard University

Preventing the Dispute Before It Begins offers a compelling and practical guide to navigating complex conflicts with skill and confidence. Drawing on years of experience and cutting-edge strategies, the authors provide invaluable insights that go beyond resolving disputes to preventing them altogether. Whether you're a seasoned professional or new to the field, you'll find actionable advice and real-world examples that will transform your approach to negotiation. This is an essential read for in house lawyers and business professionals and for the lawyers who advise them.

Joan Stearns Johnsen
Director of the Institute for Dispute Resolution
University of Florida Levin College of Law

As a legal educator who directs an ADR program for law students, I will recommend this book to my students. My philosophy in teaching ADR to law students is to better equip them to represent clients in other than adjudicative settings. This book is a must-read for those law students who will be advising clients in transactional matters in which they ought to be thinking about advising about the prevention of disputes through problem-solving. The book urges thinking beyond simply how to draft dispute resolution clauses. Lawyers who read this book will be able to answer the question, "What should I be thinking about before drafting the dispute resolution clause in the contract?" The lawyer who has read this book will be equipped to speak to the client knowingly and practically about how to prevent inevitable problems from devolving into adversarial situations, often leading to the erosion of goodwill and trust; and thus maximizing the benefits of the contractual relationship.

Homer LaRue
Practicing Mediator
Professor of Law and Founder/Director of ADR Program
Howard Law School

This book provides a practical hands-on guide to anyone who wants to change the typical way business is conducted—and too often litigated. With sample contract language and case studies, the application of systemic thinking in order to prevent disputes becomes a feasible realistic change to adopt. Choosing a different pathway, saving money, and building relationships are all far more possible now that this book is here. Bravo!

Andrea Schneider
Director of the Kukin Program for Conflict Resolution
Cardozo Law School

Dispute prevention is worth its weight in gold—making this book a must-read for companies engaged in B2B partnerships. The authors observe that all too often, companies address conflicts only after they've escalated, leading to adversarial relationships and hefty legal bills. They make a compelling case for implementing preemptive strategies to stop disputes before they start. They present a clear, actionable framework designed to avoid the substantial financial, legal, and organizational costs associated with dispute escalation. The result: significant cost savings, stronger partnerships, a healthier bottom line, and freedom from the headaches and financial drains that accompany spiraling disputes. I strongly recommend this book for any company looking to transform conflict from a costly burden into a strategic advantage.

Daniel L. Shapiro
Founder and Director, Harvard International Negotiation Program
Author *Negotiating the Nonnegotiable*

Preventing the Dispute Before It Begins is a remarkable synthesis of decades of experience and reflection on the opportunities for businesses to avoid costly conflict through thoughtful management. The book breaks new ground in presenting a spectrum of tools and insights, including the latest applied research and case studies, in a breezy, quick-read format that makes it accessible to busy decision-makers. It should be required reading for clients and counsel, not to mention students of law and business.

Thomas Stipanowich
William H. Webster Chair in Dispute Resolution
Professor of Law
Pepperdine University

Praise from Industry Associations

Imagine, if you will, the power of getting your supplier relationships right before the contract is signed. The authors have produced an amazing book that every supply chain professional should read, as no supply chain is without supplier relationships. And those relationships are the key to success. This book takes the reader through impressive concepts that, when adopted, mean you are more likely to solve potentially critical challenges before they occur. This road map of concepts leads to a more collaborative approach that can transcend what others wish they could only accomplish. Getting it right before the contract is signed involves more than just seeking an agreement. It's about ensuring one knows how to navigate a successful working relationship to accomplish mutually beneficial goals.

Mark Baxa
President and CEO
Council of Supply Chain Management Professionals

Disputes are not about law: they are about business. Research by World Commerce & Contracting reveals that almost one in nine business to business contracts experiences one or more significant disagreements during its performance. Top performers are not only better at avoiding disagreements, they are also far better at resolving them. This reflects into financial performance, employee loyalty and market reputation. So this practical, thought-provoking book matters: it is tackling the fundamental topic of how we build and sustain positive and productive relationships with our trading partners.

Tim Cummins
President, World Commerce & Contracting
Professor, University of Leeds School of Law

For many decades, CPR has been working to focus the business community on savvier methods for managing conflict. This has meant embracing not simply the best and most advanced thinking on dispute resolution, but also promoting the wisdom of adopting a dispute prevention mindset. This new book offers sophisticated business organizations a one-stop resource for learning about and implementing state-of-the-art dispute prevention mechanisms. From the beginning of a business relationship and throughout its duration, the tools and processes detailed in this text will help keep deal partners on track and moving forward without the turmoil and waste of legal disputes. If you are searching for a way to bring your business into a less dispute-filled future, this book is for you.

Serena Lee
President and CEO
International Institute for Conflict Prevention & Resolution

This book not only introduces but also elaborates on the concept of a dispute prevention system within supplier relationships. By implementing strategies to prevent disputes from arising, organizations can avoid the significant costs and disruptions that disputes often bring, leading to stronger, more resilient supplier relationships and a more stable business environment.

Dawn Tiura
President and CEO
Sourcing Industry Group

Praise from Practicing Lawyers

It is often difficult to communicate properly what it means to prevent disputes (despite the long-standing history of the concept itself) and how to implement the specific techniques and resources leading to prevention. The authors got the job done in their brand-new book: they encapsulated brilliantly the concept of dispute prevention and its nuances, turning them into a user-friendly, business-oriented framework (with illustrative examples and figures as a bonus). Now, we can all understand, explain, and put the new ideas into practice!

Rafael Alves
Partner
Souto Correa Advogados

This is a transformative book for legal professionals seeking more proactive dispute prevention practices. If you're looking for a better way to manage business problems before they become disputes, this is the perfect book for you.

Lucy Bassli
Founder and Principal, InnoLaw Group, PLLC
Former Asst. General Counsel, Legal Operations and Contracting for Microsoft

Disputes and friction in commercial relationships are value eroding, time consuming and unnecessary. This seminal book describes the clear business case for avoiding commercial disputes in the first place and then moves on to provide a concrete guide for how to do it in practice, from choice of business partner to writing of contracts, to living in a "What's In It For We?" mindset, adopting dispute preventing mechanisms is a better way. I wholeheartedly recommend this book to anyone interested in how to do better business in a market environment too often plagued by friction.

David Frydlinger
Partner
Cirio Advokatbyrå AB

Praise from the Consulting and Professional Neutral Community

Preventing the Dispute Before It Begins is a highly practical and engaging book. For too long, lawyers and others have been overly focused on how to resolve disputes—often with tired boilerplate language—and not spending enough time thinking creatively about how to more cost effectively address emerging misalignments and differences before they escalate into lamps being thrown across the room, arbitration, and litigation. This book is a huge contribution.

James Bamford
Co-Founder of Water Street Partners and
Former Co-Lead of the Joint Venture & Alliance Practice at McKinsey & Co

The book *Preventing the Dispute Before It Begins* is a go-to-guide for understanding the various mechanisms that allow business and legal professionals to work proactively to prevent and resolve conflicts and disputes—mitigating not only financial losses and costs, but also psychological and social costs. The book is a breeze to read with simplified and fluid language supported with excellent case studies that demonstrate the authors' pragmatism which go well beyond theory.

Anna Luiza Etchalus
Founder
Etchalus Advocacia

Disputes can leave contracting parties exhausted and dissatisfied with outsourcing. This book champions dispute prevention through collaboration, communication, and relationship-building, offering a timely approach to navigating some of our current contract challenges.

Julian Fris
Founder and Principal Consultant
Neller Davies

Anyone involved in a complex relationship who has experienced a serious dispute knows that conflicts have no winners—only someone who loses less than the other guy. The expense of engaging in a conflict resolution process can be very high, and often not worth the results. But worse than that, the collateral damage to the business and the relationship, along with the reputational implications to both parties, can be devastating. After nearly three decades of experience working with companies in all phases of their relationships, this book is a welcome addition to the literature. It's well thought-out, thorough, and does a great job of shedding light on this area of relationship management. It drives home the idea that the best way to win a fight is not have the fight in the first place.

Ed Hansen
Founder
Transformation Enablement

Preventing the Dispute Before It Begins is a huge and groundbreaking contribution. It will help dispute prevention finally become standard business practice, which is long overdue. The authors have boiled down decades of hard-won practical experience, as well as a great deal of research, into a remarkably efficient treatment of the complex subject of prevention. And they have geared the result specifically to the central concerns in business contracting. Highly readable and highly recommended.

Chris Honeyman
Managing Partner
Convenor Conflict Management

Having established disputes centers of excellence for both government and large corporations, and now designing cutting-edge technology in this space for organizations of all shapes and sizes, I can confidently say this book is outstanding. If your role involves managing customer or supplier relationships, this book is a must-read. It is brimming with valuable and practical information, and the insights are all spot-on. This book will rapidly take you along the path to best practice.

Fayola-Maria Jack
CEO and Founder
Resolution

Mediators and arbitrators frequently concentrate on resolving disputes. This book offers outstanding examples of how to move the dispute resolution process further "upstream" and provides insights that enable parties to communicate effectively, align their perspectives, collaborate, and discover solutions. A standout feature of this book is its expert mapping of 18 Dispute Prevention and 15 Dispute Resolution mechanisms along the Dispute Management Continuum, presented with unparalleled detail. I highly recommend it!

DeAndra Roaché, FCIArb.
Arbitrator, Mediator, Adjunct Professor
Cynergis Dispute Resolution Services

Table of Contents

Acknowledgments

When we wrote *Preventing the Dispute Before It Begins,* we stood on the shoulders of many talented pioneers who imagined and then developed mechanisms for dispute prevention. First and foremost, we'd like to honor Louis M. Brown who, in his groundbreaking 1950 text *Manual of Preventive Law*, advocated that lawyers take a preventive approach when advising their clients, pointing out that "it usually costs less to avoid getting into trouble than to pay for getting out of trouble." Next, we salute those construction industry pioneers who invented the concept of having parties to a relationship proactively agree to use mechanisms that would prevent disputes—the concept that continues to guide the development of the dispute prevention movement.

As we pause to formally recognize those others who have helped make this book a reality, it is important to point out the spirit of collaboration that infused our journey in writing this book. To say this book is by the authors would only be partially true. Without the significant insights and contributions of others, this book simply would not exist.

We'd like to start by thanking those organizations whose thought leadership has produced the research and scholarship that comprise much of the substantive material underpinning the text of our book. We want to recognize the International Institute for Conflict Prevention and Resolution (CPR) for its consistent leadership in the area of dispute prevention since its founding in the 1970s. We also want to recognize the Construction Industry Institute (CII), for its practical research into dispute prevention mechanisms. Finally, we recognize the continuing scholarship of the University of Tennessee's Haslam College of Business for its groundbreaking research into highly collaborative business relationships and practical approaches for driving better alignment that advances dispute prevention.

We want to recognize all of the innovative organizations that provided us with case studies and examples of how dispute prevention works. This includes Island Health/South Island Hospitalist Inc., Walmart, Newfoundland Labrador Health Services, EY, ISS, bp, BuyCo, Loudoun County Sanitation Authority, Microsoft, and the Olympics. Unfortunately, some company names must remain unnamed due to corporate publicity rules, but we could not have brought dispute prevention concepts to life without you or achieved progress without you. You know who you are, and you have our deepest gratitude.

We would also like to thank the following thought leaders who reviewed our work along the way and provided valuable feedback, support, and endorsements to convince us that we were on the right track:

Rafael Alves
Lucy Bassli
Thomas D. Barton
Lisa Bernstein
Howard Carsman
Tim Cummins
Bill Dodero
Anna Luiza Etchalus
Julian Fris
David Frydlinger
Rachel J. Goedken
Helena Haapio
Oliver Hart
Ed Hansen
Chris Honeyman
Fay Jack
Joan Stearns Johnsen
Homer LaRue
Serena Lee
Val Paverd
DeAndra Roaché
Laura Robertson
Andrea Schneider
Tom Stipanowich
Dawn Tiura

We proudly want to call out a few individuals who worked behind the scenes to make this book come to life. At the top of the list is the American Bar Association (ABA). This book grew out of a podcast the ABA sponsored with CPR in 2023 on dispute prevention, "Avoiding the Dispute Before It Happens." The ABA's self-proclaimed "content guy," Richard Paszkiet, immediately seized upon the transformative potential of dispute prevention and encouraged us to publish this book. Rick has continued to encourage us to get to the finish line. With the ABA, we truly have a powerful partnership in bringing visibility to dispute prevention! We also want to highlight the work of the ABA's Caitlin McCauley and Katrina Krause for their insights in helping us successfully produce and launch this book.

We'd like to recognize Dan Good—who served as the crucial glue in editing the book. Dan, you are masterful at integrating the voices of four authors. And it is not lost on us the time and attention you paid to ensuring every endnote and citation were perfectly compliant with the ABA's standards. We'd also like to thank Elizabeth Kanna and Tricia Principe who supported us in conceptualizing and producing the graphics/images for the book.

We would like to thank our colleagues at CPR, the Haslam College of Business, and DLA Piper for their support and patience during this endeavor.

And last, but certainly not least, we would like to thank our families for all their encouragement in pursuing our passion:

Greg and Austin Picinich
Ann Williams Groton
Brina Waxman
Lois Waldman and Harold Abramson

Introduction

Intellectuals solve problems; geniuses prevent them.

—Albert Einstein

Bad things happen.

Throughout history, humans have sought ways to stop bad things from happening—the classic definition of the word "prevention." There are hundreds, if not thousands, of preventive efforts to stop bad things from happening: fire prevention, disease prevention, accident prevention, crime prevention, and violence prevention, just to name a few.

One overlooked and untapped prevention measure involves contract dispute prevention.

Contract disputes cost untold amounts of money in attorneys' fees and transaction costs for both parties, interfere with business productivity, result in economic waste, and have the power to destroy once-promising business relationships. Legal and contracting professionals have wrestled with the problem of how to resolve disputes more efficiently for ages. Sadly, even successful resolutions are typically adversarial in nature and often fall short of regaining the lost value.

But do they have to? Is there a better way?

IS THERE A BETTER WAY?

The effort to find a better way propels the business and science worlds forward. It drove people like Albert Einstein and Thomas Edison to challenge the status quo to create better products and solutions.

Finding a better way prompted the music industry to reinvent how users listen to music, shifting from albums to eight-track tapes to cassettes to CDs to MP3 files to digital streaming services that put millions of songs at the listener's fingertips anywhere and anytime. But finding a better way is not just a question that inventors, technologists, and engineers ask. It also drives entrepreneurs to solve complex problems to meet customer needs. And it should drive the legal and business community to adopt ways to prevent contractual disputes rather than simply trying to find better ways to resolve them.

Adopting a better way does not mean the end of all disagreements or even conflicts. Disagreements and conflicts are essential to human nature and, thus, business relationships. As we note in the coming pages, those disagreements and conflicts often lead to greater creativity and productivity. Instead, we are calling for ways to prevent those disagreements or conflicts from turning into value-depleting disputes.

Our goal for this book is to distill our collective knowledge—from our perspectives in the academic, corporate, think tank, and practitioner's worlds—to provide a comprehensive guide on dispute prevention mechanisms to help legal and business professionals better control and even eliminate contract disputes.

Why are we so passionate about this topic? We have seen firsthand the potential of dispute prevention and have personally witnessed the power of implementing proven dispute prevention mechanisms. And we are excited to share that power with you.

OUR VISION FOR THIS BOOK

Thanks to the great work around alternative dispute resolution (ADR) over the past fifty years, most people quickly grasp the concept of dispute resolution. Many organizations already use ADR techniques such as mediation and arbitration and have seen the value of resolving disputes to avoid going to court. Unfortunately, many don't realize there are proven dispute prevention mechanisms that have the power to stop disputes before they ever start. This is where this book comes in.

Our vision for this book is simple—to help legal and business professionals understand and adopt more proactive dispute prevention practices.

Purpose of the Book

We have purposefully chosen to keep this book very focused.

First, we focus on dispute *prevention* rather than dispute resolution. The primary reason is dispute prevention can radically change how organizations and individuals approach business relationships and contracts—*for the better*. We have seen how the insights shared in this book can save millions of dollars, euros, and yen in economic value. We want to make it clear **this book is *not* about how to *resolve* disputes**. The concept of dispute resolution is already well-established and practiced. There are hundreds of articles and many books advocating for and educating organizations and individuals on the diversity of choices that exist for resolving disputes and the merits of each.

Second, we focus on business-to-business (B2B) contractual disputes. While many of the dispute prevention mechanisms we share can be applied outside B2B commercial relationships, we believe starting with preventing commercial disputes will have the most significant impact in the shortest time frame.[1] The

1. The authors recognize that scholars in the field of dispute prevention have explored the value of dispute prevention concepts and mechanisms outside the context of B2B relationships. *See* James Groton et al., *Pro Dispute and Pre-Escalation Techniques to Improve New Business Relationships, in* Negotiation Essentials for Lawyers 341–46 (Andrea Kupfer

potential benefit is massive. Take, for example, one sector where B2B contracts are essential: outsourcing of business processes. The global business process outsourcing market was valued at US $280 billion in 2023 and is projected to grow at a Compound Annual Growth Rate (CAGR) of 9.4 percent from 2023 to 2030.[2] Couple this with the fact that contract disputes are the second most common reason for disputes, and it is easy to see there is a huge opportunity to create value by preventing disputes.[3]

Last, this book is not an academic book; rather, it is a practitioner's guide to help individuals and organizations better understand and use dispute prevention mechanisms. While we start with the theoretical underpinnings of *why* the shift to dispute prevention is essential for businesses in today's economy, the bulk of this book is about *what* and *how*.

As you read this book, you will notice many of the examples come from the construction industry and procurement practices. Why? These areas—in our research and opinion—provide some of the best examples of how organizations are putting dispute prevention to use. The book's subtitle reads *Proven Mechanisms for Fostering Better Business Relationships* because we aim to share the best existing examples of dispute prevention's effectiveness. We hope as you read them, you are inspired, and consider how these examples can apply and relate to your industry, versus having a "not invented here" mindset.

Structure of the Book

This book is divided into three parts.

Part I, consisting of two chapters, introduces the why and what of dispute prevention. Chapter 1 starts by challenging organizations to view disputes through a different lens. We profile a case study from an organization that is shifting from reactive dispute resolution to applying proactive dispute prevention. We share research supporting the concept of dispute prevention and highlight the growth of the dispute prevention movement. In chapter 2, we propose a Dispute Management Continuum classified into five categories ranging from the most preventive to the most adversarial. We also provide high-level descriptions of thirty-three dispute mechanisms that fall along the continuum.

Schneider & Christopher Honeyman eds., 2019). *See also* James Groton et al., *Thinking Ahead, in* The Negotiator's Desk Reference 265–80 (Chris Honeyman & Andrea Kupfer Schneider eds., 2d ed. 2017).

2. *U.S. Business Process Outsourcing Market Size, Share & Trends Analysis Report By Service Type (Customer Services, Finance & Accounting), By End-Use (IT & Telecommunication, BFSI), And Segment Forecasts, 2023–2030*, Grand View Research, https://www.grandviewresearch.com/industry-analysis/us-business-process-outsourcing-market-report.

3. *The State of Corporate Litigation Today Survey Report*, Ass'n Corp. Couns., https://www.acc.com/state-corporate-litigation-today-survey-report.

In part II, which consists of three chapters, we shift to help you better understand the detailed workings of prevention-focused mechanisms. Chapter 3 details mechanisms applicable to entering the relationship, chapter 4 involves formalizing the relationship, and chapter 5 covers managing the relationship. Part II also provides a deeper dive into each mechanism we have encountered in our research or personal practices. We share an overview of each mechanism, *why* it helps prevent disputes, and *how* it works in practice. We then share case studies relating to how organizations are putting the mechanisms into practice.

Part III has two chapters and is for those who are serious about implementing proactive dispute prevention. Chapter 6 shares our suggestions for designing a Dispute Management System while chapter 7 presents a compelling business case for why you should make the shift upstream to dispute prevention. Chapter 7 also addresses and answers reservations organizations have expressed when trying to adopt dispute prevention.

We end the book with a call to action challenging lawyers and business professionals to join the dispute prevention movement.

As you read this book, consider it a guidebook rather than a novel. Feel free to jump ahead to the parts of the book that interest you, especially if you are already familiar with a concept or mechanism we share. In addition, many of the concepts we introduce have generated considerable scholarly discussion and research that is impossible to include in a book of this nature. If you find yourself wanting to learn more, we encourage you to consult the information provided in the footnotes as a launching pad for further learning.

A NOTE ON TERMINOLOGY

As you read this book, it is important to familiarize yourself with a few key concepts and terms.

As contracting parties interact during the natural course of their relationship, it is not uncommon for problems to arise. If not promptly addressed, these problems can escalate into differences of opinion, arguments, and full-fledged disputes. We, therefore, define a ***problem*** as a perplexing situation or question that requires attention and solution.

In some cases, a problem can turn into a conflict. We define a ***conflict*** as an active disagreement between individuals or organizations with opposing opinions, principles, or objectives. Conflict can be productive or destructive. If skillfully managed, conflict can give voice to new perspectives, unleashing greater creativity and productivity.[4] In a 2018 article in *Harvard Business Review*, Amy

4. Ginka Toegel & Jean-Louis Barsoux, *How to Preempt Team Conflict*, HARV. BUS. REV., June 2016, at 78.

Gallo cites five advantages of conflict in the workplace: better work outcomes, opportunities to learn and grow, improved relationships, higher satisfaction, and a more inclusive environment.[5]

However, if left to fester, conflict can destroy trust and goodwill and harden into a dispute. We define a ***dispute*** as a condition of escalated disagreement in which the parties have adopted adversarial positions that trigger the need for a dispute resolution process such as mediation, arbitration, or even litigation.

The primary focus of this book is on ***dispute prevention***. Dispute prevention is the purposeful use of a suite of mechanisms (processes, tools, and practices) that can reduce, if not altogether avoid, disputes entirely.

Some of the most popular dispute prevention mechanisms are used while the parties are formalizing their business relationships and while managing the relationship. However, dispute prevention techniques can also be deployed even before a business relationship begins by helping contracting parties lay the foundation for a strong relationship.

On the other end of the spectrum is ***dispute resolution***, which requires a process to resolve questions of fault, liability, damages, or other legal exposure. Dispute resolution mechanisms include litigation and well-documented ADR processes such as mediation and arbitration.

The ***Dispute Management Continuum*** (which we present in chapter 2) identifies thirty-three mechanisms ranging from preventive to adversarial in nature.

The concept of a ***Dispute Management System*** (described in detail in chapter 6) is a purposefully designed program that organizations put into place incorporating various dispute prevention and resolution mechanisms. We use the term "system" because when combined, the mechanisms interact and work together logically to reduce friction and transaction costs between contracting parties by optimizing working relations, preventing disputes where possible, and resolving disputes effectively and efficiently when they arise.

IS THIS BOOK FOR YOU?

You might be asking yourself if this book is for you.

If you play a role in contracting or managing B2B relationships and are looking for a better way to manage business problems before they become claims and disputes, then this book is for you. This book also targets individuals who procure, contract, and manage business relationships, including commercial and supply chain professionals who manage supplier relationships. It includes sales and business development specialists who lead their companies through negotiating

5. Amy Gallo, *Why We Should Be Disagreeing More at Work*, HARV. BUS. REV., Jan. 3, 2018, https://hbr.org/2018/01/why-we-should-be-disagreeing-more-at-work.

contracts, as well as account executives and alliance managers who run the strategic facets of business relationships. And it, of course, includes the lawyers and contracting professionals who support the business community—regardless of the type of business relationship and the type of contract.

Maybe the better question is whether you are ready for this book. Are you ready to reconsider how you contract and manage business relationships? Are you willing to take a more proactive stance—and actions—to prevent disputes before they occur? If not, put the book back and save your money.

GETTING READY FOR A SHIFT IN THINKING

Making the shift in attention from dispute resolution to dispute prevention demands a new approach. Conventional ADR mechanisms focus on resolving disputes rather than preventing and mitigating them. Instead of promoting a collaborative business philosophy, existing ADR techniques still may create a costly and protracted "us-versus-them" adversarial mindset. While there is no debate that conventional ADR processes have had a huge positive impact on reducing the cost and time of resolving disputes over traditional litigation, far more can and should be done.

To understand the power of the dispute prevention paradigm shift, you must start with an open mind. Keep it open, and you will surely see new opportunities around you! We wish you well as you take the road less traveled and learn how to harness the power of dispute prevention.

Part I

The Why and What of Dispute Prevention

Chapter 1

Viewing Disputes through a Different Lens

Olivia Operations (not her real name) sat through plenty of adversarial supplier disputes over her 25-year career at SemiCo. As a Vice President managing SemiCo's construction projects, Olivia was well aware of how construction contracts were fraught with change orders and claims. The process followed a classic cycle, with problems turning into formal claims. Each round of discussion left claims unresolved and led to increasing escalations, with lawyers, mediators, and outside counsel getting more and more involved. While virtually all claims were resolved—often in the 11th hour before arbitration or litigation—the vicious cycle was costly and exhausting.

After a particularly tough round of dispute resolutions, Olivia was at her wit's end. SemiCo's internal data supported the need for change. Even the best subcontractors and suppliers seemed to have claims stemming from unexpected changes in the project. For example, one construction project valued at $220 million had $30 million in claims. Another $1.3 billion project had $50 million in claims.

One thing consistent across all of the claims: as the life of a claim stretched out, the costs to manage and resolve it grew exponentially. For example, one group of unresolved claims went to arbitration that was expected to last six weeks. While SemiCo and the contractor settled in week three, the total costs of outside counsel for the protracted process up through and including arbitration exceeded $15 million. And, as Olivia further noted, this did not include the internal cost of employee time spent dedicated to supporting the arbitration.

People within SemiCo, as well as its contractors and subcontractors and suppliers, were tired of the lost time, effort, and money, as well as the frustration and stress of protracted adversarial negotiations. Olivia described the situation: "Claims would simply escalate, escalate, escalate until it was unbearable. And it happened again and again. We all dreaded it, but that was simply how the process worked. We needed to rethink the process if we wanted to change things."

It became clear to Olivia that the missing element was a spirit of collaboration and a process designed to work through problems and misalignment in real time as they arose.

Olivia reflected, "In construction projects, there is always new information that comes up causing minor (or major) scope changes. But on the business side, there are pressures to keep projects on schedule. There is capital allocated, and in many cases, if a project is not completed on time, it can negatively impact revenue. So, the typical mantra is *'Let's not make a big deal out of it, we can't lose progress, we'll deal with it when the project is done.'*"

This kick-the-can-down-the-road mindset, while being a welcome relief in the short term, results in even bigger misalignments downstream. When the time came to settle the claim, it was natural for the contractor to want to recoup its costs and lost profit. However, for many companies, the contractor's moves appeared opportunistic. This created emotionally charged environments, with each party feeling the other party was not being fair—making it even harder to resolve differences.

SemiCo was not the only one frustrated. Suppliers (primarily contractors and subcontractors) also dreaded going through traditional dispute resolution. Simon Supplier described the dispute resolution process as a "hostile affair." He added, "We were constantly escalating problems upstairs. A claim would escalate within SemiCo to their procurement manager and then to their worldwide procurement manager. We'd get stuck, and most of the time, the businesspeople involved had no understanding of what the law might actually say. So, we'd escalate to the lawyers. But, the lawyers would only get our company's perspective, so they were operating with a partial view of the facts and a selective understanding of the business situation. There was never full transparency to see problems from all angles. While my company never had to get external counsel involved, the dispute resolution process was painful and protracted."

Simon was quick to point out that SemiCo was not really any different from other companies when it came to handling construction contract claims: "It's a systemic problem—not a SemiCo problem."

Olivia Operations's frustration prompted her to act. She started by pondering a simple question: *Was there a better way?* She asked Billy Buyer (the Director of Procurement) for SemiCo's permission to create a pilot program. Together, Olivia and Billy began researching alternative approaches to resolving disputes. SemiCo was already using alternative dispute resolution (ADR) techniques such as mediation and arbitration. While significantly better than litigation, these lawyer-led processes were falling short. They turned to Danny Dispute Manager, a construction lawyer, for advice. Danny was familiar with ADR practices and had worked as a mediator and arbitrator in the construction industry for several years.

Danny's outside perspective validated Olivia's hunch: the traditional ADR process of using a neutral party was valuable—but the neutral party was brought in too late. SemiCo needed a process that would shift the focus of claims management from dispute resolution to dispute prevention.

Billy Buyer had the idea to hire Danny Dispute Manager and challenge him to transform SemiCo's dispute resolution practice to focus on dispute prevention. Danny ultimately went on not only to design the new program but also to become the internal champion and owner of the program.

Danny Dispute Manager reflected on the importance of that early conversation: "Truly—the *if-you've-got-a-better-idea* moment—became an extraordinarily important milestone. That's what gave the green light to challenge the *status quo* and gave birth to what is now SemiCo's Dispute Prevention system."

Danny joined SemiCo and worked on the procurement team, reporting directly to Billy Buyer. Danny remembered, "When I started the job, SemiCo had two major projects already on track for arbitration. In both projects, outside counsel had already been involved for almost two years. In these projects, I originally acted more like in-house counsel than anything else, functioning as the primary contact with (and member of) the legal team. While the immediate focus was these two projects, I knew the bigger task was to design a more proactive and preventive dispute management system to not only resolve disputes quickly at the project level but also help prevent disputes altogether."

As Danny began to think about the attributes of a good dispute management system, he pulled together various concepts he had seen work in practice as a mediator and arbitrator to find a better way to prevent disputes. Danny wanted to create a system that would:

- Create a culture for proactive and constructive dialogues with more frequent discussions aiming to provide continuous alignment and addressing problems as they arise, not after they escalate.
- Leverage professionally facilitated problem-solving expertise in a timely/cost-effective manner.
- Help SemiCo and contractors see each other's perspectives—encouraging a sense of reasonableness and a willingness to resolve issues quickly rather than letting them fester into a formal claim.

The shift to a preventive approach led to significantly fewer claims and formal disputes, saving millions of dollars. Six years after Olivia Operations's "ah-ha" moment and SemiCo's adoption of preventive approaches, SemiCo's dispute prevention system has expanded to include five prime contractors with a value of almost $20 billion in construction projects. Since the program started, only one claim has escalated to a predetermined formal arbitration process.

For comparison, before the shift, two of SemiCo's larger construction contracts suffered from a stifling stack of claims. As noted above, the resolution of these claims was expensive, both in terms of the cost of counsel and indirect transaction costs.

Simon Supplier is ecstatic with the system: "The SemiCo dispute prevention program is a complete paradigm shift to managing claims. The one issue that did go to resolution was managed quickly and fairly. If anything, the prevention focus proves how much faster problems can be de-escalated even if they happen to flare once a decade."

Danny Dispute Manager reflects on the dispute prevention system's success: "The program has taught SemiCo and our suppliers the power of a preventive approach. The typical dispute resolution process promotes a 'We want to be right. We want to win.' mindset. This creates a zero-sum game when it doesn't have to be that way."

Olivia Operations is pleased with the shift that happened on her watch and summed up why organizations around the world should care: "The shift to a preventive focus is brilliant. Risks are identified upfront, and people openly talk about them. Transparency and collaboration completely change the dynamics of what is inherently a risky business. The shift is truly transformational."

WHY THE NEED FOR DISPUTE PREVENTION?

An ounce of prevention is worth a pound of cure. A stitch in time saves nine.
Fortune favors the prepared mind. Blessed are the peacemakers.

These common-sense maxims have been around for hundreds of years. However, these age-old adages are rarely considered when managing contractual conflicts.

Contracts can be similar to buying a new pair of shoes; they are often great at first, but as they get worn in, they either become as comfortable to walk in as a slipper or begin to cause friction that can turn into a blister.

Left unchecked, what starts as friction or misaligned interests can turn into a full-blown dispute—or worse, end up in court. While the vast majority of conflicts avoid litigation, the time and cost associated with traditional lawyer-led negotiation, mediation, and arbitration can be protracted and expensive. Even if the issue does not go to a formal dispute, the friction can result in lost opportunity, value leakage, and transaction costs, which is what economist and Nobel Laureate Oliver Williamson calls Transaction Cost Economics.

The simple fact is that friction should be expected in any complex contract. Why? In the words of Oliver Williamson: "All complex contracts will be incomplete. There will be errors, omissions, and the like."[1] The very nature of complex contracts means it is impossible to predict every "what if" scenario given today's global and dynamic business environment.

Another Nobel Laureate in economics—Oliver Hart—echoes Williamson's sentiments regarding the friction resulting from inevitably incomplete contracts. Hart's research with longtime collaborator John Moore suggests you really should not be surprised by what appears to be opportunistic behavior from "the other guy." Why? What may seem like opportunistic behavior is often a predictable reaction to earlier unmet expectations, which Hart calls *shading*.[2]

1. Oliver E. Williamson, *Outsourcing: Transaction Cost Economics and Supply Chain Management*, 44 J.S.C.M. 5–16 (2008) (friction in complex contracts).

2. Oliver Hart & John Moore, *Contracts as Reference Points*, 123 Q.J.E. 1, 3–4 (2008) (definition of "shading").

Shading is retaliatory behavior in which a party stops cooperating, ceases to be proactive, or makes aggressive countermoves because of disappointment. Shading happens when a party doesn't get the expected outcome from the deal and feels the other party is to blame for failing to act reasonably to preserve value or mitigate losses.

For example, consider the all too contentious "scope-creep" debate. A supplier projects its business case based on the information shared during a competitive bid process. Let's assume the supplier estimates it will make a 15 percent profit margin. If demand is lower than expected or unexpected extra work is required (e.g., scope creep), the supplier will have a lower-than-expected profit. This disappointment will cause the supplier to ask for approval for scope changes. And if the buying organization makes it difficult to get a contract change through, the supplier may be tempted to reduce service levels or replace the expensive A-team with the less costly C-team and quality will likely suffer which may result in a contractual dispute.

In short, when a problem or misunderstanding occurs, each party's action leads to the other party's reaction, creating a negative tit-for-tat cycle. One disappointment leads to another, and the vicious cycle begins. This problem is so systemic in large and complex contracts that it can lead to a death spiral because once the cycle starts, it often ends with an incumbent supplier losing the work to a competitor during the next bid cycle. Sadly, the root cause is often not opportunism but disappointment based on the parties' misaligned expectations.[3]

Unfortunately, traditional contracts rarely contain proactive alignment mechanisms to avoid disappointments. In far too many situations, the need to begin a process for dealing with disputes isn't recognized until after those disappointments have led to real pain and frustration. The reality is that many issues do not resolve themselves easily and they drag on. However, most problems can be prevented while they are still small. This book details how eighteen dispute prevention mechanisms can help organizations better align interests and collaboratively address differences in "real-time" when misalignment is still manageable.

Organizations adopting proactive dispute prevention practices acknowledge the reality that no relationship is perfect, and no contract can cover every eventuality. Rather, businesses operate in dynamic environments that require frequent adjustments. Dispute prevention embraces this reality and provides mechanisms to help the parties maintain alignment as their relationship evolves. This is especially important when working in more strategic and longer-term business relationships such as strategic outsourcing agreements, large construction projects, franchise agreements, critical supply contracts, and joint ventures.

---

3. Kate Vitasek et al., *Unpacking the Standing Neutral: A Cost Effective and Common-Sense Approach for Preventing Conflict*, Univ. Tenn., 1–71 (2019) (negative tit-for-tat cycles).

WORKING "UPSTREAM": FROM RESOLUTION TO PREVENTION

The concept of ADR is well grounded in practice. In fact, 2025 marks the 100th anniversary of the Federal Arbitration Act. ADR got a boost in 1976 after the first Pound Conference (inspired by Harvard law professor Roscoe Pound) which promoted the use of mediation and arbitration as adjuncts to the traditional legal system.[4] The Pound Conference marked the beginning of a much broader movement encouraging the business world to actively embrace out-of-court processes for managing conflict. The movement attempted to shift the dispute resolution process farther "upstream," closer to the origins and sources of disputes.

In 1977, on the heels of the Pound Conference, the Center for Public Resources (now more aptly named the International Institute for Conflict Prevention and Resolution or CPR) was established as a think tank for improving ADR processes. In 1984, then-Supreme Court Chief Justice Warren Burger advocated for lawyers to increase their use of ADR during an address to the American Bar Association. He acknowledged that while trials may be the only way to resolve some disputes, the legal system is too adversarial, painful, destructive, and inefficient to effectively manage all disputes.[5]

Today there are numerous ways to resolve disputes outside of litigation. While the deployment of ADR since the Pound Conference has been substantial, it is important to note that the "R" in ADR stands for Alternative Dispute ***Resolution***. As such, conventional ADR methods focus on resolving disputes versus preventing or actively managing problems as they arise. We argue that today's business leaders need to launch a formal movement to help organizations expand their focus beyond dispute resolution to dispute prevention. And with this shift, organizations need to create a dispute management system leveraging a spectrum of mechanisms to help them not only resolve disputes but try to prevent them in the first place.

Recall from the introduction, where we define dispute prevention and a dispute management system as follows:

4. *About the 2016–2017 Global Pound Conference*, INT'L MEDIATION INST. (2016), https://imimediation.org/research/gpc/gpc-about/; Brian Farkas & Lara Traum, *The History and Legacy of the Pound Conferences*, 18 C.J.C.R. 677, 692–96 (2017) (the use of mediation and arbitration).

5. Mary Dunnewold, *What Every Law Student Should Know*, STUDENT LAW., October 2009, at 1.

Dispute Prevention	The purposeful use of a suite of mechanisms (processes, tools, and practices) that can reduce, if not eliminate, disputes altogether. Some of the most popular dispute prevention mechanisms are used while the parties are formalizing the business relationships and while managing those relationships. However, dispute prevention techniques can also be deployed even before a business relationship begins by helping contracting parties lay the foundation for a strong relationship.
Dispute Management System	A purposefully designed program that organizations put into place incorporating various dispute prevention and resolution mechanisms. We use the term "system" because when combined, the mechanisms interact and work together in a logical manner to reduce friction and transaction costs between contracting parties by optimizing working relations, preventing disputes where possible, and resolving disputes effectively and efficiently when they arise.

The Advent of Proactive Prevention Practices

The good news is that forward-thinking lawyers, business leaders, and academics have been pushing to shift to more preventive approaches. In 1950, long before ADR was taking hold, business attorney Louis M. Brown highlighted the need for lawyers to take a preventive approach when counseling their clients, famously writing, "It usually costs less to avoid getting into trouble than to pay for getting out of trouble." He called this "preventive law."[6]

Twenty-five years later, the construction industry, historically fraught with disputes, led the way in pioneering a variety of dispute prevention mechanisms. In 1975, a group of innovative construction practitioners conceived the idea of convening a "dispute review board" of geological engineers to immediately solve, in "real-time," difficult rock and soil problems on a major tunneling construction project to keep these problems from becoming disruptive disputes.[7] This was the first in a series of dispute prevention mechanism that evolved, such as realistic risk allocation, incentives to encourage cooperation, and partnering.[8]

---

6. Louis M. Brown, Manual of Preventive Law (1950).

7. *History of the Dispute Board process and the DRBF*, DRBF, https://www.drb.org/history.

8. *Id;* David B. Ashley & Wayne B. Workman, *Incentives in Construction Contracts* (CII Source Document SD-8, 1986); *Construction Industry Institute Contracts Task Force* (CII Source Document RS5-3, 1988).

The 1990s initiated more formal studies into preventive techniques. The Construction Industry Institute (CII) and CPR led the pack with significant research between 1990 and 1994.

CPR, one of the first organizations to support ADR, undertook a study in 1990 "to take a fresh look at both dispute prevention and dispute resolution" as it had developed in the construction industry. The work led in 1991 to the seminal publication *Preventing and Resolving Construction Disputes*, which was the first compilation of the newly developed dispute prevention techniques used in the construction industry.[9] The report urged further education, the signing of a pledge to use preventive practices, and experimentation and research into newly developed prevention techniques.

Next, CII kicked off research looking into ways to improve dispute management. It emphasized the importance of always having one or more agreed-upon preventive processes available to help parties deal with possible conflict as it arose. It also experimented with expanding the use of Dispute Review Boards beyond projects involving single-issue technical disciplines into multi-disciplinary projects such as high-rise office buildings.[10]

While the construction industry was having early successes with preventing practices, other industries were still stuck in "resolution" which was growing more complicated and costlier. A 1994 *Harvard Business Review* article critiqued ADR in the pointedly titled article "Alternative Dispute Resolution: Why It Doesn't Work and Why It Does," stating: "The bad news is that ADR as currently practiced too often mutates into a private judicial system that looks and costs like the litigation it's supposed to prevent."[11] This trend has only worsened over the years.[12]

Following the CPR 1991 book, lawyers and practitioners experimented with using the construction dispute prevention mechanisms in other kinds of business relationships. In 2010, CPR went on to develop a "Prevention Initiative" supported by "Prevention Practice Materials" that demonstrated how prevention mechanisms could help prevent disputes.

The value of preventive practices was recognized during a series of conferences organized by the International Mediation Institute in 2016 and 2017. The conference series—titled the Global Pound Conference in honor of the original 1976 conference that birthed the modern ADR movement—was held in twenty-eight cities around the world and brought together thousands of users, providers,

9. *Preventing and Resolving Construction Disputes*, 9 ALT. TO THE HIGH COST OF LITIG. 182–87 (1991) (dispute prevention techniques in the construction industry).

10. M. C. Vorster, *Alternative Dispute Resolution in Construction with Emphasis on Dispute Review Boards* (CII Source Document SD-95, 1993).

11. Todd B. Carver & Albert A. Vondra, *Alternative Dispute Resolution: Why It Doesn't Work and Why It Does*, 72 HARV. BUS. REV. 120 (1994).

12. Thomas J. Stipanowich, *Arbitration: The "New Litigation,"* U. ILL. L. REV. 1 (2010) (discussing worsening trends in resolution).

and advisors to discuss the future direction of ADR.[13] During each event, delegates voted on which dispute "resolution" processes should be prioritized to improve dispute resolution. In an ironic but prescient twist, the worldwide delegates—by a substantial margin—voted that "pre-dispute or pre-escalation processes to prevent disputes" constituted the preferred processes over all other dispute "resolution" processes to improve future dispute management.

The Causes of Disputes

There are currently dozens of proven dispute prevention mechanisms that expand well beyond the construction industry. As the art, science, and practice of dispute prevention have evolved, one theme emerges: organizations are seeking ways to design dispute prevention mechanisms to respond to underlying causes of contractual disputes.

So just what are the causes of contractual disputes? As noted in the Introduction, contractual disputes arise from conflicts that go unidentified and/or unaddressed; so, to understand the cause of contractual disputes, it is worth first understanding the underlying conflicts that may give rise to those disputes. Legal scholars provide useful frameworks that organize the various causes of contractual conflict.[14] One such framework categorized conflict into five types.

- *Interest Conflicts*: those arising from perceived or actual competition over the parties' substantive, legal, or procedural interests.
- *Relationship Conflicts*: those arising from difficulties in communication or behavior.
- *Structural Conflicts*: those arising from imbalances in control, ownership, or resources.
- *Data/Information Conflicts*: those arising from a perceived or actual lack of data or information.
- *Value Conflicts*: those arising from different ideas, values, or principles guiding parties' behaviors.

The scholars acknowledged there is often an overlap between the categories and the patterns of conflict. Also, root causes will vary in different contexts and industries. For example, contracting parties in highly regulated industries may have conflicts arising over the interpretation of contractual provisions related to

---

13. *About the 2016–2017 Global Pound Conference supra* note 4.

14. Christopher W. Moore, The Mediation Process: Practical Strategies for Resolving Conflict (2014); Petra Hietanen-Kunwald & Helena Haapio, *Effective Dispute Prevention and Resolution through Proactive Contract Design*, 5 J.S.C.A.N. 3, 6–7 (2021); Carrie Menkel-Meadow, Dispute Processing and Conflict Resolution: Theory, Practice and Policy (2003).

compliance requirements while less regulated industries may have conflicts arising from a lack of clarity over expectations.[15]

Recall from our earlier discussion that not all conflicts are bad.[16] Thus, a conflict over the clarity of expectations may lead to greater alignment on expectations. However, regardless of what causes conflict, if left unidentified or unattended, conflicts can turn into legal disputes. One research study that systematically reviewed the literature on the causes of construction disputes identified the eight most often cited causes:[17]

1. Poor contractual arrangements
2. Scope changes
3. Unforeseen site conditions
4. Poor contract understanding and administration
5. Quality of work
6. Inability to achieve time targets
7. Non or delayed payments; and
8. Poor quality of design.

Looking at these causes of dispute alongside the categories of conflict identified above it becomes clearer to see how the conflicts can lead to contractual disputes. Take for example the most cited cause of construction disputes—*poor contractual arrangements.* These poor arrangements often involve contracts not assigning risks among the parties reasonably.[18] Such poor arrangements can trigger the *structural* conflict described in which one party, perhaps due to its superior power, imposes more risk-taking on the other. If left unattended, it is not surprising how such an imbalance would lead to a contractual dispute. With this understanding, the mechanism for attending to the underlying conflict and for avoiding the dispute then becomes apparent; in this instance, it is the dispute prevention mechanism sensibly called realistic risk allocation, which we discuss in chapter 4.

Figure 1 provides an illustrative example using the above logic to map dispute prevention mechanisms which can address the other most cited causes of construction disputes (column A). For each, we offer potential underlying conflict categories (column B) that, if left unidentified or unattended, may lead to the corresponding dispute. With this connection in mind, we then propose relevant

15. *Id.*

16. *See Introduction* note 5 regarding the work of Amy Gallo identifying five advantages of conflict in the workplace. Amy Gallo, *Why We Should Be Disagreeing More at Work*, Harv. Bus. Rev., Jan. 3, 2018, https://hbr.org/2018/01/why-we-should-be-disagreeing-more-at-work.

17. Pramod Malak Silva et al., *Causes of Disputes in the Construction Industry—A Systematic Literature Review*, 28 J.F.M.P.C. (2023) (eight most often cited causes of disputes).

18. *Id.*

dispute prevention mechanisms, to be discussed later in this book, that are best designed to address the conflict and prevent the dispute (column C).

A Cause of Dispute	B Illustrative Underlying Conflict Category(s)	C Dispute Prevention Mechanism
Poor Contractual Arrangements	Structural, Relationship	Realistic Risk Allocation (Chapter 4), Partnering (Chapter 5)
Scope Changes	Relationship, Data/Information	Contractual Clauses (Chapter 4)
Unforeseen Site Conditions	Data/Information, Structural	Relationship Governance (Chapter 5)
Poor Contract Understanding and Administration	Relationship, Interest	Contract Design (Chapter 4)
Quality of Work	Value, Data/Information, Relationship	Modern Standing Neutral (Chapter 5)
Inability to Achieve Time Targets	Structural, Value, Relationship	Incentives (Chapter 4)
Non or Delayed Payments	Structural, Value	Relational Negotiation (Chapter 5)
Poor Quality of Design	Relationship, Structural	Traditional Standing Neutral (Chapter 5)

Figure 1: Illustrative Map of Dispute Prevention Mechanism to Cause of Dispute

A LOOK AHEAD

In this chapter, we set out to help you view disputes through a different lens: a lens of preventing disputes rather than just resolving them. In chapter 2, we introduce a Dispute Management Continuum with thirty-three dispute prevention and dispute resolution mechanisms. We also provide a high-level overview of each mechanism to show the breadth of dispute prevention mechanisms and how they augment more traditional dispute resolution mechanisms. As you read chapter 2, you will see that many of these "upstream" mechanisms in the Dispute Management Continuum are used to help organizations get to the root causes associated with conflict.

Chapter 2

The Dispute Management Continuum

The concept of a Dispute Management Continuum is not new. In 1991, the International Institute for Conflict Prevention and Resolution (CPR) introduced this concept in their publication *Preventing and Resolving Construction Disputes.*[1] The concept was a simple way to classify a diversity of mechanisms ranging from dispute prevention to dispute resolution. Over the years the continuum has evolved.[2]

This book provides a fresh update to the previous versions, which spans five categories, from the most preventive options to the most adversarial options (Figure 2).

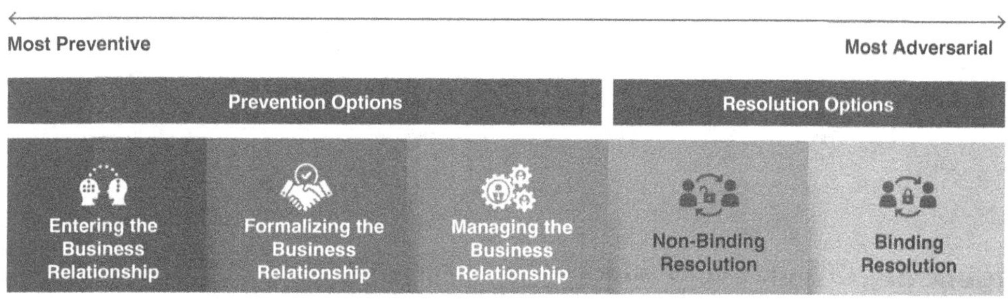

Figure 2: Dispute Management Continuum

The first three categories of the Dispute Management Continuum focus on dispute prevention. They cover the evolving stages of the business relationship: from the pre-contract relationship development stage (entering the business relationship), to the negotiations stage (formalizing the business relationship), to

1. James Groton, *Preventing and Resolving Construction Disputes*, CPR Legal Program Constr. Disp. Comm. (1991) (introduction of the concept of Dispute Management Continuum).

2. James P. Groton & Helena Haapio, *From Reaction to Proactive Action: Dispute Prevention Processes in Business Agreements*, 9 IACCM EMEA Academic Symposium (2007); Kate Vitasek et al., *Unpacking the Standing Neutral: A Cost Effective and Common-Sense Approach for Preventing Conflict*, UNI Scholarworks 1–70 (2019) (Dispute Management Continuum).

managing the business relationship. It is during these three stages that the parties can most effectively deploy dispute prevention mechanisms.

The last two categories of the Dispute Management Continuum cover the two kinds of dispute resolution mechanisms: non-binding dispute resolution (which includes mechanisms such as assisted resolution and mediation where an outcome is not dictated to the parties), and binding dispute resolution (which includes mechanisms such as arbitration and litigation where a third party mandates the result).

Figure 3 provides a more detailed view of the Dispute Management Continuum, which includes thirty-three mechanisms across the five categories.

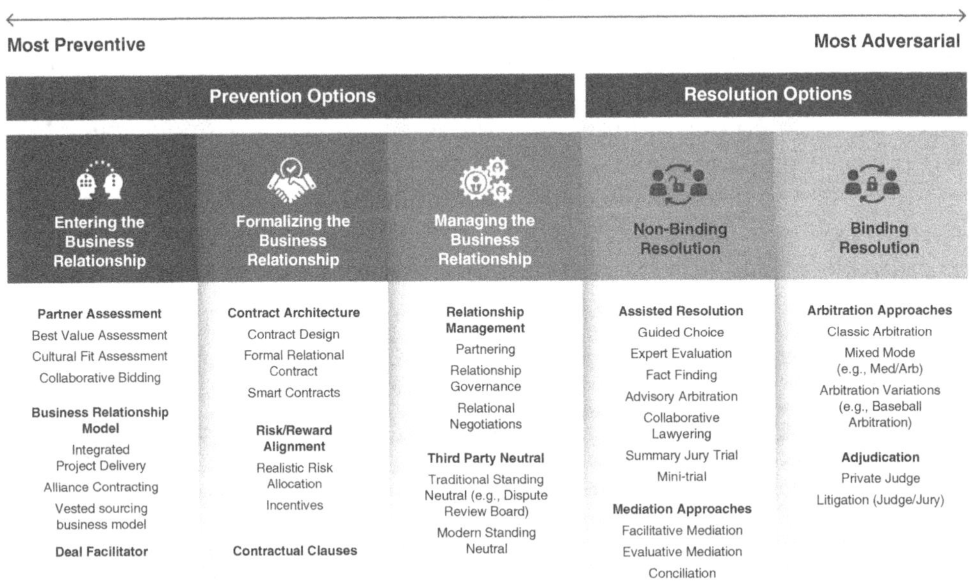

Figure 3: Detailed Dispute Management Continuum

We want to stress the thirty-three mechanisms called out in figure 3 and discussed in this book are not a finite list of mechanisms. Rather, we have chosen to include these mechanisms due to their popularity and success in practice.

The rest of this chapter provides a ***high-level overview*** of each of the listed dispute prevention and resolution mechanisms. Chapters 3, 4, and 5 provide a deep dive into each dispute prevention mechanism covering the *what*, *why*, and *how* of each. In addition, a case study illustrates how organizations are putting each mechanism into practice to prevent disputes.

You might be asking, if the purpose of the book is dispute prevention, why do we include dispute resolution items in the continuum? The answers are simple: First, we want to provide context into how dispute prevention relates to dispute resolution. Second, in chapter 6 of this book we will outline the essentials of a Dispute Management System, which necessarily requires both prevention and resolution mechanisms.

As you read this book—especially this chapter—we want to emphasize that you should think of this book as a guidebook. For example,

- If you are already an expert in dispute resolution feel free to skip through the high-level descriptions we provide in this chapter.
- If you are already familiar with dispute prevention, you may want to skip this chapter entirely and visit chapters 3, 4, and 5, choosing to focus on the dispute prevention mechanisms that may be new to you and also review part III of this book as it showcases how to develop a Dispute Management System and overcome barriers to adopting dispute prevention.

ENTERING THE BUSINESS RELATIONSHIP

Some dispute prevention mechanisms are intended to be used well before parties even begin to put pen to paper and formalize their business relationship in a contract. For example, this book devotes chapter 3 to showing how three promising mechanisms are utilized when entering a business relationship: partner assessment, business relationship model, and use of a third-party neutral to assist in deal facilitation. While some of these mechanisms will find their way into a formal contract, many do not. Nonetheless, their impact is often significant in terms of preventing and mitigating the results of misalignment that often leads to disputes.

Partner Assessment

Partner assessment is often viewed as a procurement practice and not something lawyers should care about. However, when organizations select an optimal business partner with aligned priorities and goals, there is a higher likelihood that the partners will be able to work together more successfully. This in turn reduces the likelihood of disputes after the contract is signed. While lawyers may not participate in applying these mechanisms, we are sharing these proven approaches to show how progressive organizations are shifting attention upstream in the pre-contract stage to strengthen the alignment with business partners at the earliest phase of doing business. In this book, we profile those three partner assessment mechanisms that help organizations select the best business partner for their unique needs.

Business Relationship Model

Over the years, organizations have challenged the traditional transactional contracting approach when entering more complex and risky contracts (e.g., long-term outsourcing agreements and complex construction contracts). The result is alternative contracting models (often called hybrid contracting models or alternative delivery models) that aim to align the interests of commercial partners. They are: integrated project delivery (IPD), alliance contracting, and a Vested sourcing business model.

Deal Facilitator

Using a neutral party to resolve disputes is commonplace today. But an interesting spin proving to be effective at preventing disputes is to leverage a third party for help in deal development, too. The third party—often referred to as a deal facilitator or deal mediator—is engaged by contracting parties to help them collaboratively negotiate the specific deal terms.[3]

Deal facilitators may or may not be lawyers. Even if they are lawyers, they do not operate in the capacity of a lawyer. Rather, they operate as a coach or consultant for business partners instead of representing just one party as their client. A goal of the deal facilitator is to help the parties optimize the value of their business relationship during the contracting process. Parties to contract negotiations typically use a deal facilitator with the focus on helping them to collaboratively create specific deal points (e.g., develop a statement of work, the economic model, align on the right metrics for the partnership, and governance mechanisms).

A key benefit of using a deal facilitator is to ensure the contracting parties create a fair and balanced agreement that works for both parties. This, in turn, helps reduce the contractual shading we previously discussed, which is when one party engages in opportunistic actions to get even when they perceive they have been treated unfairly.[4]

FORMING THE BUSINESS RELATIONSHIP

Once contracting parties have agreed to formally enter a business relationship, there are several proven dispute prevention mechanisms parties can embed into their contractual relationship. Embedding preventive techniques in the formal contract can help manage the parties' expectations and feelings of entitlement and reduce the risk of misunderstandings, by incentivizing cooperation and better defining the parties' roles.[5] This book devotes chapter 4 to showing how

3. For a good history of Deal Facilitation, *see Deal Mediation*, INT'L MEDIATION INST., https://imimediation.org/resources/deal-mediation/.

4. David Frydlinger & Oliver Hart, *Overcoming Contractual Incompleteness: The Role of Guiding Principles*, 66 J.L. ECON. & ORG. 1, 5–9 (2023) (contractional shading).

5. Henry Allen Blair, *Anticipating Procedural Innovation: How and When Parties Calibrate Procedure through Contract*, 72 O.L.R. 797–855 (2020) (reduce risk of misunderstandings by incentivizing cooperation).

organizations are using contract architecture, risk/reward alignment, and contractual clauses to prevent disputes. Some of these mechanisms are more conventional in nature and are standard in contracts, while others are more modern and have evolved over the last two decades.

Contract Architecture

Contract architecture refers to the framing or scaffolding of how a contract is designed. Ideally, the chosen contract architecture supports the business relationship model the parties have selected. Contract architecture differs from contract drafting, as it uses social and computer science to ensure an effective contract design, develop formal relational contracts, and create smart contracts.

Contract Design

Proactive contract design applies good process, content and document design to contracting processes and documents.[6] Good contract design makes contracts easier to understand—and, therefore, easier to follow. Designing contracts for usability serves the needs of the contracting parties and of the people who work with contracts so the parties reach their objectives and avoid unnecessary problems.[7] There are many contract design techniques that help contract users find what they need, understand what they find, and use the information. The most common contract design techniques are plain language contracts[8] and visualization[9] techniques.

Formal Relational Contract

The concept of relational contracting dates to the 1960s with the work of legal scholars Ian Macneil and Steward Macauley. However, the concept of using

---

6. Petra Hietanen-Kunwald & Helena Haapio, *Effective Dispute Prevention and Resolution through Proactive Contract Design*, 5 J.S.C.A.N. 1–22 (2021) (proactive contract design).

7. Thomas D. Barton et al., *Reframing Contract Design: Integrating Business, Legal, Design, and Technology Perspectives*, *in* Research Handbook on Contract Design 33–54 (Marcelo Corrales Compagnucci et al. eds., 2022) (avoiding unnecessary problems in contract design).

8. Shawn Burton, *The Case for Plain-Language Contracts*, Harv. Bus. Rev., Jan.–Feb. 2018, at 134.

9. Helena Haapio & Stefania Passera, *Contracts as Interfaces: Visual Representation Patterns in Contract Design*, *in* Legal Informatics 213–38 (2021) (importance of visualization techniques in contract design); Stefania Passera, *Flowcharts, Swimlanes, and Timelines: Alternatives to Prose in Communicating Legal–Bureaucratic Instructions to Civil Servants*, 32 J. Bus. Tech. 229–72 (2018) (visualization techniques in contract design).

formal relational contracts began to get traction after *Harvard Business Review* published an article in 2019 by David Frydlinger, Oliver Hart, and Kate Vitasek. Formal relational contracts have the parties document the relational elements of the agreement into the actual contract to create a contractual commitment for the parties to apply relationship-building practices designed to keep the parties in continual alignment of interests.

A well-drafted relational contract embeds a formal "Statement of Intent" into the contract that includes a jointly developed shared vision, Guiding Principles, and a model set of behaviors that both parties agree to be part of their relationship.[10] It also formally incorporates relational governance mechanisms obliging the parties to effectively manage the relationship proactively, addressing any gaps, errors, or omissions in their agreement in the manner outlined in their Statement of Intent and governance.[11] The result is a formal commitment to use fair, balanced, and proactive approaches for managing the relationship when "business happens." This, in turn, can reduce disputes.

Smart Contracts

Smart contracts are built on computer programs or transaction protocols that automatically execute contractual events and actions according to the terms of a contract. Smart contracts are an emerging practice. A *smart legal contract* is emerging as a legally binding contract in some jurisdictions and is intended to be both executable by a machine and legally enforceable.[12] Smart contracts built on blockchain technology are a powerful tool business partners can use to prevent disputes. An excellent example is how Walmart and its major trucking supplier collaborated with a blockchain consultant to devise a system to solve freight

10. David Frydlinger et al., Contracting in the New Economy: Using Relational Contracts to Boost Trust and Collaboration in Strategic Business Relationships (2021).

11. The authors have chosen to focus on formal relational contracts for this book. However, it is important to note the concept of using informal "networked" governance has also been researched and proven effective. For example, *see* Lisa Bernstein, *Private Commercial Law in the Cotton Industry: Creating Cooperation through Rules, Norms, and Institutions*, 99 Mich. L. Rev. 1724–90 (2001) (cooperation in cotton industry); *see also* Lisa Bernstein, *Opting Out of the Legal System: Extralegal Contractual Relations in the Diamond Industry*, 21 J. Leg. Stud. 115–59 (1992) (networked governance in the diamond industry).

12. CleanApp, *Crypto's Founding Fallacy: How Mistakes in the "Smart Contract" Genesis Block Weaken the Whole Chain*, Crypto L. Rev. (2019) (smart legal contracts); Daniel Drummer & Dirk Neumann, *Is Code Law? Current Legal and Technical Adoption Issues and Remedies for Blockchain-Enabled Smart Contracts*, 35 J. Inf. Technol. 337–60 (2020) (legality of smart contracts); Nataliia Filatova, *Smart Contracts from the Contract Law Perspective: Outlining New Regulative Strategies*, 28 I.I.L.I.T. 217–42 (2020) (smart legal contracts).

payment problems, reducing freight claim disputes by 98.5 percent. The blockchain solution was released across sixty-nine more freight carriers to join this highly effective dispute prevention system.[13]

Risk/Reward Alignment

When parties enter a commercial agreement, there is often risk involved. One way to prevent disputes is to align interests around risks and rewards. Two mechanisms have evolved as ways to align contracting parties around risks: using realistic risk allocation and incentives.

Realistic Risk Allocation

Risks are inherent in virtually all commercial activities. Realistic risk allocation is an integral part of risk management that starts at the planning phase in any business relationship and includes the process of fairly allocating risks among the parties. When businesses identify, understand, anticipate, assess, analyze, and learn to manage risks, they can create a significant source of value for the contracting parties through risk reduction. The goal is to consciously not shift risk to the "weaker" party to "win" the negotiation, but rather to intentionally identify and analyze potential risks in a relationship and assign each risk to the party that is most capable of managing, controlling, or insuring against that risk. Each time a risk is appropriately allocated, a source of potential conflict diminishes.

Incentives

When applied appropriately, incentives can be a valuable tool to align interests, encourage superior performance, and discourage disputes. When used effectively, incentives align behaviors toward a common goal, even when one or more parties might otherwise be motivated solely by their limited perception of their short-term interests rather than the success of the enterprise. For example, the leader of a multi-party transaction may establish a bonus pool that, upon attainment of specific goals, will pay out a sum to each of the transaction participants. Importantly, the bonus is payable only if these participants as a group meet the assigned goals; either everyone or no one receives the bonus. Incentives also

13. Kate Vitasek et al., *How Walmart Canada Uses Blockchain to Solve Supply-Chain Challenges*, Harv. Bus. Rev. (Jan. 5, 2022), https://hbr.org/2022/01/how-walmart-canada-uses-blockchain-to-solve-supply-chain-challenges; Kate Vitasek, *How Walmart Used Collaboration and Co-Creation to Build the World's Largest Industrial Blockchain Solution*, World Fin. Rev. (May 19, 2022), https://worldfinancialreview.com/how-walmart-used-collaboration-and-co-creation-to-build-the-worlds-largest-industrial-blockchain-solution/.

align interests between buyers and suppliers in performance-based and Vested agreements.[14]

Contractual Clauses

Organizations can embed a variety of clauses into their contracts to signal the business partner's intent to deal with problems and disputes when they arise.[15] Some of the most well-known and widely used contractual clauses to help prevent disputes include:

- A *Covenant of Good Faith and Fair Dealing Contract Clause* obligating contracting parties to deal with each other honestly, fairly, and in good faith with the intent not to destroy the right of the other party or parties to receive the benefits of the contract.[16]
- A *Contract Changes Clause* enabling contracting parties to make changes to their contract, which helps keep the parties aligned.
- A *Dispute Management Clause* providing guidance on how the parties should handle a contract dispute.
- A *Notice and Cure Agreement* signaling a warning when there is a serious issue between contracting parties—typically a potential breach of contract. The logic behind this clause is to allow the parties to send a warning signal before issuing a termination. This lets the offending party respond and address any issues to get back into compliance with the contract.

In chapter 4, we will share how these contractual clauses are used to help organizations prevent disputes by laying the groundwork for the "rules" of how the parties manage any potential disputes.

MANAGING THE BUSINESS RELATIONSHIP

Business is dynamic. Even the most mature contracting process and a well-developed contract can fall into misalignment. As previously noted, the concept of

14. BONNIE KEITH ET AL., STRATEGIC SOURCING IN THE NEW ECONOMY: HARNESSING THE POTENTIAL OF SOURCING BUSINESS MODELS IN MODERN PROCUREMENT (2016).

15. While this book illustrates contractual approaches, organizations can also signal their intent to deal with problems informally, such as through informal social norms or networked governance. *See* Bernstein, *Opting Out of the Legal System: Extralegal Contractual Relations in the Diamond Industry supra* note 11, at 115–59 (informal social norms or networked governance).

16. Note that this clause is not recognized as legally binding in all jurisdictions.

contractual misalignment is so prevalent that Nobel laureate Oliver Williamson stated, "all complex contracts will be incomplete; there will be errors, gaps, omissions and the like."[17]

The reason is simple. Business conditions often change, financial pressures arise, and personnel come and go. Any of these circumstances may create friction in the relationship even amongst the most well-intentioned parties. That is why it is critical to consider implementing mechanisms for managing the relationship after signing a contract. We dedicate chapter 5 to sharing five dispute prevention mechanisms falling into two categories: relationship management and the use of third-party neutrals. The goal is to help parties solve problems and conflicts *before* they turn into disputes.

Relationship Management

The concept of relationship management is a relatively new discipline. Much of the original work on relationship management stems from managing complex outsourcing and strategic alliances. Relationship management seeks to do exactly what the name implies: help parties manage their ongoing relationship effectively following contract signing. In this book, we profile three relationship management mechanisms that have shown success is helping to prevent disputes: partnering, relationship governance, and relational negotiations.

Partnering

Partnering uses team-building tactics to help build a strong, collaborative working relationship among contracting parties. Partnering is a deliberate undertaking between parties to ensure they align on the purpose of the contract, their mutual objectives, expectations and values, the risks they are likely to confront, conflicts that may arise, or any other issues that will portend a better relationship.[18] Partnering often involves workshops with key stakeholders. For example, contracting parties may hold a retreat among key personnel involved in the project/relationship. The expected benefits from partnering activities include improved efficiencies and cost-control, increased possibilities for innovation, continued quality improvement of goods and services, and reduced likelihood that conflict will escalate to dispute.

17. Oliver Williamson, *Outsourcing: Transaction Cost Economics and Supply Chain Management*, 44 J.S.C.M. 5–16 (2008) (prevalence of contractual misalignment).

18. *Joint Best Practice Approaches to Dispute Prevention in Business Arrangements*, CPR, https://assets-002.noviams.com/novi-file-uploads/cpr/pdfs-and-documents/Joint-Best-Practices-Outline-for-Dispute-Prevention.pdf.

Traditionally, partnering is considered a post-contract signing mechanism. However, in recent years, partnering has extended to pre-contract signing with the use of a deal facilitator, who helps contracting parties develop their contract.

Relationship Governance

Relationship governance includes a variety of tools and tactics contracting parties can use to manage their relationship post-contract signing. Examples include a tiered structure for decision-making and managing escalations, a regular cadence of reviews (e.g., quarterly business review, monthly operation review, and annual relationship health check), defined continuity of resource protocols, and collaborative "two-in-a-box" peer-to-peer mapping of key personnel working in the relationship.[19] When applied, sound relationship governance helps keep parties aligned and prevents unwanted surprises.

While many longer-term and strategic relationships intuitively use relationship governance to manage their relationship, there is a trend for contracting parties to formally include governance mechanisms into the parties' contract—typically in the form of a schedule or appendix. As such, the protocols become a contractual obligation for the parties to apply sound governance practices.

Relational Negotiations

Negotiation is a common mechanism contracting parties can use to prevent a problem from becoming a formal dispute. Interest in collaborative negotiation approaches increased after the launch of the Harvard Negotiations Project by Roger Fisher, William Ury, and Bruce Patton. In chapter 5, we explain how interest-based negotiations and step negotiations are being used as ways to maintain a positive focus on contracting parties' relationship when negotiating.

Third-Party Neutral

Independence and neutrality are key reasons why organizations turn to third-party neutrals to resolve disputes. By the same token, these qualities lead more and more businesses to retain an independent third party to help them identify potential problem areas and work through them *before* they turn into a dispute.

To be effective, contracting parties engage the neutral at the beginning of their relationship, and the neutral is embedded into the party's ongoing governance structure. Contracting parties determine the roles and nature of how they will use the neutral and split the cost between them.

19. Kate Vitasek et al., *Unpacking Outsourcing Governance*, UNIV. TENN., 1–45 (2022) (governance mechanisms).

In this book, we profile two types of third-party neutrals: a traditional standing neutral and a modern standing neutral.

Traditional Standing Neutral (e.g., Dispute Review Board)

As mentioned above, the parties appoint a standing neutral at the beginning of the relationship and embed it within the party's governance. An excellent example of a traditional standing neutral is a Dispute Review Board (DRB) used in the construction industry. DRBs—first emerging in the 1970s—regularly meet with contracting parties to review problems and/or claims and resolve them on a near real-time basis before they become a contested dispute. DRBs have been highly successful in the construction industry[20] and the sector birthed the Dispute Review Board Foundation to educate and promote the use of DRBs.[21]

Modern Standing Neutral

Over time, the concept and application of using standing neutrals has evolved into what we coin a "modern" standing neutral. We use the term modern standing neutral because of the more proactive approach in which the neutral supports the business partners. While a common role is to support the contracting parties with advice on how to work through problems and conflict (like a traditional standing neutral), a modern standing neutral will almost always provide support in areas that are far more proactive and preventive in nature. For example, a modern standing neutral facilitates ongoing risk assessment monitoring, supports the parties in dealing with contract changes in a fair and balanced manner, and performs relationship health checks.

NON-BINDING RESOLUTION

Organizations unable to prevent conflicts from escalating into disputes will find themselves seeking more formal ways to manage their misalignment. In this phase of the Dispute Management Continuum, the parties still have many non-binding dispute resolution mechanisms they can use to resolve a claim or dispute, which enables parties to have control over resolving the dispute. This typically yields a faster and more cost-effective resolution than binding resolution options.

As this book focuses on dispute prevention, we are choosing to limit our discussion of existing dispute resolution mechanisms to only the high-level overview found in this chapter. Below we provide two categories of non-binding

20. Cyril Chern, Chern on Dispute Boards (3d ed. 2015).
21. *Dispute Resolution Board Foundation*, DRBF, https://www.drb.org.

dispute resolution mechanisms: assisted resolution and mediation approaches.[22] The good news for readers who want to learn more about resolution mechanisms is there is significant research, books, articles, and others resources that are widely available with a simple internet search.

Assisted Resolution

Guided Choice

Guided choice is a process where contracting parties work with a person who acts as a "guide" or facilitator when the parties find themselves at the threshold of a dispute. This person assists the parties in choosing the most appropriate, practical, and economical method for resolving their dispute. There are several terms used to describe guided choice, with the most common being "guided choice mediation." Guided choice allows for customization to fit the unique needs of a dispute with the goal of finding the best solution for parties to resolve their commercial disputes quickly, fairly, and least expensively and to the parties' satisfaction.

If the parties are using a standing neutral, the standing neutral may fill the role of a guided choice mediator.

Expert Evaluation

Expert evaluation is a process in which the parties use a mutually chosen expert (or experts) who provides a balanced and unbiased evaluation of the dispute and offers an opinion and/or recommendation. The expert evaluator is a professional in the specific field where the parties have a dispute (e.g., construction, facilities management, or IT) and may or may not be an attorney. The expert evaluator listens to each party present its interests and positions along with a summary of its evidence. The expert evaluator gives the parties and their counsel a preliminary opinion on the merits of the dispute. In essence, the process operates as a reality check.[23]

The evaluation is confidential, advisory only, and generally not admissible at trial. The expert evaluator usually does not mediate the dispute but returns the parties to their own negotiation.[24]

---

22. The authors have opted for practicality over completeness. Much has been written about each of the below items—often with debate on the details of how each mechanism works. We encourage anyone wanting to learn more about any mechanism discussed here to delve into one of the many excellent resources that exist focusing entirely on non-binding consensual dispute resolution.

23. Lisa Blomgren Amsler et al., Dispute System Design (2020).

24. *Id.*

Fact Finding

The American Arbitration Association defines fact finding as "a process by which both parties present the arguments and evidence to a neutral person who then issues a non-binding report on the findings, usually recommending a basis for settlement."[25] Parties can opt to use a fact finder themselves, or the fact finder might be appointed by a judge prior to a trial. The goal is to clarify the situation, provide guidance in resolving a dispute, and determine next steps. Fact finders differ from mediators because they are not concerned with involving the parties in the solution and only focus on the substance of the case. Their job is to sort out objective reality from each party's interpretation or version of it and then apply that reality to a non-binding recommendation.

Advisory Arbitration

Advisory arbitration is a form of arbitration, but it is non-binding. (See "Arbitration Approaches" in this chapter for definitions and types of binding arbitration.) As the decision is merely advisory, it allows the parties to exercise more control over the resolution and to pursue a resolution informed by the non-binding decision of the panel.

Collaborative Lawyering

Collaborative lawyering is a bottom-up movement spearheaded in 1990 by Stu Webb, a Minneapolis family lawyer who refused to remain as counsel if the opposing party in a divorce case resorted to taking the dispute to court.[26] CPR defines collaborative law as a process that requires the parties and their lawyers to execute a "four-way agreement" or "participation agreement" as independent parties. This agreement limits the lawyers' participation only to the negotiation and facilitation of a settlement without the threat of litigation. If the parties decide to use the court system, they must hire lawyers other than those who participated in the collaborative law process.[27]

The process itself usually involves a series of meetings with all the parties (often called four ways) designed to foster a team approach to creative problem-solving that encompasses elements such as open and honest communication, cooperation, good faith, and willingness to listen. In this respect, the collaborative

---

25. *A Guide to Commercial Mediation and Arbitration for Business People*, Am. Arb. Assoc. 1–30 (2023) (fact finding definition) https://www.adr.org/sites/default/files/document_repository/A_Guide_to_Commercial.pdf.

26. *Judges Love Collaborative Law—Here's Why*, ABA (Jul. 2018), https://www.americanbar.org/news/abanews/publications/youraba/2018/july-2018/neither-mediators-nor-negotiators--collaborative-lawyers-emphasi/.

27. *ADR Primer*, CPR Inst., https://www.cpradr.org/adr-primer##.

law process focuses on the parties' future relationship. By taking the adversarial element out of resolving a dispute, the collaborative law process lets the parties settle the dispute in a manner that leaves them with a new productive relationship.

Summary Jury Trial

In a summary jury trial, the parties impanel an actual jury, the members of which usually believe they are participating in an actual trial. However, the parties present condensed versions of the evidence. The jury deliberates and makes findings of fact and liability, after which they are released. The parties use the jury's findings to negotiate a settlement. The parties are not bound by the jury's findings; the findings are merely advisory (though the jury may believe otherwise).[28] Summary jury trials are rarely used to resolve complex civil litigations.

Mini-Trial

A mini-trial is a structured settlement procedure that treats the dispute more as a business problem than a legal one. A mini-trial is not a real trial. Rather, it is a settlement process used as a vehicle to help the parties arrive at a solution.

CPR defines a mini-trial as a hybrid process by which the parties present their legal and factual contentions to a panel of representatives selected by each party, or to a single third-party neutral, or both. The presentations are limited, and at the end of the presentations, the party representatives and/or neutral meet and confer. The benefit of a mini-trial is that it allows parties to balance the strength of their claims against the contentions of their adversary, with an eye to resolving the matter.[29]

Mini-trials differ from expert evaluation in that the panel and/or neutral will not give an opinion on the likely outcome of the dispute unless the parties reach an impasse and they are asked to become an evaluator. Mini-trials are effective when complex issues are at stake, and the parties need or wish to maintain a friendly relationship.[30]

Mediation Approaches

Mediation, as defined by CPR, is a form of alternative dispute resolution in which a neutral party (a mediator) selected by the parties seeks to determine the interests

28. Lisa Blomgren Amsler et al., *supra* note 23.

29. *ADR Primer supra* note 27.

30. Wesam S. Alaloul et al., *A Comprehensive Review of Disputes Prevention and Resolution in Construction Projects*, 270 MATEC Web of Conferences 1–7 (2019) (the benefits of mini-trials); Lisa Blomgren Amsler et al., *supra* note 23.

of the parties, discover shared interests, and alert them to a resolution that may further those interests.[31] The two most common forms of mediation are facilitative mediation and evaluative mediation.

Facilitative Mediation

In facilitative mediation, the mediator's role is limited to facilitation. At times, the mediator draws the parties toward a mutually satisfactory way to "split the pie"; at other times, the mediator assists the parties in inventing ways to "make the pie bigger" before splitting it. Communications during mediation may be ex-parte and are always strictly confidential and, to the extent provided by law, inadmissible as settlement negotiations.

Evaluative Mediation

For evaluative mediation, the mediator provides an opinion on the dispute. The evaluation is triggered only if the mediator is competent to offer an opinion and only if both parties request it. Under evaluative mediation, the mediator may eventually offer (1) an opinion on the parties' likelihood of success in an adjudicated proceeding and/or (2) a proposed "best resolution" that the mediator considers is the fairest, most commercially rational outcome to the dispute. However, the mediator has no authority to impose an outcome on the parties and controls only the mediation process, not its result.

Conciliation

Conciliation often gets confused with mediation and arbitration, but it is neither. In mediation, the mediator works with the parties to help them develop an agreement that is mutually acceptable. In conciliation, however, the conciliator meets with the parties, who present their viewpoints separately. The conciliator may ask the parties to make concessions to arrive at a resolution. Ultimately, the conciliator drafts a resolution they consider beneficial to both parties, but the proposed resolution is non-binding, and the parties may accept or reject it as they wish.[32]

---

31. *ADR Primer supra* note 27.

32. *Three Surprising Facts about Conciliation*, L. Dictionary, https://web.archive.org/web/20160613012424/https://thelawdictionary.org/article/three-surprising-facts-conciliation/ (noting that conciliation, like mediation, is private and not a matter of public record, which encourages parties to be forthright and reveal underlying interests).

BINDING RESOLUTION

Binding dispute resolution is an adjudication process. Adjudication, as defined by CPR, is the resolution of the dispute by a third-party neutral vested (by law or agreement) with authority to bind the disputants to the terms of an award. Common adjudicative processes are arbitration and litigation.[33]

The main differences between binding and non-binding dispute resolution lie in the enforceability of the decision and the finality it provides. Below we provide a high-level overview of five binding dispute resolution mechanisms.[34] Once again, we encourage anyone wanting to learn more about dispute resolution to explore the many great books, articles and other resources found with a simple internet search.

Arbitration Approaches

Arbitration is an ancient practice, dating back at least as far as Roman law and the medieval merchant courts.[35] Arbitration is a voluntary dispute resolution mechanism in which an independent, impartial, third-party neutral (an arbitrator or arbitral panel) considers arguments and evidence from disputing parties and then renders a decision or award. Almost without exception, arbitration is a creature of contract and both the powers of the arbitrator and the conduct of the arbitration process are determined by the parties at the time of their agreement. Absent an agreement to the contrary, arbitral awards cannot be judicially appealed except on very limited statutory grounds.[36] A benefit of arbitration is also that it is often shielded from the public or conducted more privately.

Classic Arbitration

Classic arbitration is a private process where disputing parties agree in writing that one or several individuals can decide about the dispute after receiving evidence and hearing arguments. The American Arbitration Association (AAA) requires arbitrators to have at least ten years of experience and

33. *ADR Primer supra* note 27.

34. The authors have again opted for practicality over completeness in our high-level overview of each mechanism. Much has been written about each of the below items—often with debate on the details of how each mechanism works. We encourage anyone wanting to learn more about any mechanism discussed here to explore the wealth of resources available on these topics. For a law school text discussing various varieties of dispute resolution, including arbitration, *see* Carrie Menkel-Meadow et. al, Dispute Resolution: Beyond the Adversarial Model (3d ed. 2018).

35. Lisa Blomgren Amsler et al., *supra* note 23.

36. *ADR Primer supra* note 27.

appropriate education and training in arbitration to join the AAA National Roster of Arbitrators.[37]

The arbitration process is similar to a trial because the parties make opening statements and present evidence to the arbitrator. It is typically conducted under the procedural rules of an established dispute resolution organization such as the AAA, CPR, Judicial Arbitration and Mediation Services, Inc. (JAMS), or a similar international organization. Compared to traditional trials, arbitration is usually less formal and takes less time. For example, often, the parties do not have to follow state or federal rules of evidence, and if the parties agree, the arbitrator is not required to apply the governing law. After the hearing, the arbitrator issues an award, which under the Federal Arbitration Act is legally enforceable.

Mixed Mode (e.g., Med/Arb)

Over the years, organizations have been combining mediation and arbitration to create tailored dispute resolution processes. The concept of "med/arb" was developed by the Associated Soil and Foundation Engineers (ASFE) in the 1970s to streamline dispute resolution.[38]

Today, there are a variety of mixed-mode methods. The general premise is that disputing parties engage in mediation with the intention of submitting all unresolved issues to final and binding arbitration, or they engage in an arbitration with an opportunity for the arbitrator to facilitate resolution through a mediation before an award is issued.[39]

Typically—and unlike in most mediations—parties must agree in writing that the outcome of the process will be binding and the same neutral plays the role of both mediator and arbitrator.[40] In med/arb, the parties start using mediation and, if they cannot settle the dispute, they move on to arbitration.[41] As all parties have agreed to work through the process until all issues are resolved, the med/arb method can be thought of as a binding mediation.[42]

---

37. Clayton Browne, *Do Arbitrators Have to Be Lawyers?*, CHRON (Oct. 3, 2022), http://work.chron.com/arbitrators-lawyers-14405.html.

38. Wesam S. Alaloul et al., *A Comprehensive Review of Disputes Prevention and Resolution in Construction Projects*, 270 MATEC Web of Conferences 1–7 (2019) (benefits of mini-trials).

39. *ADR Primer supra* note 27.

40. Katie Shonk, *What Is Med-Arb?*, HARV. L. SCH.: PROGRAM ON NEGOT. (June 10, 2024), https://www.pon.harvard.edu/daily/mediation/what-is-med-arb/.

41. J. Richard Cheeks, *Multistep Dispute Resolution in Design and Construction Industry*, 129 J. PROF. ISSUES ENG. EDUC. PRACT. 84–91 (2003) (concurrent arbitration and mediation); Edward J. Costello, *ADR: Virtue or Vice?*, 54 DIS. RES. J. 54–62 (1999) (med/arb procedure).

42. Thomas Stipanowich, *Contract and Conflict Management*, 3 WIS. L. REV. 831–916 (2009) (med/arb and binding mediation).

In arb/med, the parties begin arbitrating a dispute and, once the arbitrator(s) have drafted an award and by agreement of the parties, the arbitrator(s) act as mediators to try and facilitate a resolution before the award is issued. If the parties do not agree upon a resolution, the award is issued.

CPR also provides for a concurrent arbitration and mediation process.[43] The benefit of this process is that it does not prolong the proceedings in a step-wise fashion but, instead, allows the parties to mediate while arbitrating with two different sets of neutrals. Arbitration often informs the mediation process.

A hybrid process provides more flexibility and options for resolving the dispute. However hybrid approaches have come under scrutiny when the mediator is to become an arbitrator because it is difficult for a mediator to be a neutral party during the arbitration stage after learning confidential information during mediation.[44] In addition, there are those who contend hybrid approaches are less meaningful because, with the parties knowing there is a possibility of going into arbitration, they might hold information back that might otherwise emerge if only mediation is used.[45]

Arbitration Variations

As ADR has taken hold, more and more organizations are seeking to adopt variations for their unique situation. A good example is "baseball arbitration." Baseball arbitration gets its name from the process used for salary negotiation between a Major League Baseball team and a player.[46] As part of the arbitration process, each party submits a proposed monetary award to the arbitrator. After the hearing, the arbitrator selects one of the proposed awards without modification. This approach, sometimes called "last offer arbitration" or LOA, severely limits the arbitrator's discretion. A common consequence of baseball arbitration is to incentivize the parties to conduct their negotiations diligently and submit a reasonable proposal to the arbitrator, hoping it will be adopted.[47]

In a related variation, "night baseball arbitration," the parties agree privately to conform the arbitrator's award to the last offer closest to it. Thus, the arbitrator is unaware of the parties' intention and renders an award based on the merits, without restriction, which the parties then privately convert to an agreement.

---

43. *Concurrent Mediation-Arbitration Clause and Protocol*, CPR (July 2020), https://drs.cpradr.org/rules/protocols-guidelines/concurrent-mediation-arbitration-clauses-and-protocol.

44. *ADR Primer supra* note 27.

45. Katie Shonk *supra* note 40.

46. Not all player salaries are determined via arbitration. Players who have three or more years of Major League service but less than six years of Major League service become eligible for salary arbitration if they do not already have a contract for the next season. *See Salary Arbitration*, MLB, https://www.mlb.com/glossary/transactions/salary-arbitration

47. *ADR Primer supra* note 27.

Today, the number of arbitration variations is quite broad and is a testament to the creativity ADR offers.

Adjudication

Private Judge

Private judges were first introduced in the United States in the late 1970s in New York. The American Bar Association (ABA) defines private judging[48] as: "A process where the disputing parties agree to retain a neutral person as a private judge. The private judge, who is often a former judge with expertise in the dispute, hears the case and makes a decision in a manner similar to a judge. Depending on court rules, the decision of the private judge may be appealable in the public courts."

When using a private judge, the parties' attorneys select the private judge, and the cost is split between the disputing parties. Private judges typically hear domestic relationship, breach of contract, and other types of civil cases. They would not hear criminal cases such as murder or a case that requires a jury.

The benefits of using a private judge are primarily the speedy timeline, the ability to choose the judge, and privacy. There is also a benefit for the taxpayers because the disputing parties pay for the cost.

Litigation (Judge/Jury)

Litigation is an adversarial proceeding in public court to determine and enforce legally cognizable rights and defenses. Litigation results in a judgment that awards a remedy in conformance with statutory or common law. With few exceptions, judgments resulting from litigation are appealable on a variety of legally cognizable grounds.[49]

Litigation is the most expensive and adversarial dispute resolution technique. A key cost driver, especially in the United States, is the extensive discovery which typically includes interrogatories and depositions of parties and witnesses made available in the judicial process. This adversarial process takes a less extreme form in other common law jurisdictions (i.e., the United Kingdom and the former British colonies of India, Australia, New Zealand, and parts of Canada). However, there are benefits to this process, including its public nature if a party wants to set a precedent for others.

---

48. *Private Judging*, ABA: Section of Disp. Resol., https://web.archive.org/web/20200924191940/https://www.americanbar.org/groups/dispute_resolution/resources/DisputeResolutionProcesses/private_judging/.

49. *ADR Primer supra* note 27.

A LOOK AHEAD

In this chapter, we have provided a high-level overview of eighteen dispute prevention and fifteen dispute resolution mechanisms mapped to the Dispute Management Continuum. In part II, chapters 3, 4, and 5, we shift to help you better understand each of the more prevention-focused mechanisms by providing a deeper dive into each. For each mechanism, we share the what, why, and how. In addition, we provide a case study to illustrate how the mechanism is being used in practice to prevent disputes.

Part II

Understanding Dispute Prevention Mechanisms

Chapter 3

Entering the Relationship

Every day companies seek to enter new business relationships. For some, the process starts with business leaders having strategic discussions about new opportunities. For others, it begins when a company's procurement team sends a tender seeking competitive bids for a specific scope of work. In either case, the expected result will be the establishment of a viable business relationship that adds value to each participant. How viable and enriching that relationship will be depends primarily on how aligned the participants are in their goals and values, cultural compatibility, and ability to function in a collaborative, flexible, and innovative fashion.

In this book, we profile three categories of dispute prevention mechanisms for use when entering a business relationship: partner assessment, business relationship model, and using a neutral deal facilitator (Figure 4).

While some form of these mechanisms will find their way into a contract, others may not. Nonetheless, each of these dispute prevention mechanisms can offer significant benefits in preventing or mitigating disputes.

Figure 4: Prevention Mechanisms for Entering the Business Relationship

PARTNER ASSESSMENT

Business professionals are increasingly turning to approaches that lay the foundation for dispute prevention during partner assessment. The most common mechanisms used during partner assessment are best value assessment, cultural fit assessment, and collaborative bidding. While lawyers may not participate in applying partner assessment mechanisms, it is important to understand how these mechanisms are contributing to dispute prevention.

Why

As discussed in chapter 1, the source of conflicts that arise between parties in contractual relationships often stems from a misalignment in their interests, communications, power, and/or values. By focusing their attention further "upstream" before they enter into contracts, parties can anticipate these conflicts and ensure better alignment on scope and goals right from the outset, which can avoid or better address the conflicts as they arise and prevent any resulting disputes. Partner assessments foster this alignment and can prevent disputes downstream.

How It Works

In this book, we profile three broad categories of partner assessment: best value assessment, cultural fit assessment, and collaborative bidding.

Best Value Assessment

Often companies are lulled into basing their selection on the lowest bid when selecting a supplier. The result, however, can be counterproductive and lead to disputes. For example, in one study when organizations selected a contractor with a bid price of 10 percent below average, they were over 40 percent more likely to have a claim. The results are even more dramatic when the contractor bid price was 20 percent lower than the average bid price—resulting in a 70 percent increase in the likelihood of having a claim.[1]

To counter this, procurement professionals have eschewed an overreliance on low bids and turned to "best value" approaches for selecting suppliers. For example, Section 2.101 of the U.S. Federal Acquisition Regulation now recognizes that best value can help the government get "the expected outcome which provides the greatest overall benefit in response to the requirement."[2]

Definitions of "best value" vary widely. The one consistent feature of "best value" is the recognition that factors other than price should figure prominently in partner selection. As defining best value is flexible based on the given needs of each situation, organizations can define other key factors they deem important. Typical criteria include quality, past performance, schedule, customer satisfaction, and risks/risk mitigation ability.

The Minnesota Department of Transportation (MnDOT) was an early adopter of best value when it selected a supplier to rebuild the I-35 bridge after its

1. Paul Barshop, *Methods for Reducing Claims*, *in* Reducing Construction Costs: Uses of Best Dispute Resolution Practices by Project Owners: Proceedings Report, Nat'l Acad. Sci., Eng'g, Med. 37–42 (2007), https://nap.nationalacademies.org/read/11846/chapter/9.

2. *Best Value Continuum*, DAU, https://www.dau.edu/acquipedia-article/best-value-continuum.

collapse in 2007. The chosen supplier far exceeded expectations—coming in under budget, ahead of schedule (the bridge was built in just thirteen months), and winning almost two dozen quality awards. Today, MnDOT promotes best value as "innovative contracting" with the ability to "minimize impacts and enhance the long-term performance and value of construction."[3]

Cultural Fit (Compatibility) Assessment

Cultural fit in a business relationship means the degree to which partners are compatible on management philosophy, organizational values, decision-making, and communication patterns and behaviors.[4] Cultural fit between businesses has been a focus of academic study since the 1990s.[5]

Many organizations identify cultural fit as a key ingredient in the success of their strategic business relationships. Procter & Gamble (P&G), for example, cites cultural fit as a critical factor in the success of its facilities management outsourcing relationship with Jones Lang Lasalle (JLL).[6] Research suggests that poor cultural fit between business partners results in lower productivity, lower financial performance outcomes, lower relationship satisfaction, and higher levels of conflict.[7] These conditions often lead to disputes between culturally discordant business partners.

It is important to understand that cultural fit does not mean "sameness," but rather avoiding incompatibilities that can create conflict from incongruent management philosophies. Do the business partners have a similar view on transparency? Or do organizations make decisions using a top-down hierarchical approach or a bottom-up collaborative approach?

---

3. *Best-Value Contracting*, Minn. Dept. Transp., https://www.dot.state.mn.us/const/innovative-contracting/best-value-contracting.html.

4. Douglas M. Lambert & A. Michael Knemeyer, *We're in This Together*, 82 Harv. Bus. Rev., Dec. 2004, at 114; Geert Hofstede, Culture's Consequences: International Differences in Work Related Values (1980); Vijay Pothukuchi et al., *National and Organizational Culture Differences and International Joint Venture Performance*, 33 J. Int. Bus. Stud. 243–65 (2002) (cultural fit between businesses); Kate Vitasek et al., *Unpacking Trading Partner Trust*, Univ. Tenn., 1–59 (October 2022) (cultural fit in a business relationship).

5. Susan Cartwright & Cary L. Cooper, *The Role of Culture Compatibility in Successful Organizational Marriage*, 7 Acad. of Mgmt. Exec. 57–70 (1993) (culture fit as a focus since the 1990s).

6. Kate Vitasek et al., *Vested for Success Case Study; How P&G and JLL Transformed Corporate Real Estate*, Univ. Tenn., 1–47 (2011) (importance of culture fit in P&G and JLL relationship).

7. Susan Cartwright & Cary L. Cooper *supra* note 5; Vijay Pothukuchi et al., *supra* note 4; Roberto A. Weber & Colin F. Camerer, *Cultural Conflict and Merger Failure: An Experimental Approach*, 49 Mgmt. Sci. 400–15 (2003) (impacts of poor culture fit between partners); Kate Vitasek et al., *supra* note 4.

While you might not think of cultural fit as a critical variable, organizations recognize that poor cultural fit contributes to failed business relationships. The consequences of a cultural fit mismatch became excruciatingly evident in the case of a medical device company that outsourced its workplace services and maintenance operations to a culturally incongruent supplier.[8]

The medical device company's operating culture valued collaborative decision-making, flexibility, and innovation, while the supplier's culture was hierarchical and process-oriented. Employees of the medical device company often joked they suffered from attention deficit disorder because they needed dozens of people in every meeting to make a decision. In contrast, the service provider—noted for their high quality and reasonable pricing—had an operational culture that valued standardization and frowned on flexibility; contrary to the medical device company, excessive meetings were considered a waste of time. The service provider had a hard time keeping people on the "high maintenance and schizophrenic" medical device company's account. The A team turned into the C team, service levels dropped, and the parties found themselves in back-and-forth tit-for-tat actions of petty claims. Ultimately, the medical device company triggered the termination for convenience clause to terminate the contract early—something that was costly and frustrating for both parties.

Collaborative Bidding

The collaborative bidding process illustrates how partner assessment itself can, from the very earliest of discussions between potential business partners, encourage innovation, build trust, align interests, and eliminate disputes. Collaborative bidding emphasizes parties working together from inception in defining common goals and approaches to foster a more synchronized relationship.

The University of Tennessee (UT) is a leader in researching collaborative bidding methods. UT research on collaborative bidding maps the various types of bidding methods (called RFx methods) along a continuum (Figure 5). There are two types of collaborative bidding methods: a Request for Solution (RFS) and a Request for Partner (RFPartner).

A *Request for Solution* (also known as a *request for proposed solution or competitive dialogue*) is a collaborative bidding process in which a buying organization has a dialogue with supplier finalists to collaborate and determine the best solution to meet the buyer's needs. The buyer shifts from giving pre-described requirements to providing insight into the problems they are trying to solve. The parties then go through a collaborative dialogue process to define/refine the solution, and the supplier develops a formalized proposal that includes their solution.

8. *Id.*

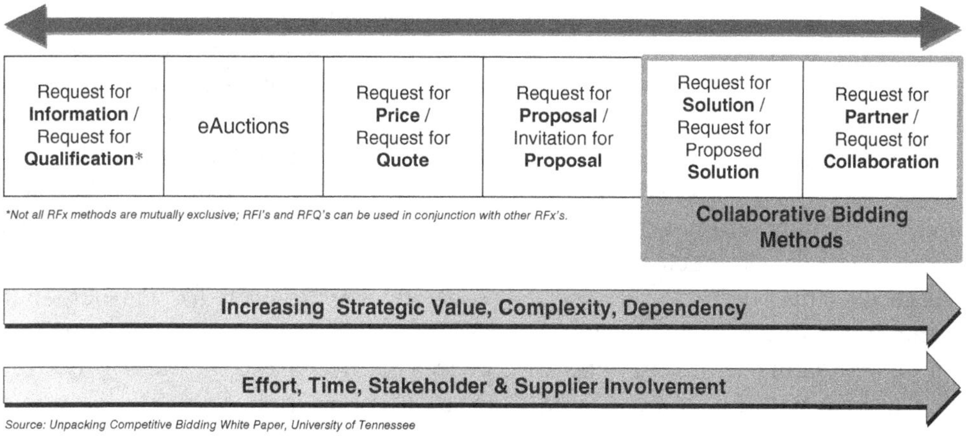

Figure 5: Continuum of RFx Approaches

Request for Partner (also known as a *request for collaboration* or a *request for mutual value solution*) is similar to an RFS in which the buyer seeks to collaborate with potential partners on a solution. A key difference is the buyer is actively seeking not just a solution but also a supplier with a high degree of "cultural fit" and compatibility. A Request for Partner process is typically useful when selecting a supplier for a long-term relationship—such as a large outsourcing initiative requiring significant investment and alignment by the buyer and supplier.

A well-structured collaborative bidding process is transparent. Transparency is essential because it allows the supplier to seek (and get) the needed information to properly develop their solution. When a buyer uses collaborative bidding methods, they provide prospective suppliers with information such as:

- Business goals and objectives
- Any known or perceived constraints
- Operating data to provide a general landscape of the current situation. This includes relevant operational information, existing service levels, high-level cost structures or estimated budget, and desired legal requirements.

Suppliers then use the information to create a high-level concept proposal.

A major part of a collaborative bidding process includes interactive "dialogue" workshops where a buying organization works with each supplier to define and refine the supplier's concept and align more deeply on things like goals and scope. These workshops enable the buyer to "test drive" suppliers through in-depth and informative discussions. An additional benefit is that team members from both the buyer and supplier organizations begin to work together during the process and build trust.

Another key difference between RFS and RFPartner processes is the latter brings commercial team members into the process early to ensure the contractual terms support the solution. For example, UT's collaborative RFPartner process suggests selecting the best-fit supplier based on a concept proposal. Once the supplier is selected, the details of the solution are co-created alongside the commercial and legal teams. This enables the contractual terms to tightly align with the desired solution rather than having the buyer and supplier negotiate the terms after the supplier is selected.

Collaborative bidding processes—especially the Request for Partner—help contracting partners to: (1) align interests on scope and goals and (2) bring commercial teams into the contracting process early—avoiding the top two pitfalls cited by World Commerce and Contract (WCC) report on value leakage in contracts.[9]

Case Study

Eastern Health Authority (now Newfoundland Labrador Health Services) used all three of the above partner assessment mechanisms when selecting a partner for a large multi-year support services contract.

Newfoundland Labrador Health Services (NLHS) provides community, hospital, and long-term health care in Newfoundland and Labrador Canada as part of the Canadian government's public health care services. NLHS has extensive experience in outsourcing, and one of its largest spending areas was "support services." The support services were critical and extensive—including patient/resident food, retail food, environmental services/housekeeping, laundry, portering, and call center services.

To reduce its risk, NLHS had a strategy to split its support services work with two suppliers. With the contracts expiring, NLHS executives questioned if they could gain efficiencies by shifting to work with one supplier. Executives ultimately issued a bid seeking a partner who would work under a more strategic Vested sourcing business model.

In 2019, NLHS sent a collaborative RFPartner to potential suppliers. The bid document stated NLHS was "interested in receiving proposals from qualified suppliers that are capable of delivering the scope of the opportunity—providing creative, innovative, effective, and best value solutions."

Both of NLHS's existing suppliers passed the down-selection process where they participated in collaborative dialogue workshops to determine how each

9. *Commercial Excellence: Ten Pitfalls to Avoid in Contracting*, IACCM, https://s3.eu-central-1.amazonaws.com/iaccmportal/resources/files/8414_j11652-10pitfalls-16pp-2015-06-08-web.pdf.

supplier best aligned with the goals of NLHS. The evaluation included thirty-six criteria across five categories (Figure 6).

An evaluation team graded each criterion using a formal scoring rubric, ranging from 0 (no response provided) to 10 (fully satisfied requirement).

Criteria	Weight
Cultural Fit/Compatibility with Newfoundland Labrador Health Services. The workshops will be a good venue to validate align and fit. We will use the Compatibility and Trust (CaT) assessment developed by Gerald Ledlow Ph.D. and Karl Manrodt Ph.D. to measure the compatibility and trust.	35%
Vision on Statement of Intent/Desired Outcomes by Business line/Guiding Principles	35%
Vision on difference of current solution to proposed solution	20%
Risk Mitigation Plan/Guardrails	5%
Vision for addressing Guardrails for each Business Line	5%

Figure 6: Evaluation Criteria

Selecting a strategic partner with a good cultural fit was important to NLHS; thus, eleven of the thirty-six assessment criteria related to cultural fit. To help NLHS determine cultural fit, both NLHS and each supplier completed a Compatibility and Trust (CaT) assessment to determine their baseline compatibility and trust levels. A CaT Assessment works very well when assessing existing business relationships, such as those in the NLHS scenario. Figures 7 and 8 illustrate one of the analyses from the CaT assessment for each supplier.

Figure 7 shows a tight alignment with Compass (the winning supplier) across five dimensions—focus, trust, team orientation, innovation and communication—tested in the CaT assessment. Figure 8 indicates there is a gap in cultural fit between NLHS and Supplier B (the losing supplier).

The assessment showed Compass had a higher cultural fit. How? As part of the CaT assessment, team members score both how well they believe their own organizations perform (a self-score) against each of the five dimensions as well as scoring their *perception* of their partner (partner perception score). A tell-tale sign of cultural fit is when the CaT self-assessments have small gaps across the five CaT dimensions. For example, taking a closer look at the innovation dimension, NLHS (noted with a grey line in both figures 7 and 8) scores its own organization as quite innovative. This aligns tightly with Compass's self-scores (black line in figure 7) while Supplier B scores its organization as much less innovative (noted with a black line in figure 8). It is easy to see the significant gap in cultural fit regarding how the parties view innovation in figure 8.

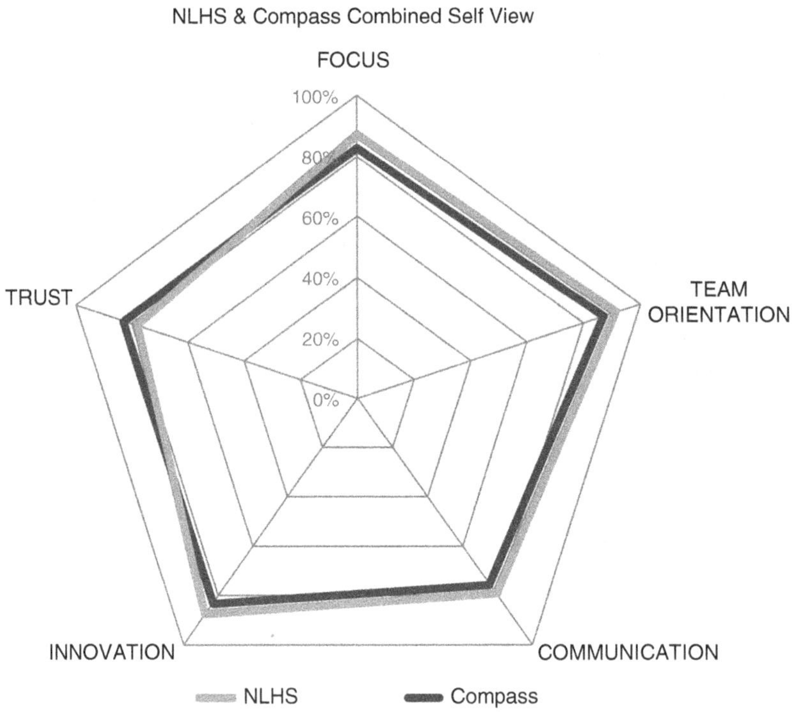

Figure 7: NLHS & Compass Combined Self View

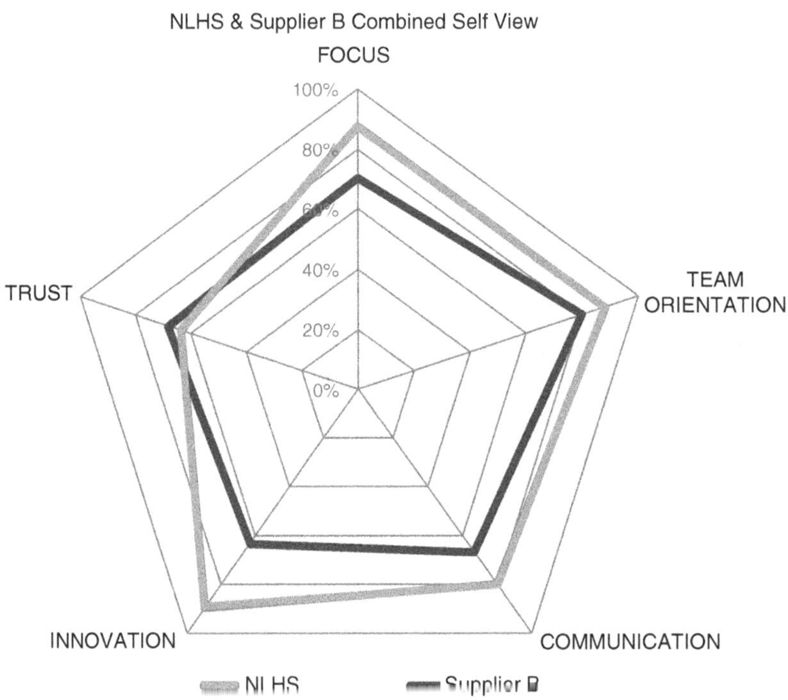

Figure 8: NLHS & Supplier B Combined Self View

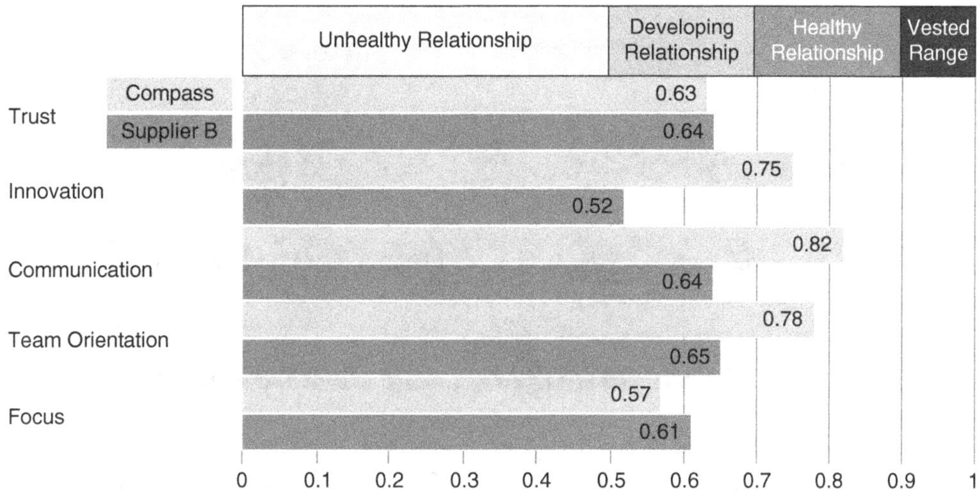

Figure 9: CaT Index Comparison—Compass and Supplier B

The CaT Index is calculated from the self-scores and the partner perception scores. The better the alignment (few gaps) the higher the CaT Index. Once again, the CaT assessment revealed a much healthier business relationship for the Compass relationship, with an aggregate CaT Index of 0.71 for Compass versus 0.61 for Supplier B. Three out of five dimensions scored in the "healthy" range for Compass, whereas supplier B's scores on the CaT fell short of "healthy" in all five dimensions (Figure 9).

As part of the bid process, NLHS used the CaT assessment data as the foundation for dialogues with each supplier. The dialogue workshops challenged the suppliers to address how they would close gaps in their cultural fit by addressing the cultural fit criteria in the scoring rubric.

NLHS ultimately picked Compass as their provider of choice. UT researchers interviewed both suppliers as part of their research. Both suppliers loved the collaborative bidding process and felt selecting the winning supplier with a combination of best value and cultural fit was a superior way to run a bidding process. The losing supplier did not protest—something that is common in large public procurement outsourcing tenders.

An interesting aspect of the NLHS–Compass relationship is that they agreed to continue to monitor relationship health with an annual CaT assessment. The parties have seen consistent improvements in relationship health as measured by the CaT assessment with a CaT Index rising from a baseline aggregate score of 0.71 to an aggregate score of 0.86 (Figure 10).

Scott Bishop, NLHS's Vice President of Corporate Services and Chief Financial Officer, is proud to report no disputes related to the contract: "The effort we put in up front to ensure alignment has made the Compass contract one of the best contracts we have. The focus on dispute prevention using mechanisms like collaborative bidding and culture fit assessment is brilliant."

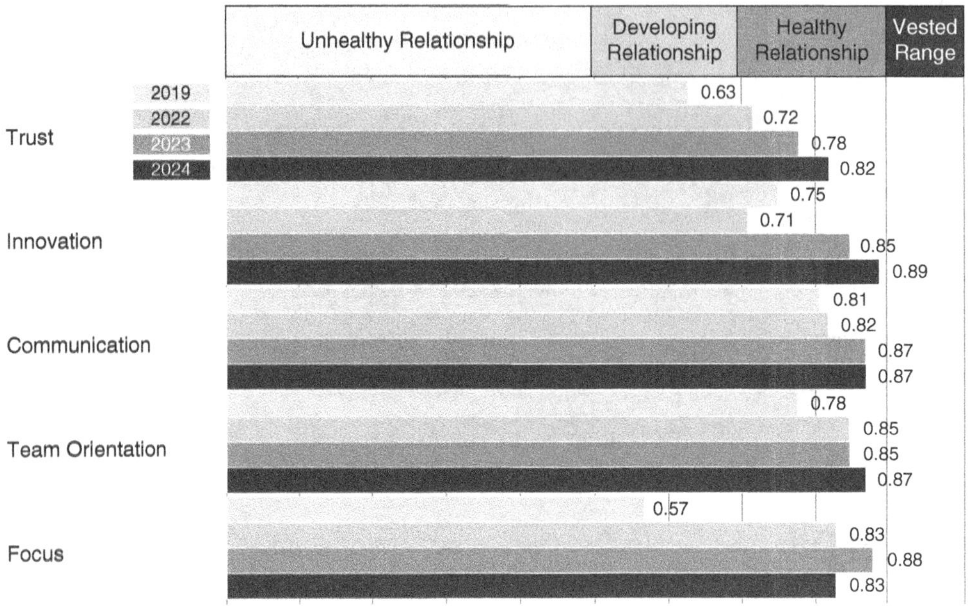

Figure 10: Improvements in Relationship Health

BUSINESS RELATIONSHIP MODEL

Once the parties have identified and chosen each other through the partner assessment process, they need to focus on the structure and mechanics of their business relationship. Paramount among their concerns from a dispute prevention standpoint will be selecting a business relationship model that aligns the economic interests of the business partners and promotes a collaborative approach to conducting the business.

Why

The structure contracting parties use as the foundation for their relationship plays a significant role in helping the parties manage their interaction and any resulting conflicts. Research shows that relying on market dynamics and traditional transactional contracts is inadequate for more complex relationships (e.g., outsourcing agreements, franchise agreements, and distribution agreements), where the parties are interdependent and confront high switching costs.[10] This is because

10. Richard Makadok & Russell Wayne Coff, *Both Market and Hierarchy: An Incentive-System Theory of Hybrid Governance Forms*, 34 A.M.R. 297–319 (2012) (differences between markets and hierarchies).

traditional transactional contracts provide very little in the way of mitigating structural or other kinds of conflicts, as they generally proceed from one party seeking to maximize its interest at the expense of the other.

As business environments have grown more complex with greater interdependencies (e.g., outsourcing deals, strategic alliances, and complex public works initiatives), contracting professionals have devised alternative contracting models to better align the parties' interests around the objectives of the contract.

Alternative contracting models often use a shared risk and incentive pool to align interests which helps the parties shift behaviors away from maximizing their own short-term benefit to behaviors that promote collaboration.

Some models go so far as to require contracting parties to waive or limit claims against each other while allowing only certain claims, like claims for intellectual property violations or willful default, to be preserved.[11] In so doing, these alternative contracting models help reduce disputes. Case in point is research on large urban infrastructure projects using a particular type of alternative contracting model, called integrated project delivery (IPD) model. The research shows a correlation with reduced disputes due to improved organization, leadership, and strengthened planning aimed at managing and mitigating risk.[12] In addition, UT's research indicates contracting parties using a Vested sourcing business model have not reported a dispute since the model's introduction in 2010.[13]

Below we highlight various relationship models and profile three that we have seen work well in practice.

How It Works

Performance-based agreements, Integrated Project Delivery (IPD), alliance contracting, a Vested sourcing business model and public-private partnerships (PPPs) have all emerged as credible alternative contracting models. In this book we profile three models we believe have the most promise for preventing disputes: IPDs, alliance contracting, and the Vested sourcing business model. We share a brief overview of how each of these three models works.

---

11. Andrew Wong & Ethan McCarthy, *Integrated Project Delivery Model in Canada: What You Need to Know*, Osler 1–4 (Nov. 23, 2018), https://www.osler.com/en/resources/transactions/2018/integrated-project-delivery-model-in-canada-what-you-need-to-know.

12. Meisam Mahboubi Niazmandi et al., *Integrated Project Delivery (IPD) Capabilities on Reducing Claims in Urban Underground Projects: A Hybrid FAHP-FTOPSIS Approach*, 7 Sustainable Futures 1–19 (2024) (traditional approaches and complex relationships).

13. UT only tracks contracting parties that have gone through UT's Vested program. As there are books on the Vested methodology, it is possible some contracting parties have adopted a Vested approach without doing the formal training and these contracts could have disputes.

Integrated Project Delivery Agreements (IPDs)

IPD agreements, used in the construction industry, create a temporary, virtual, or formal organization with management and decision-making processes. IPDs motivate collaboration throughout the design and construction process, tying stakeholder success to project success. The first IPDs emerged in the 1960s. The American Institute for Architects (AIA) has created an "authoritative guide that walks you through the principles of Integrated Project Delivery so you can advocate for, set up, and deliver integrated projects."[14]

A successful IPD contract has decision-making methods and processes that each team member must accept and agree to abide by. In a fully integrated project, ultimate decision-making abilities are not vested in a single team member. Rather, all decisions are unanimous and made by the defined decision-making body. In an integrated project, one overriding principle directs the decision-making body: all decisions represent the best interest of the project.

Alliance Contracting

Alliance contracting, or alliancing, is also used for complex construction contracts. Alliancing originated in the United Kingdom in the early 1990s to improve the delivery method of complex construction projects such as offshore oil and gas rigs.[15] Alliancing is an alternative delivery model that aims to achieve project goals through collaboration and teamwork. With alliance contracting, designers, constructors, clients, and suppliers work in an integrated team under an alliance contract using a legal framework consisting of an owner and one or more non-owner participants (NOPs) to deliver capital works projects. These parties operate as a single entity, collectively sharing project risks.

Alliance arrangements have three common principles:[16]

1. All alliances are agreements between two or more separate firms that involve ongoing resource contributions from each to create joint value (including technology, staff, customers, brands, capital, and equipment).
2. All alliances are considered to be an "incomplete contract," a phrase from the economics of law that refers to an agreement in which the terms cannot be completely specified and agreed to at the outset.
3. All alliances share joint decision-making to manage the business and share the value.

---

14. *Integrated Project Delivery: A Guide*, AIA, https://www.aia.org/resource-center/integrated-project-delivery-guide.

15. Karl Wieneke, *Engaging SME Subcontactors on Alliance Delivered Infrastructure Projects*, Unitec Inst. Tech. (2010) (background on alliancing).

16. James D. Bamford et al., Mastering Alliance Strategy: A Comprehensive Guide to Design, Management, and Organization (2003).

Alliance contracting is becoming increasingly popular in the Australian and U.K. construction industry. The Australian government has even issued *National Alliance Contracting Guidelines*.[17]

Vested/Vested Outsourcing Agreements

The Vested sourcing business model was born from research by the University of Tennessee (UT) in 2010 as a way to create highly collaborative win-win outsourcing agreements.[18] A Vested agreement combines a formal relational contract (see more in chapter 4) with an outcome-based economic model where the parties create and share value above and beyond the conventional buy–sell economics of a transaction-based agreement. In short, the parties are equally committed—vested—in each other's success.

While Vested agreements can be used for construction projects, they are typically used for longer-term complex business-to-business (B2B) relationships such as strategic partnerships, strategic supplier and outsourcing relationships, and critical labor services agreements.

Contracting parties wanting to create a strategic Vested partnership establish a joint (cross-functional and cross-company) deal architect team (DAT) that co-creates the contract following Five Rules and ten contractual elements. The goal is to align interests in all aspects of the business and contract. Much of UT's work on the Vested model is open source, making it attractive for companies to learn more, and if desired, they can formally train team members through UT's Certified Deal Architect program.

Vested agreements are similar to alliances and IPDs because contracting parties rely on shared risk/shared reward economics. However, Vested differs from alliances and IPDs in that it creates a formal relational contract. The contract represents a flexible contract framework that helps the parties better navigate changing business conditions. While parties can create physical co-ownership (e.g., a joint venture), they typically do not. Rather, they align interests through a win-win outcome-based economic model and manage the relationship with relational contracting principles, which the parties formally agree to.

Case Study

bp (formerly the British Petroleum Company and BP Amoco) set out to transform its workplace contracts when Wendy Cuthbert—bp's Global Head of Workplace Solutions—encouraged bp's workplace leaders to explore UT's Vested

17. *National Alliance Contracting Guidelines*, Austl. Gov't 1–166 (2015) (popularity of alliance contracting in Australia).

18. Kate Vitasek et al., Vested Outsourcing: Five Rules that will Transform Outsourcing (2d ed. 2013).

methodology. In the spring of 2020, bp selected JLL to help them reimagine their workplace solutions across the globe.

This meant big changes. For starters, bp would shift from four primary suppliers to having one global supplier. In addition, it would mean completely reimagining how they outsourced their workplace services. A joint bp–JLL DAT set out to create a win-win Vested agreement with the goal for bp to win by reducing cost, increasing service, and achieving workplace sustainability goals while JLL would win with earned incentives to increase their business and profits.

The DAT began to work through the Vested methodology starting in late April 2020. Over the next five months, the joint DAT challenged every aspect of how bp and JLL would work by following the Vested methodology's Five Rules.

Rule 1: Outcome-Based Business Model

The first transformation was a fundamental shift in the underlying business model of how bp outsourced. The parties would make the leap from a tried-and-true transactional business model (i.e., paying per transaction) to an outcome-based business model. A key step was to define the endgame: a shared vision and six mutually defined desired outcomes (Figure 11).

Figure 11: Six Mutually Defined Desired Outcomes

Rule 2: Focusing on the What, Not the How

Next, the parties set out to address the scope of work. The scope was vast—spanning ninety-two sites in thirty-two countries. Facility types ranged from bp's expansive corporate campuses and the sprawling Pangborn Research and Development (R&D) facilities to strategic data centers to a one-story childcare facility.

bp and JLL applied Rule 2 by flipping the conventional concept of a Statement of Work (SOW) on its head by challenging bp to leverage the fact that JLL was the true expert in the services they would provide. Rather than bp write a SOW, the DAT co-created a taxonomy and workload allocation to define the scope. The taxonomy is an end-to-end inventory of the work needed to achieve the shared vision and desired outcomes, while the workload allocation outlined not only JLL's responsibilities, but also bp's responsibilities in supporting the partnership. As the parties rethought the delivery of workplace services, they created a list of transformation initiatives that would help the partners achieve their shared vision and desired outcomes.

Rule 3: Clearly Defined and Measurable Outcomes

Next, the DAT set out to rethink how bp measured success. Shifting to an outcome-based business model meant conventional service level agreements (SLAs) would be too narrowly focused because they would only measure how well JLL performed its tasks and not how well the parties collaborated to achieve the desired outcomes. The result was a complete reimagining of success measures where the parties defined success not against tasks but against the mutually defined desired outcomes. The parties linked eleven strategic metrics to the six desired outcomes. The shift was a radical refocus—measuring success against where they were going versus measuring performance against tasks JLL performed.

Rule 4: Pricing Model with Incentives to Optimize the Business

A key part of the party's ability to deliver on the desired outcomes would mean investing in transformation initiatives. The pricing model was designed so that the more successful JLL would be in earning incentives, the parties would be more successful in delivering on bp's transformation goals. This meant shifting from having a transactional "price" to having a "pricing model" with incentives to optimize the business. Some of the key design principles of the pricing model include:

- *Fully transparent "cost-is-the-cost" mantra*: Full transparency enabled the parties to identify the true cost drivers for both organizations and to create a model that incentivizes investments that will help achieve the desired outcomes.
- *Both monetary and non-monetary incentives*: Incentives reward JLL for achieving success against the desired outcomes. For example, monetary incentives reward JLL for driving down costs and non-monetary incentives reward JLL for achieving non-cost-related desired outcomes such as helping bp achieve its zero-emissions goal.
- *Ensure cost savings are not prioritized over quality and safety*: The pricing model included "unlock" targets based on certain conditions; a safety lock meant that JLL must achieve a certain safety threshold to unlock other incentives.

Rule 5: Insight versus Oversight Governance

The last thing the DAT needed to reimagine was how the parties would manage the relationship and keep in continual alignment when "business happens." The governance framework included comprehensive processes for managing the relationship, managing transformation initiatives, and managing dynamic compliance and regulatory needs. The companies embedded formal governance mechanisms such as those outlined in chapter 5. To help operationalize the agreement, the parties adopted "2-in-a-Box" teams where bp and JLL team members would work closely around the world.

The Results

bp and JLL agree that a Vested sourcing business model fundamentally changed the way bp works with JLL. The parties have created a highly collaborative culture versus the previous buyer-supplier approach typical of most outsourcing relationships. Innovation is at the heart of their culture. This shift produces real benefits as team members challenge the status quo and continue to implement transformation initiatives. The team members call the results the power of *and*—lower costs for bp's procurement organization *and* better operational results for bp's workplace groups *and* higher profits for JLL. Figure 12 highlights a sampling of the results just two years after signing the contract.

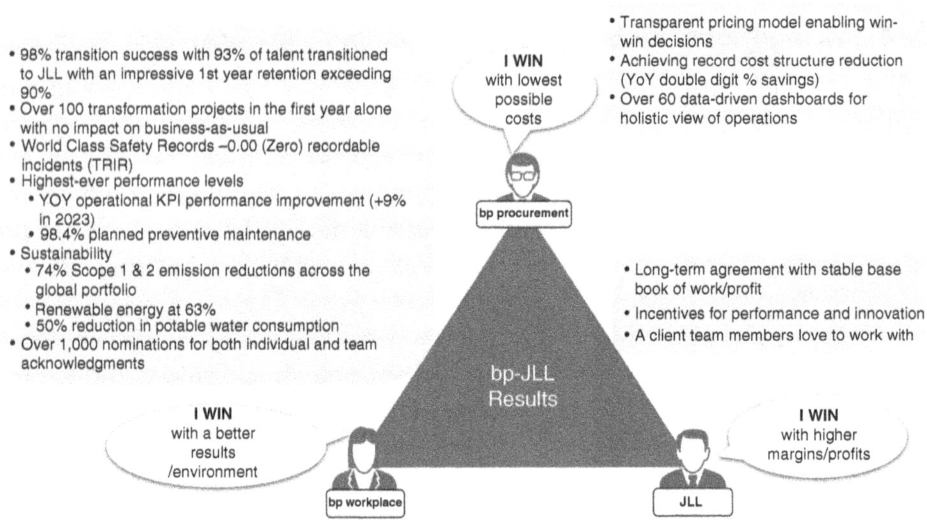

Figure 12: bp-JLL Results from the Vested Relationship Model

In the first year alone, the companies delivered over one-hundred transformation initiatives designed to create value against the desired outcomes. By the end of the third year they had logged over 500 innovations. While the results are rewarding, one thing team members are most proud of is the cultural shift. For example, the parties used a CaT assessment, which quantifies the soft side of a win-win approach, with a remarkable 95 percent score for "team orientation" and 86 percent score for "innovation"—considered world-class. With such a collaborative win-win business model, the parties proudly report no contract claims or disputes after four years.

DEAL FACILITATOR

One innovative approach to help parties create a contract that is good for both parties is using a deal facilitator. A deal facilitator is a trained professional facilitator employed jointly by contracting parties to assist in negotiating and/or drafting a fair and balanced agreement on behalf of contracting parties.

L. Michael Hager and Robert Pritchard introduced the idea of using a third-party neutral to assist with deal development in a 1999 *Foreign Investment Law Journal* article.[19] The paper states using a third-party neutral is a "potentially powerful tool for lawyers who negotiate global deals for parties who seek wise and fair agreements in complex environments. It has as much to do with issues of culture, values, trust, and adaptability as it has to do with law and contracts."[20]

Why

Negotiations of any business deal, especially large and complex deals, can be fraught with a myriad of difficulties. For example, one study found at least 40 percent and up to 70 percent of all joint ventures are estimated to fail.[21] Key reasons are miscommunication and misunderstandings between the parties, which lead to mistrust and cause the negotiations to reach an impasse.[22] The use of deal facilitators is intended to overcome these obstacles.

Joan Stearns Johnsen, an expert in deal facilitation and a Master Lecturer and Master Legal Skills Professor at the University of Florida Levin College of Law,

---

19. L. Michael Hager & Robert Pritchard, *Deal Mediation: How ADR Techniques Can Help Achieve Durable Agreements in the Global Markets*, 14 F.I.L.J. 1–15 (1999) (using a third party neutral to assist with deal development).

20. Scott R. Peppet, Associate Professor of Law at the University of Colorado School of Law, contributed a compelling article on the topic, *Contract Formation in Imperfect Markets—Should We Use Mediators to Make Deals?* 19 Ohio St. J. Disp. Resol. 283 (2004) (deal facilitation). For a good history on Deal Facilitation, *see Deal Mediation*, International Mediation Institute, https://imimediation.org/resources/deal-mediation/.

21. Patricia E. Farrell & Dan Bova, *The 7 Deadly Sins of Joint Ventures*, Entrepreneur (Sep. 2, 2014), https://www.entrepreneur.com/business-news/the-7-deadly-sins-of-joint-ventures/236987.

22. *Id.*

suggests the beauty of using a neutral deal facilitator is that they have no stake in the outcomes and can apply their skills "in an evenhanded manner to serve the interests of the deal rather than those of any party in interest."[23] She argues that when contracting parties use agents (e.g., outside or in-house counsel or consulting advisory firms working on behalf of only one party), the agent is subject to the same self-serving psychological bias that their client has.[24]

When contracting parties use a deal facilitator, the neutral has no incentive to obtain any specific terms of benefit to a particular party. For this reason, the deal facilitator can engage in "reality testing" of proposals and positions. For example, a deal facilitator can help a party who is opportunistically seeking terms that may generate distrust or resentment to see the benefit of adopting more evenhanded terms that promote business harmony and the long-term health of the relationship.

How It Works

The general idea of a deal facilitator is similar to that of a mediator, except the third-party neutral supports contracting parties during the design and architecting of the deal rather than supporting the parties in resolving a dispute after they sign the contract. Like a mediator, a deal facilitator should be neutral and have excellent facilitation skills to help bridge misalignments between contracting parties. Professor Johnsen suggests that a deal facilitator is ideal for complex deals or cross-cultural negotiations where regional differences and divergent bargaining styles complicate the effort to reach an agreement.[25]

Using a deal facilitator starts with contracting parties engaging the deal facilitator. For the deal facilitator to remain neutral, the parties should split the cost. When selecting a deal facilitator, it is important to check any country or state-specific guidelines that might limit a lawyer acting as a third-party neutral. For example, the State of Washington has guidelines for lawyers wishing to work as third-party neutrals.[26]

Deal facilitators should facilitate communication, manage difficult dynamics and conversations, use relationship-building skills, and generate options to help the parties reach a successful, fair, and balanced agreement.

---

23. Joan Stearns Johnsen, *Alternative "Deal" Resolution: The Facilitated Negotiation of Transactions*, 30 Windsor Rev. Leg. Soc. Iss. 1–33 (2011) (benefits of using a neutral deal facilitator).

24. For example, endowment effect, optimistic overconfidence, and reactive devaluation.

25. Joan Stearns Johnsen, *supra* note 23.

26. *Washington Rules of Professional Conduct*, Wash. St. Bar Ass'n 1–105 (2021) (guidelines for lawyers who work as third-party neutrals). The concept of lawyers needing to adhere to guidelines to be a neutral applies much more broadly than just deal facilitation.

Ideally, deal facilitators are knowledgeable in the contracting parties' business area or industry. Typical roles of a deal facilitator include:

- Facilitating communications that build relationship trust.
- Keeping contracting parties focused on the objective versus parochial self-interest.
- Helping the parties to determine, sooner rather than later, whether a deal is possible.
- Assisting the parties in identifying what they need instead of what an individual party may want.
- Helping the parties work through problems that may arise during the negotiation.
- Making sure that the parties allocate risks realistically so that each risk is allocated to the party best able to manage, absorb, or insure against the risk.
- Engaging in reality testing of proposals with impartiality and objectivity and, when appropriate, assisting in generating options.
- Helping the parties to create a Dispute Management System as part of their relationship.
- Encouraging the parties to establish a separate negotiating committee of representatives of the parties, which would design a Dispute Management System and would continue as a champion for relationship strengthening throughout the course of their relationship.

Case Study

Vancouver Island Health Authority (Island Health) and South Island Hospitalists Inc. (SIHI) provide a good example of how the parties engaged a third-party neutral to help them resolve a contract standstill.[27] Between 2000 and 2014, Island Health and SIHI had gone through contentious contract negotiations four times. Despite attempts at negotiation, the contract expired in July 2014; ultimately, the sides reached an interim agreement with the hopes of reaching a long-term agreement that fall. However, almost one year later, in April 2015, the *Times Colonist* summed up the situation with the headline, "One year later, no sign of deal for Greater Victoria Hospitalists."[28]

The parties—recognizing the critical need to build a new relationship—changed personnel in the fall of 2015. However, the relationship was so broken

27. Kate Vitasek & William DiBenedetto, *The Island Health—Hospitalist Journey to Vested: A New Day, A New Way*, Univ. Tenn. (2018).

28. Cindy E. Harnett, *One Year Later, No Sign of Deal for Greater Victoria Hospitalists*, Times Colonist (April 8, 2015), https://www.timescolonist.com/local-news/one-year-later-no-sign-of-deal-for-greater-victoria-hospitalists-4621075.

that contract negotiations remained at an impasse; neither side knew how to proceed. Simply put, both sides were stuck.

Both parties agreed to send key leaders and stakeholders to engage a neutral deal facilitator from The Forefront Group (TFG). The deal facilitator—Bonnie Keith, a Certified Deal Architect—recommended the parties participate in a three-day "alignment" workshop to get the contract negotiations back on track.

To prepare for the workshop, TFG had Island Health and SIHI complete a CaT assessment. TFG also did a contract review to determine if structural flaws in their existing agreement could be causing misalignment and perverse incentives. Lastly, TFG interviewed both parties to better learn about their background and situation.

The parties held the alignment workshop at an offsite location in May 2016, away from the hospital campuses. The offsite location was selected because there were no clinical or administrative distractions. But equally important, it offered a "neutral" territory. Twelve Island Health administrators and nine SIHI hospitalists attended the workshop.

The workshop kicked off with a light-hearted ice-breaker to set the tone and to help the parties get to know each other on a more personal level. TFG then shared the results of the CaT assessment—starting with a Word Cloud of the adjectives team members used to describe the relationship, which included words such as toxic, distrustful, adversarial, and opaque.

Courtney Peereboom, Director of Special Projects and In-Facility Care at Island Health, was disheartened by what she saw.

"Seeing the words on the Word Cloud from that survey was very disturbing. When you look back at it, we were in a terrible place," she said.

Before going into the detailed CaT results, TFG asked workshop attendees to write down three adjectives describing an ideal relationship between Island Health and SIHI. Each participant wrote down three words. During a break, a second Word Cloud was prepared, but this time, the words represented hope for a "future state" in the relationship, with words like collaborative, trusting, respectful, and honest. The "Today" and "Future State" Word Clouds were posted at the front of the room, with TFG challenging the parties to think about how they might change their behaviors and begin to "live into" the future state.

Dr. Milvi Tiislar, an SIHI hospitalist, describes her reaction to seeing the words. "It was very powerful to see a graphical depiction of all the negative emotions. There was a huge contrast describing what we all wanted the relationship to be. It was both eye-opening and nice to see that we had all described the same fundamental things that we wanted."

A key part of the workshop was for the parties to understand the perception gaps uncovered in the CaT assessment and why the parties had such deep-seated mistrust. SIHI hospitalist and lead negotiator Dr. Jean Maskey explains, "It was very freeing to think that we could kind of ditch all the negativity and old history and choose to go with the new in the space of six hours. It was a miracle."

The second day of the workshop focused on creating a "Statement of Intent," a two-page document that laid the foundation for a future relationship by establishing a shared vision, Guiding Principles, and mutual desired outcomes. Dr. Mann, an Island Health administrator, described the workshop as "therapeutic," helping the parties "have a strong feeling of empathy."

After the workshop, the parties continued to work with their deal facilitator to develop a formal relational contract. All agree they could not have broken the stalemate without a deal facilitator.

Dr. Slobodian credits using a deal facilitator with bringing "a completely different approach to traditional contract negotiations in turning around a situation that seemed, at the time, beyond repair."

Dr. Smith believes, "There was no way to create those relationships—the trust and the communication—without a third party with significant experience coming in and helping."

Janet Grove, legal counsel for Island Health shares, "The advantage is it (using a deal facilitator) creates a safer environment than at the arbitration or a court process. There is also an element of neutrality that is quite helpful because the facilitator can call a spade a spade when people are taking ridiculous positions or extreme positions or unfounded or are not following the Guiding Principles they agreed to."

Since signing their agreement, the parties have continued to tap into the neutral deal facilitator, but in the form of a modern standing neutral (see chapter 5 for more detail on a modern standing neutral) who continues to work with the parties to measure their relationship health using a CaT assessment and act as a sounding board for the parties. The parties have not had any disputes.

A LOOK AHEAD

In this chapter, we profiled three categories of dispute prevention mechanisms used when *entering* a business relationship: partner assessment, alternative business relationship models, and using a neutral deal facilitator. In the next chapter, we shift further along the Dispute Management Continuum and explore dispute prevention mechanisms contracting parties can use when they are *forming* their business relationship.

Chapter 4

Formalizing the Relationship

Once contracting parties have agreed to formally enter a business relationship, there are several proven dispute prevention mechanisms they can embed into their contractual relationship. Embedding preventive mechanisms in a parties' formal contract can help the parties manage their expectations and feelings of entitlement and reduce the risk of misunderstandings.[1] This book covers six such preventive mechanisms.

In this chapter, we look at how contract architecture can prevent disputes by making contracts easier to understand with good contract design and easier to execute with smart contracts. We also explore how formal relational contracts create a flexible contract framework and embed relational contract constructs to help parties stay in continual alignment when internal or external changes in the business environment require modification. We then consider how companies use risk/reward alignment to create fair and balanced contracts that motivate good performance. Lastly, we explore contractual clauses organizations can use to guide the management and escalation of problems to prevent disputes (Figure 13).

Contract Architecture
Contract Design
Formal Relational Contract
Smart Contracts

Risk/Reward Alignment
Realistic Risk Allocation
Incentives

Contractual Clauses

Figure 13: Prevention Mechanisms for Formalizing the Relationship

1. Henry Allen Blair, *Anticipating Procedural Innovation: How and When Parties Calibrate Procedure through Contract*, 72 Okla. L. Rev. 797–855 (2020) (preventive mechanisms in formal contracts).

CONTRACT ARCHITECTURE

Contract architecture refers to the framing or scaffolding of how a contract is put together. Contract architecting is different from contract drafting. In this book, we cover three preventive mechanisms classified as contract architecture: contract design, formal relational contracts and smart contracts.

Contract Design

Contract design is the art, science, and practice of developing contracts that are easy to use and execute. Two contract design techniques gaining traction are plain-language contract drafting and using visualization and design patterns to make it easier for readers to understand and use contracts.

Plain language contracting represents a conscious decision to move away from a more formal and legalistic style of writing contracts. The non-profit Plain Language Association International (PLAIN) notes that with plain language drafting principles, "wording, structure, and design are so clear that the intended audience can easily find what they need, understand what they find, and use that information."[2]

Visualization is also growing in popularity. Visualization relies on diagrams, images, and visually structured layouts to make contracts more searchable, readable, and understandable. Research on contract visualization shows people can read contracts faster and make fewer comprehension mistakes. In addition, good visualization also makes it easy to find and interpret critical information when there is a difference of opinion.

Why

Studies reveal contracts are getting longer,[3] more complex,[4] and are harder to read.[5] Contracts that are hard to read or contain ambiguities are likely to lead to misunderstandings and disputes.[6] Research in the construction industry found

---

2. *Who We Are*, PLAIN, https://plainlanguagenetwork.org/about/who-we-are/.

3. John C. Coates, IV, *Why Have M&A Contracts Grown? Evidence from Twenty Years of Deals*, 333 E.C.G.I. 1–65 (2016) (length of merger and acquisitions contracts).

4. Albert Choi & George Triantis, *Multi-Stage Contracting* (Working Paper, on file with authors) (2014) ("some agreements are simply too complex to be completed in a single stage").

5. John C. Coates, IV, *Why Have M&A Contracts Grown? Evidence from Twenty Years of Deals*, 333 E.C.G.I. 1–65 (2016) (contracts are harder to read).

6. Petra Hietanen-Kunwald & Helena Haapio, *Effective Dispute Prevention and Resolution through Proactive Contract Design*, 5 J.S.C.A.N. 3, 6–7 (2021) (contracts fueling misunderstandings and disputes); Thomas D. Barton et al., *Reframing Contract Design: Integrating Business, Legal, Design, and Technology Perspectives*, *in* RSCH. HANDBOOK CONT.

that poorly drafted and incomplete documents and parties' failure to understand their contractual obligations were among the leading causes of disputes.[7] Contract design is emerging as a strategy to help organizations make their contracts easier to read, understand, and comply with.

Why should organizations care? An overly legalistic style can put off businesspeople who need to implement the contract requirements without distractions brought on by inaccessible legal jargon. If the language is unclear or dense, businesspeople may misunderstand requirements and fail to comply with the contract terms, which can lead to a dispute. While some organizations may not initially care, we argue they will likely need to start caring because, increasingly, government policies and regulations mandate using plain language. For example, did you know that today, there are over 500 statutes and regulations requiring plain language in contracts or contract-related documents?[8] While many of the laws are focused on consumer contracts, some apply to commercial contracts as well.[9]

How It Works

Companies like General Electric Company (GE) are behind the movement to use plain-language contracts and profiled their experience and success in a *Harvard Business Review* article.[10] GE's Shaun Burton refers to a plain-language contract as "a contract that a high schooler could understand with zero context or explanation."[11] Advocates for plain-language contracts suggest writing short paragraphs and adding examples to help users understand the point. This means eliminating legalese such as "herein," "hereinafter," "the aforementioned," and "pursuant to."

Software is making it easy for organizations to use plain language. Gary Kinder, a lawyer by training, developed WordRake software to "rake" documents of the legalese that clogs and obscures meaning.[12] Rudolph Flesch, a supporter of the Plain English Movement, created the Flesch Reading Ease and Flesch-Kincaid

---

Design 33–54 (Marcelo Corrales Compagnucci et al., eds., 2022) (misunderstandings and disputes).

7. *Construction Disputes Reporter 2023*, Arcadis, https://www.arcadis.com/en-us/knowledge-hub/perspectives/north-america/united-states/2023/construction-disputes-report-2023.

8. Michael Blaise, *496 U.S. Laws Require Plain-Language Contracts*, Cont. Nerds (Mar. 15, 2023), https://web.archive.org/web/20230325205543/https://contractnerds.com/496-u-s-laws-require-plain-language-contracts/.

9. *Id.*

10. Shawn Burton, *The Case for Plain-Language Contracts*, Harv. Bus. Rev., Jan.–Feb. 2018, at 134.

11. *Id.*

12. *About WordRake*, WordRake, https://www.wordrake.com/editing-software-for-writing-professionals-about.

Grade Level tests, both of which analyze a document and provide a readability score.[13] World Contracting and Commerce (WCC) recommends having a Flesch Reading Ease target of 55–60 (with the higher being the better) and a Flesch-Kincaid Grade Level at no more than eleventh grade (with a lower score the better). Microsoft Word has integrated the Flesch reading statistics into their software making it easy to test a contract's readability.

WCC provides some of the best thinking on contract visualization and offers a free "contract design pattern library" that includes examples of various contract design patterns.[14] Some design patterns can help explain contract information better. For example:

- *Emphasis* highlights key information and focuses readers' attention on it. You can emphasize things (e.g., bold font) to give visual prominence to things you don't want the reader to overlook, such as key terms/defined words, deadlines, and exceptions. Emphasis patterns should be used sparingly and limited to only the key information.
- *Explainers* help users better understand difficult information. An explainer could be simply providing more detail to properly frame the information. For example, a contract may have an incentive formula the parties use to determine incentive payouts to a supplier. An explainer will add additional information or even profile a scenario or example.
- *Visualization* techniques (the use of maps, diagrams, illustrations, and photos) are good to use when text alone does not clearly convey the message. Visualization techniques can clarify complex information. These techniques are also helpful when readers of the content are unfamiliar with the vocabulary or phraseology of the contract text. For example, it may be easier for business or technical people to grasp the information if it appears with a familiar diagram.

Other contract design patterns help contracting parties structure and organize their contract to make them easier to navigate. Design patterns are especially useful for busy businesspeople who strategically read a contract (e.g., skimming, scanning, and previewing) when trying to find important information. WCC suggests using the following contract design patterns to improve the structure and organization of their contract:

- *Navigation* patterns help readers find their way through the document and access necessary information. They offer a visual and logical access

13. *Learn How to Use the Flesch-Kincaid Grade Level Formula*, Readability Formulas, https://readabilityformulas.com/learn-how-to-use-the-flesch-kincaid-grade-level/.

14. *Explore Library*, WorldCC Found., https://contract-design.worldcc.com/library.

structure, with clear and well-organized headings, sections, pages, cross-references and indexes, tables of contents, and menus.

- *Layering* creates a visual hierarchy, which can prevent information overload. *Layout patterns* help organize content on document pages so it is easily readable, legible, and searchable. This enables readers to find the information they want more easily.

WCC recommends organizations pick and mix the various techniques that work best for their situation. For example, a visualization technique may work for one clause while an explainer technique might work better for a different clause.

Case Studies

The Support Structure Agreement between Rogers Communications Inc. and Bell Aliant Regional Communications Income Fund is a widely cited case study on how contract design can prevent disputes.[15] Rogers contracted with Aliant for support of their telephone poles in Canada. Aliant terminated the agreement after a rate disagreement—believing they had the right to terminate with a one-year notice. However, Rogers—believing the contract was still valid—objected to the termination because it would result in a rate hike.

The parties engaged in an eighteen-month dispute over the meaning of the following wording in their termination clause: "This agreement shall be effective from the date it is made and shall continue in force for a period of five (5) years from the date it is made, and thereafter for successive five (5) year terms, unless and until terminated by one-year prior notice in writing by either party." Interestingly, neither party drafted the clause. Instead, their agreement was based on the English language standard form issued by the Canadian Radio-Television and Telecommunications Commission.

In figure 14, contract design experts and scholars Stefania Passera and Helena Haapio illustrate how a simple graphic visualization would have prevented confusion.[16]

15. Ian Austen, *The Comma that Costs 1 Million Dollars (Canadian)*, N.Y. Times, Oct. 25, 2006, https://www.nytimes.com/2006/10/25/business/worldbusiness/25comma.html; Helena Haapio, *Contract Clarity through Visualization—Preliminary Observations and Experiments*, 15th Int'l Conf. on Info. Visualisation 337–42 (2011) (Rogers Communications Inc. and Bell Aliant Regional Communications Income Fund); Helena Haapio & George J. Siedel, A Short Guide to Contract Risk (Short Guides to Business Risk) (2013); Petra Hietanen-Kunwald & Helena Haapio, *Effective Dispute Prevention and Resolution through Proactive Contract Design*, 5 J.S.C.A.N. 3, 6–7 (2021) (Rogers Communications Inc. and Bell Aliant Regional Communications Income Fund).

16. Stefania Passera & Helena Haapio, *Facilitating Collaboration through Contract Visualization and Modularization*, ECCE '11: Proceedings of the 29th Annual European Conference on Cognitive Ergonomics (2011) (how graphic visualizations can prevent confusion).

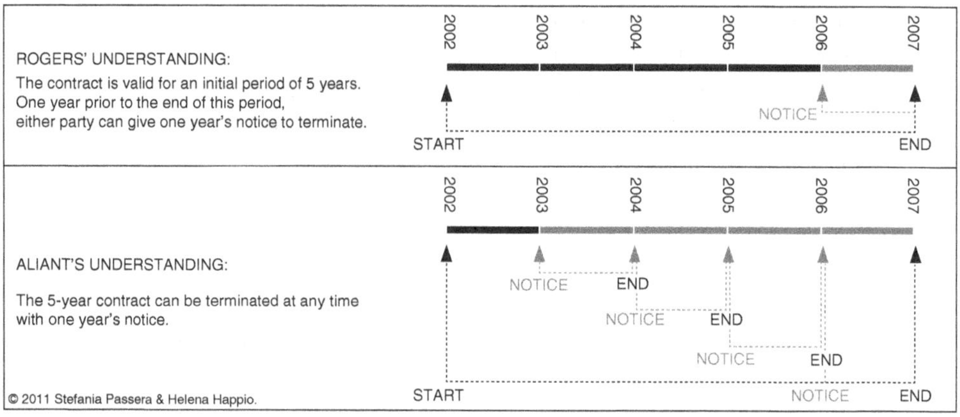

Figure 14: Visualization of Contract Termination Clause

The two graphics show how each party's interpretation led to different understandings of the clause. Haapio argues, "Had the parties or their lawyers drawn two simple timelines on a flipchart, they could have seen the gap between their understandings. Had they discovered this, discussed their needs and expectations and articulated their interpretation of the meaning of the clause, they could have come to a mutual understanding and removed the ambiguity—or they would have realized that they had no basis for a deal and walked away."[17]

The case study proves that sometimes a picture is worth 1,000 words—or, in the case of Rogers and Aliant, can prevent an eighteen-month contract dispute.

A *Havard Business Review* article on GE's shift to using plain-language contracts provides an excellent example of what it looks like to recast contract clauses with plain language.[18] The following before and after examples show how an indemnification clause for a services contract was revised for clarity and conciseness:

> BEFORE
>
> Customer shall indemnify, defend, and hold Company harmless from any and all claims, suits, actions, liabilities, damages and costs, including reasonable attorneys' fees and court costs, incurred by Company arising from or based upon (a) any actual or alleged infringement of any United States patents, copyright, or other intellectual property right of a third party, attributable to Customer's use of the licensed System with other software, hardware or configuration not either provided by Company or specified in Exhibit D.3, (b) any data, information, technology, system or other Confidential Information disclosed or made available

17. Petra Hietanen-Kunwald & Helena Haapio *supra* note 15.
18. Shawn Burton *supra* note 10 at 134.

by Customer to Company under this Agreement, (c) the use, operation, maintenance, repair, safety, regulatory compliance or performance of any aircraft owned, leased, operated, or maintained by Customer of (d) any use, by Customer or by a third party to whom Customer has provided the information, of Customer's Flight Data, the System, or information generated by the System.

AFTER

If an arbitrator finds that this contract was breached and losses were suffered because of that breach, the breaching party will compensate the non-breaching party for such losses or provide the remedies specified in Section 8 if Section 8 is breached.[19]

Formal Relational Contracts

Legal scholars Ian Macneil and Stewart Macaulay began studying the concept of relational contracts in the 1960s. Relational contracts embrace the fact that many business dealings are not once-and-done deals but rather consist of ongoing business relationships where deal partners have a series of interactions over a long period (e.g., franchise agreements, outsourcing agreements, and long-term distribution partnerships). The idea is that business is dynamic, and contracting parties need to create a flexible contract framework in which they put the relationship first.

Macaulay and Macneil's concept of relational contracts never gained traction in practice, primarily because the "relational" aspects of contracting happened outside of the written contract. Lawyers eschewed relational contracts as "fluffy" and akin to a "handshake deal"—something most lawyers and commercial businesspeople see as risky.

The book *Contracting in the New Economy: Using Relational Contracts to Boost Trust and Collaboration in Strategic Business Relationships* distinguishes between an *informal relational contract* and a *formal relational contract*. A key difference is that a formal relational contract formally incorporates the relational elements into a party's physical contract. The book defines a formal relational contract[20] as: "A legally enforceable written contract establishing a commercial partnership within a flexible contractual framework based on social norms and jointly defined objectives, prioritizing a relationship with the continuous alignment of interests before commercial transactions."

A key goal is to create a flexible contracting framework that supports the dynamic nature of the business partner relationship and formalizes the relational constructs to help keep the parties stay in continual alignment when "business happens."

19. *Id.*

20. David Frydlinger et al., Contracting the New Economy: Using Relational Contracts to Boost Trust and Collaboration in Strategic Business Relationships (2021).

The University of Tennessee (UT) has been studying and teaching formal relational contracting since 2010. Today, major organizations such as the Canadian government, Intel, DHL, AstraZeneca, Compass, Boeing, bp, Discovery Health, Jones Lang Lasalle, and the Swedish telecommunications firm Telia are successfully using formal relational contracts.

Why

A *Harvard Business Review* article, "A New Approach to Contracts," articulates why formal relational contracts are an excellent alternative to larger and more complex traditional purchasing contracts.[21]

The problem, the cause, and the solution

The Problem	The Cause	The Solution
Traditional purchasing contracts don't work in complex strategic relationships where the parties are highly dependent on each other, future events are unpredictable, and flexibility and trust are required. Instead of promoting the partnership-like relationships needed to cope with uncertainty, conventional contracts undermine them.	Companies have traditionally used contracts as protection against the possibility that one party will abuse its power to extract benefits at the expense of the other. This adversarial mindset creates a downward spiral of negative tit-for-tat behaviors.	A formal relational contract lays a foundation of trust, specifies mutual goals, and establishes governance structures to keep the parties' expectations and interests aligned over time.

When organizations seek to protect themselves from their contractual counterpart, it stems from a fear known as the *hold-up problem*: the fear that one party will exploit the other. The hold-up problem is exacerbated because complex contracts are by nature incomplete: it is impossible to predict the future, and inevitable changes in the business environment often require partners to revisit their contracts and make changes.

In a supply contract, for example, organizations use a range of tactics to ensure their counterpart doesn't take advantage of them after the contract signing. These

21. David Frydlinger et al., *A New Approach to Contracts*, Sept.–Oct. 2019, Harv. Bus. Rev., https://hbr.org/2019/09/a-new-approach-to-contracts.

include contracting with multiple suppliers, forcing suppliers to lock in prices, using termination for convenience clauses, or obligating suppliers to cover unanticipated tasks that arise after the initial contracting phase (scope sweep clause).[22] Some companies go so far as to install a "shadow organization" to micromanage the supplier.

"Contractual shading"—the term discussed in chapter 2 and introduced by Harvard University's Oliver Hart (the 2016 Nobel Prize winner in Economics for his work on contract theory)—occurs when a party isn't getting the outcome it expected from a deal and feels the other party is to blame or has not acted reasonably to mitigate the losses. The aggrieved party often cuts back on performance in subtle ways, sometimes even unconsciously, to compensate.

To help understand how contractual shading happens, imagine that a supplier of engineering services submits a proposal in a competitive bidding process and wins the contract. If demand is lower during the contract term than the buyer stated in the request for proposal or the scope expands in an unanticipated area, the supplier's profit will suffer. If the buyer refuses to adjust the supplier's fee or the Statement of Work (they have a scope sweep clause), the supplier may try to recoup losses by replacing the expensive A team on the project with its less costly C team.[23] This may lead to lower quality performance, which will tempt the buyer to retaliate by evoking a penalty clause. When left unchecked, shading leads to negative tit-for-tat behavior that can become a death spiral and lead to disputes.

A formal relational contract seeks to prevent a death spiral by committing the parties to a flexible contractual framework based on social norms and jointly defined objectives with a vow to prioritize the relationship health before the details of the commercial transaction. This is done by embedding relational constructs into the actual contract (versus having them reside outside of the contract).

How It Works

Researchers at UT developed a simple five-step relational contracting process that, when applied, creates a formal relational contract.[24]

---

22. Bonnie Keith et al., Strategic Sourcing in the New Economy: Harnessing the Potential of Sourcing Business Models in Modern Procurement (2016).

23. A scope sweep clause—used in outsourcing agreements—supplement statements of work by obligating a supplier to perform functions that may not be described in the statement of work description but are an inherent part of the services provided. For example, if a service provider takes over a company's in-house work, the scope sweep clause assumes if the work was being done in-house before outsourcing, the scope would appear in the contract even if the statement of work was silent on the task.

24. The five steps were originally proposed in UT coursework. They were later explained in the book *Getting to We: Negotiating Agreements for Highly Collaborative*

Step 1: Lay the foundation

Step 1 focuses on negotiating the foundation of the relationship before proceeding to the details of the actual deal. This includes having discussions about trust, transparency, and cultural fit between the trading partners. For example, one effective approach is to openly discuss transparency and agree on the types of information that should be transparent between the parties. A second example is addressing potential cultural fit issues (recall the Newfoundland Labrador Health Services case study in chapter 3). Consciously laying a strong foundation of trust, transparency, and cultural fit helps establish a "partnership mentality" that can prevent an adversarial mindset from eroding the relationship.

Step 2: Co-create a shared vision and objectives

Step 2 starts with contracting parties expressing what they want to achieve from their contractual relationship. It is important that all parties (not just the one with the upper hand) explain their desired outcomes and goals. Step 2 concludes with the parties agreeing on a shared vision and specific goals for the relationship.

Step 3: Adopt Guiding Principles

Once parties have clearly defined what they are trying to achieve, step 3 is adopting the Guiding Principles to which the parties commit. Guiding Principles are social norms that, when adopted, can help preemptively steer away from potential potholes. UT research shows six Guiding Principles, when combined, can help parties create a fair and balanced contract that helps prevent opportunism. The six Guiding Principles—reciprocity, autonomy, honesty, loyalty, equity, and integrity—form a framework for resolving potential misalignments when unforeseen circumstances occur.

> Steps 1–3 are combined into a "Statement of Intent." The parties typically embed the Statement of Intent into the contract at the beginning, which sets the tone for the entire contract. In addition, the parties develop the bulk of the agreement under the guidance of the Statement of Intent to ensure the actual contract terms and clauses support the intent of the relationship.

Step 4: Align expectations and interests

In step 4, the parties align expectations and interests as contractual clauses and schedules. Here, the parties negotiate the specific deal points such as

---

Business Agreements and further codified in the book *Contracting in the New Economy*. (*See* Jeanette Nyden et al., Getting to We: Negotiating Agreements for Highly Collaborative Business Agreements (2013); Frydlinger et al., *supra* note 20.)

responsibilities, pricing, metrics, etc. Getting step 4 right is where the rubber hits the road. Why? Unfortunately, many traditional transactional contracts—especially those written on form agreements—use clauses typically breaching one or more of the Guiding Principles. While the *concept* of the clauses themselves is *not* in breach of the Guiding Principles, the exact wording often favors the party with the most power. Take, for example, the below termination for convenience clause required by the state of Alabama:[25]

> The Owner may terminate this contract at any time by giving at least ten (10) days' notice in writing to the Contractor. If the contract is terminated by the Owner as provided herein, the Contractor will be paid for the time provided and expenses incurred up to the termination date.

A termination for convenience clause such as the one cited above creates an inherent perverse incentive for suppliers not to invest in a business relationship that one party can terminate so cavalierly.

Let's revisit the termination for convenience clause through the lens of relational contracting. Relational contracting experts suggest contracting parties replace a termination for convenience clause with a *termination for justified reason* clause. The parties can then specify under what justified conditions to terminate the contract early.

In addition, relational contracting experts suggest drafting exit provisions to align with the Guiding Principles. For example:

- The parties would turn to the reciprocity principle, creating bilateral termination rights for both the buyer and the supplier.
- Using the loyalty principle, the parties would agree on an appropriate off-ramp period, allowing ample time and support for the parties to unwind their relationships. This may or may not be symmetrical based on the dependency and ease of unwinding the relationship.
- The parties would rely on the equity principle when determining how to compensate the supplier for any asset-specific investments they may have made on behalf of the buying company that may not be fully amortized.

Using the Guiding Principles forces the parties to adopt a fresh view on common contractual clauses, shifting from using market or state power to working together to develop more fair and balanced contract clauses that are more fit for purpose. A key benefit is both parties align on more realistic expectations and are likely to work more collaboratively and reduce shading after the contract's signing.

There is seldom one "right" answer or solution with clauses. For example, a one-sided termination for convenience clause might be appropriate for a contract

25. *Sample Required Termination Clauses*, Alabama.Gov, https://adeca.alabama.gov/wp-content/uploads/Sample-Required-Termination-Clauses.docx.

where there is little dependency and investment by the supplier. But in another contract where the supplier has made significant investments, it could easily be incompatible with the equity Guiding Principle because the supplier may not be able to fairly recoup its investments.

Step 5: Stay aligned

In step 5, the contracting parties define the governance mechanisms they will use to stay aligned after signing the contract. This can involve regular check-ins, follow-ups, and feedback to track progress toward the parties' shared vision and goals. A key point in a relational contracting process is for the parties to define their governance and commitments to good governance practices before signing the contract. These governance mechanisms are formally embedded into the parties' contract (typically in the form of a governance schedule) and become a contractual commitment. For example, in a strategic outsourcing agreement, the parties may agree to Monthly Operations and Performance Reviews and Quarterly Business Reviews that are more strategic.

When to Use a Relational Contracting Process

It is important to understand that relational contractings are not for every business relationship. First, going through a relational contracting process takes time and effort. A typical organization has hundreds, if not thousands, of contracts. Investing in the process will not be worthwhile for smaller and low-risk contracts.

So, when should you invest the time? The choice to use a relational contracting process should be based on the characteristics of the deal and the relationship between the parties. At a high level, the two most important features to focus on are the *dependency* between the parties and the *risks* involved in the deal and relationship. The overall logic is simple: the higher the dependency and risk, the more crucial it is to apply a relational contract designed to continuously align the interests and expectations of the parties. The book *Contracting in the New Economy* suggests relational contracting is a good fit for complicated outsourcing and purchasing arrangements, strategic alliances, joint ventures, franchises, public-private partnerships, major construction projects, and collective bargaining agreements.[26]

Case Study[27]

Recall the Vancouver Island Health Authority and South Island Hospitalist, Inc. (SIHI) case study from chapter 3, where the parties engaged a deal facilitator to help them work through relationship issues causing a negotiation standstill.

---

26. Frydlinger et al., *supra* note 20.

27. Kate Vitasek & William DiBenedetto, *The Island Health—Hospitalist Journey to Toward: A New Day, A New Way*, Univ. Tenn. (2018).

As part of the discussions, the deal facilitator introduced using a relational contract. As part of the process, the parties developed a Statement of Intent (shared vision and Guiding Principles). The first two pages of the contract formally embedded the Statement of Intent into the contract. The contract reads:

> The Parties enter into this Agreement with the following Statement of Intent as our mutual-relationship philosophy and the principles under which we commit to operate. The Parties endeavor to abide by the Statement of Intent in all dealings during the term of this agreement in pursuit of our common shared vision. Together, we are a team that celebrates and advances excellence in care for all through shared responsibility, collaborative innovation, mutual understanding, and the courage to act in a safe and supportive environment.
>
> We will achieve this by building a relationship grounded in trust and respect, anchored in the following Guiding Principles and behaviors.
>
> Our **Guiding Principles** are social norms that will guide us in our actions and decision-making, especially during times of adversity.
>
> - *Reciprocity*: We conduct ourselves in the spirit of achieving mutual benefit and understanding. We recognize that this requires ongoing give and take. We each bring unique strengths and resources that enable us to overcome our challenges and celebrate our successes.
> - *Autonomy*: We give each other the freedom to manage and make decisions within the framework of our unique skills, training, and professional responsibilities. We individually commit to make decisions and take actions that respect and strengthen the collective interest to achieve our shared vision.
> - *Honesty*: We will all model truthfulness and authenticity even when that makes us vulnerable or uncomfortable. This includes honesty about facts, unknowns, feelings, intentions, perceptions, and preferred outcomes.
> - *Loyalty*: We are committed to our relationship. We will value each other's interests as we value our own. Standing together through adversity, we will achieve our shared vision.
> - *Equity*: We are committed to fairness, which does not always mean equality. We will make decisions based on a balanced assessment of needs, risks, and available resources.
> - *Integrity*: To achieve extraordinary results, our actions will be intentionally consistent with our words and agreements. Decisions will not be made arbitrarily but will align with our shared vision and principles. Our collective words and actions will be for the greater good of the relationship and the provision of patient-centered care.

The parties then worked through step 4—aligning interests with the scope, metrics, and pricing model. Dr. Jean Maskey, the lead negotiator for SIHI, points to the Statement of Intent as a key success factor in helping them shift to relational contracting and putting the concept into the contract clauses: "During the contracting workshops, we often referred to our Statement of Intent, especially during difficult conversations where people might fall back into their old 'us versus them' mindset."[28]

Lastly, the parties worked through step 5 and developed a governance structure (see chapter 6)—something that was not present either formally or informally in the previous agreements. For example, the parties established a "best value team" co-chaired by an Island Health administrator and a hospitalist that meets once a month. The team works through the budget and data to determine how to best handle external developments that pose financial challenges. For example, how would the parties address changing requirements when the Canadian government passed the law to allow Medical Assistance in Dying (MAID)? The parties adopted governance structure and protocols into their contract as part of a schedule.

As Dr. Ken Smith reflects, "The contract really did mark a profound fundamental change that has persisted in our relationship with the administration and our group. We now work together on our goals. We are actually helping each other get past the hurdles as opposed to putting up barriers. The change is quite profound."

Janet Grove, the legal counsel for Island Health, explained how the relational contract differs from a traditional contract. "The contract sets the shared vision and the Guiding Principles upfront. As such, you see more decisions referred to that are trusted to the governance framework than in a normal contract. There is a recognition that things will evolve and how you manage the evolution is entrusted to a framework."

The before and after descriptions of the relationship are nothing short of transformational—*with a shift from 84.5 percent negative words to 86.2 percent positive in less than two years* (Figures 15 and 16).

The COVID-19 pandemic put the parties' relational contract to the test. Would their flexible contract framework allow them to navigate prolonged and persistent stress and pressure?

Kim Kerrone—Island Heath's Vice President, Chief Financial Officer, Legal Services & Risk—reflected on the challenge posed by the pandemic: "When the pandemic hit, we were suddenly faced with a 60 percent reduction in the overall patient census on the one hand—yet on the other hand, physicians needed to manage higher-risk COVID-19 patients. The impact on budget and workload was drastic: physicians treated far fewer yet higher-risk patients. Questions such as who would get to work what hours and who would have to work in the new high-risk COVID-19 ward were front and center."

28. *Id.*

Figure 15: The Island Health/Hospitalist Relationship Description 2016–2018—Word Cloud Before Vested (May 2016)

Figure 16: The Island Health/Hospitalist Relationship Description 2016–2018—Word Cloud After Vested (October 2018)

Dr. Maskey explained how the parties' formal relational contract helped them be ready to address the changes fairly and flexibly: "Our Vested (formal relational contract) agreement uses Guiding Principles such as autonomy and equity. Using these Guiding Principles as the backdrop for decisions, we found an effective way to rethink schedule allocations to reduce hospitalist hours while keeping all physicians employed. Part of the process also 'banked' hours, which can be used for future surges. Without our Vested contract, this would have been arduous under the old contract."

The relationship is still going strong, and the parties continue to use their governance structure and Statement of Intent to keep the parties in continual alignment, which has let them prevent disputes.

Smart Contracts

The term "smart contract" was coined in 1996 to mean "a set of promises, specified in digital form, including protocols within which the parties perform their promises."[29] Think of smart contracts as computer code that helps companies perform part (or all) of their contract obligations. Smart contracts do not contain legal language or terms of an agreement; rather, a smart contract has code that executes actions as specified by contracting parties. For example, contracting parties may create a smart contract to trigger a payment when certain conditions are met.

Blockchain technology has helped operationalize the concept of smart contracts and has become a powerful tool contracting parties can use to prevent disputes. One of the key attributes of smart contracts is their ability to automatically execute transactions without human intervention. An excellent example is how Walmart and a major trucking supplier collaborated with a blockchain consultant to devise a system to solve freight payment problems, reducing freight claim disputes by 98.5 percent (profiled as the case study below).[30]

Why

Smart contracts reduce potential conflicts by translating the parties' agreement into automated responses to a set of agreed-upon preconditions. This automation requires the parties to agree and establish the contract's execution rules.

---

29. Nick Szabo, *Smart Contracts: Building Blocks for Digital Market*, 16 Extropy: J. Transhumanist Thought 50 (1996) (smart contracts).

30. Kate Vitasek et al., *How Walmart Canada Uses Blockchain to Solve Supply-Chain Challenges*, Harv. Bus. Rev. (Jan. 5, 2022), https://hbr.org/2022/01/how-walmart-canada-uses-blockchain-to-solve-supply-chain-challenges; Kate Vitasek, *How Walmart Used Collaboration and Co-Creation to Build the World's Largest Industrial Blockchain Solution*, World Fin. Rev. (May 19, 2022), https://worldfinancialreview.com/how-walmart-used-collaboration-and-co-creation-to-build-the-worlds-largest-industrial-blockchain-solution/.

Why is automation helpful? All too often, humans complete the work done to comply with the contract. And humans—unfortunately make mistakes. A contract may include hundreds of steps behind the scenes to comply with the contract and missing or overlooking even one of those steps can lead to a claim.

For example, in the transportation industry, companies pay their freight carriers based on pre-established business rules in their contract (price per mile, gallons of fuel used, and number of stop locations). In addition, a successful delivery is determined if a shipment arrives on time and the product is treated properly (not damaged and kept in an acceptable temperature range). This removes the chances of contract misinterpretation or poor contract understanding. The actions under the contract are pre-programmed, forcing the parties to anticipate and resolve their differences in advance.

The implications are not immaterial. The National Cargo Security Council estimates the impact of cargo loss from freight carriers surpasses $50 billion annually.[31] This means companies and their freight carriers often find themselves haggling over freight claims—claims that sometimes turn into protracted disputes. Smart contracts require the parties to address these issues upfront—when programming the smart contract. In this way, execution on the back end is automated through technology such as blockchain ledgers, which provide electronic validation when a task is met and automatically release payment per the contract terms.

The potential for using smart contracts is growing as companies succeed with them. Indeed, even in a field as dependent upon traditional contracts as arbitration, some thought leaders have used smart contract technology to overcome disputes relating to the enforcement of arbitral awards.[32] Enforcement of arbitral awards can be time-consuming and costly. As smart contracts can be programmed to automatically perform actions when certain conditions are met, they can be programmed to release funds from an escrow account to the winning party once the arbitrator issues the award. Smart contracting advocates also suggest using smart contracts to facilitate the enforcement of the award by automatically triggering certain financial transactions if the losing party fails to comply with the award. For example, a smart contract could automatically transfer ownership of a specific asset or property to the winning party if the losing party fails to pay the award within a specified timeframe. While there are many challenges—academic, legal, and ethical—to address, "considering the fact that there are instances where a winning party is denied [sic] their prize for decades even after winning a dispute, expediency may ultimately win the balance of convenience."[33]

31. *Freight Claims Management Use Cases and Software*, Freight Claims, https://freightclaims.com/freight-claims-management-use-cases-and-software/.

32. *Smart Arbitral Awards or Smart Contract Enabled Arbitral Awards*, Hong Kong Law., https://www.hk-lawyer.org/content/smart-arbitral-awards-or-smart-contract-enabled-arbitral-awards-how-smart-contracts-can.

33. *Id.*

How It Works

Developing a smart contract begins with contracting parties agreeing on the terms of the arrangement. The parties must also decide how the smart contract will work, including the conditions for how rules agreed to will be executed. There are dozens (if not hundreds) of how-to guides on the internet with instructions on developing a smart contract. The high-level steps are given below.

1. Select the Team

A smart contract is only smart if it executes what the contracting parties agree to. The team composition can vary but typically should include business, legal, and technology people.

2. Select the Strategy

Contracting parties need to make strategic decisions when setting up a smart contract. For example, will you use a public or private blockchain network? A public blockchain network—where anyone can join without asking for permission—allows unlimited viewing of information stored on it, eliminates intermediaries, and operates independently of any governing party. It is well-suited for digital consumer offerings (like non-fungible tokens [NFTs]), cryptocurrencies, and certifying information such as individuals' degrees or certificates. But private networks—those that require permission to join it—are often far better suited for business-to-business contracts because access is restricted to verified members, and only parties directly working together can see the specific information they exchange.

3. Agree on the Business Rules and Calculations

Any complex business has both fixed and variable processes and costs and they are rarely, if ever, the same for any two companies. A fundamental prerequisite for creating a blockchain-enabled system is to get the parties to agree to the calculations and business rules the network will employ.

4. Develop the Smart Contract

This is the actual development of the blockchain network and smart contract.

5. Test and Pilot

Software code can be complex, and it is imperative to test your smart contract. If the smart contract will have multiple contracting parties on the network, it is good to start with a pilot and then roll it out to the remaining organizations.

A key benefit of smart contracts is the code performs the transaction and there is no human discretion. However, this is also the downside. For example, if a supplier fails to meet commitments, the smart contract will not trigger payment even if the parties agree there should be a partial payment. For this reason, it is important to have governance protocols to address any potential agreed variances, such as releasing a partial payment.

Case Study[34]

Walmart delivers over 500,000 shipments annually to distribution centers and over 400 stores across Canada, using both its own trucking fleet and 70 third-party carriers. The essential service of moving a massive quantity of goods (much of which is perishable) across borders, time zones, and different climates is an enormous operational challenge. Each load shipped requires tracking data points, such as stop locations, gallons of fuel, and temperature updates, calculated and incorporated into each invoice.

With over 200 data points factoring into invoices, it is easy to see how vast discrepancies in data led to significant non-value-added reconciliation and claims. In fact, a whopping 70 percent of invoices had discrepancies. For Walmart, this meant substantial transaction costs, unhappy carriers feeling frustrated with an inconsistent payment process, and final payment sometimes extending weeks or even months beyond the invoice due date. For carriers, the problem was equally painful, with what seemed to be never-ending disputes revolving around "us versus them" versions of the truth that wreaked havoc on the carrier's economics.

John Bayliss, Executive Vice President, Chief Transformation Officer, Walmart Canada, explains how the initiative came about: "We had some very vocal carriers complaining about the lead times to settle accounts." Bayliss adds, "We knew the root causes were systems issues and not people problems."

Walmart selected DLT Labs to help them both think through a distributed ledger smart contract (blockchain) solution and implement it. What started as a partnership with DLT soon extended to Bison Transport—one of Walmart Canada's largest transportation providers.

To lay the foundation for the blockchain-enabled system the parties agreed to the calculations and business rules the network would employ. For Walmart and its carriers, this meant working with each carrier's unique data (vendor name, payment terms, contract duration, and general terms and conditions), which was combined with governing master tables of information such as fuel rates and tax rates. The parties then jointly agreed to the formulas that the blockchain uses to calculate each invoice.

With the rules in place the blockchain could be operationalized. The blockchain synthesizes all the data points in real-time throughout each unique delivery,

34. Kate Vitasek et al., *supra* note 29.

taking into account information such as fuel costs, offroad mileage, and delays at the delivery point. The system creates a running invoice that evolves in real time as costs accrue.

The blockchain network went live with Bison Transport in January 2020, with the remaining sixty-nine carriers in Canada onboarding in March.

By all accounts, the blockchain platform has been a tremendous success, leading to increased trust, efficiencies, and savings. The parties have reduced payment disputes by 98.5 percent. In addition, any discrepancies are easily flagged and quickly resolved.

While the original goal was to eliminate disputes and wasted resources, one of the biggest benefits of the blockchain platform is the unprecedented level of trust it has created between Walmart and its carriers due to the end-to-end supply chain visibility among all parties.

RISK/REWARD ALIGNMENT

When parties enter a commercial agreement, there is often risk involved. One way to prevent disputes is to find ways to align interests around risks and rewards. Two mechanisms have evolved as ways to align contracting parties around risks: using realistic risk allocation and incentives.

Realistic Risk Allocation

A risk is an uncertain event or set of circumstances that, if it occurs, will affect the achievement of one or more of the parties' goals. As long as there is uncertainty, there is risk.

Risks include controllable and uncontrollable actions such as weather, ground conditions, labor markets, defective work or materials, inadequate design, incorrect estimating, incorrect programming, and natural disasters. Inevitably, there are also relationship-specific risks as well, such as the inability to properly define the scope of work.

Realistic risk allocation involves intentionally analyzing potential risks in a relationship and assigning each risk to the party that is most capable of managing, controlling, or insuring against that risk. The goal is to consciously avoid shifting risk to the "weaker" party to "win" the negotiation. The best approach is to allocate risks to the party that can best eliminate them. When that is not possible, the next best approach is to allocate the risk to the party that can best manage and mitigate it in a cost-effective manner.

Why

A mistake many organizations make is blindly shifting risk to another party. One reason this happens is because lawyers often seek to protect their clients from risks and attempt to limit the liability flowing from the materialization of those risks. As one lawyer put it, "It is my fiduciary and legal responsibility to protect my client." In many cases, an organization's legal and contracting group develops "standard contract templates" that include terms designed to protect their organization. These standard contract templates are often presented as a "take it or leave it" proposition.

But legal departments are not the only ones who shift risk with costly consequences. Many large organizations have procurement departments that pressure procurement professionals to shift risk when the buying organization has more power than its suppliers. To make matters worse, many procurement professionals also have personal incentives to "win" at the negotiation table by shifting risk to suppliers. Heavy-handed approaches are usually met with the shell game, where the service provider incorporates the cost of the risk assumed into the bidding price. When the companies are not transparent in pricing, it is hard to see the impact of the risk shifting. Typically, risks are deeply buried in hidden costs, and once out of sight, the risks often also become out of mind and are not actively managed. If an event does occur, the parties' legal teams wave limitation of liability and indemnification clauses at each other.

Finance departments are also to blame for risk shifting. Take, for example, the trend of companies to push out payment terms. A *New York Times* article highlighted the trend with the headline "Big Companies Pay Later, Squeezing Their Suppliers." The article states, "The practice of implementing grossly unfair trading terms is a growing trend."[35]

The core philosophy behind realistic risk allocation is that each time a risk is appropriately allocated, a source of potential conflict disappears. The concept and benefits of realistic risk allocation were highlighted in a 1973 paper published by internationally recognized construction law expert Max Abrahamson.[36] Realistic risk allocation evolved throughout the 1980s and has since become a hot topic in the construction industry, where claims are more pervasive than in most industries.[37] However, risk shifting is not unique to the construction industry.

---

35. Stephanie Strom, *Big Companies Pay Later, Squeezing Their Suppliers*, N.Y. Times (Apr. 6, 2015), https://www.nytimes.com/2015/04/07/business/big-companies-pay-later-squeezing-their-suppliers.html.

36. Bell Gully, *The Meaning and Contestability of Fair Risk Allocation in Commercial Contracting*, Legal 500 (Sept. 20, 2019), https://www.legal500.com/developments/thought-leadership/the-meaning-and-contestability-of-fair-risk-allocation-in-commercial-contracting/.

37. 1979 landmark industry conference on "Construction Risks and Liability Sharing" (American Society of Civil Engineers, *Construction Risks and Liability Sharing*, Vol. II at 2 [1980]; *Impact of Various Construction Contract Types and Clauses on Project Performance*, Construction Industry Institute [1986]). Studies conducted by organizations interested in major construction, such as The Business Roundtable and the Construction

The University of Tennessee published a White Paper, "Unpacking Risk Shifting: A Whitepaper Challenging Unreasonable Risk-Shifting in the Transportation and Logistics Industry."[38]

Nobel Laureate Oliver Williamson strongly urges organizations to avoid power-based approaches to shift risk, stating: "Using a muscular approach is myopic and inefficient. Companies not only use their service providers—they use up their service providers."[39]

Williamson suggests that shifting risk inappropriately will only add friction and costs to business relationships. Rather than save money, companies will likely increase their total costs from an end-to-end perspective through hidden transaction costs. Inappropriate risk-shifting also creates the structural conflicts discussed in chapter 1, and when left unattended, can sow the seeds of countless potential disputes, create distrust and resentment, and establish adversarial relationships that likely will interfere with the success of the business enterprise. For example, in a classic multi-party construction project, an owner's use of superior bargaining power to shift risks unrealistically to another party typically creates a chain reaction of cost inflation, resentment, downstream risk-shifting, defensive and retaliatory tactics, and misunderstandings caused by different perceptions as to the enforceability of some risk-shifting provisions. The result is usually adversarial relationships leading to claims and disputes that could have been avoided by intelligent sharing of risks.

Organizations are turning to business relationship models (see chapter 3) that seek to share risk and reward. However, another solution is adopting realistic risk allocation.

How It Works

Risks are inherent in virtually all commercial activities. When businesses identify, understand, anticipate, assess, analyze, and learn to manage risks, they can create a significant source of value for the contracting parties through risk reduction.

Industry Institute (CII) (*Contract Risk Allocation and Cost Effectiveness*, Construction Industry Institute, Publication No. RS5-3 [1988]) have confirmed that the imposition of onerous contract conditions is not cost-effective because it: reduces contractor competition, increases bid prices due to increased contractor contingencies, causes a high-quality contractor to be replaced by a lesser-quality contractor who is more likely to unknowingly accept grossly inequitable risk allocation, creates an adversarial owner–contractor relationship, is more likely to increase requests for change orders and claims for extra compensation, and increases the likelihood of disputes; Bell Gully *supra* note 35.

38. Kate Vitasek et al., *Unpacking Risk Shifting: A Whitepaper Challenging Unreasonable Risk-Shifting in the Transportation and Logistics Industry*, UNIV. TENN., 1–27 (2016) (risk shifting).

39. Oliver E. Williamson, *Outsourcing: Transaction Cost Economics and Supply Chain Management*, 44 J.S.C.M. 5–16 (2008) (friction in complex contracts).

Realistic risk allocation is an integral part of risk management that starts at the planning phase in any business relationship and includes identifying risks and then fairly allocating them among the parties. Realistic risk allocation helps prevent problems by assigning each potential risk of the business relationship to the party best able to manage, control, or insure against the particular risk.

A four-step realistic risk allocation process involving a joint risk assessment is given below.

Step 1: Identify Risks

Step 1 begins with contracting parties identifying risk. This means collaboratively and candidly putting all potential risks on the table. It is often best to sort risks into categories. While the types of risk are likely limitless, the majority of risks fall into the following categories:[40]

- *Operational Risks*: These risks relate to the work scope and workload allocation. For example, poor service from the service provider or poor forecasting from the company creates operational risks.
- *Planning Risks*: These risks relate to overconsumption of services (poor assumptions) or inaccurate baselines impacting pricing and margins.
- *Scope Risks*: These risks result from the actual implementation of the work scope, such as unmanageable workload allocation and unforeseeable project overruns ("business happens"). For example, weather and available labor are common risks associated with the scope of a construction project. Or, in an outsourced facilities management agreement, change in requirements due to regulatory or buying organizations' desire to shift to more environmentally sustainable options.
- *Compliance and Security Risks*: These risks impact highly regulated industries and pose significant legal liability issues for both companies. For example, a Target HVAC (Heating, Ventilation, and Air Conditioning) supplier's security breach enabled a hacker to steal over 100 million pieces of credit cards or personal information from Target customers nationwide.[41]

---

40. George Kimball, *Risk Allocation Liability Limits and Disputes in Outsourcing, in* OUTSOURCING 2010: STRUCTURING, NEGOTIATION AND GOVERNANCE, Vol. 1, 257 (2010) (five types of risk).

41. Mike Lennon, *Target HVAC Contractor Says It Was Breached by Hackers*, SECURITY WEEK (Feb. 7, 2014), https://www.securityweek.com/target-hvac-contractor-says-it-was-breached-hackers/; *Settlement Reached with Target Following Major Consumer Data Breach*, PENN. ATT'Y GEN. (May 23, 2017), https://www.attorneygeneral.gov/taking-action/settlement-reached-with-target-following-major-consumer-data-breach/.

- *Business/Programmatic/Project Risks*: These risks relate to scheduling issues that may affect success. For example, permitting delays in a construction contract.
- *Technical Risks*: These risks relate to the maturity of technology and processes reliant on technology. For example, Microsoft stopped support for SQL Server 2014.[42]
- *Cost/Resource Risks*: These risks can often be planned for (e.g., inflation or attrition). However, often, there are unexpected spikes, such as when the pandemic significantly inflated material costs and delays.
- *Process Risks*: These risks are associated with the execution of processes—especially new processes—that are required to be implemented. For example, Hershey's suffered $100 million in estimated losses from "missing Halloween" due to supply chain process failures after implementing a new enterprise resource planning (ERP) system.[43]
- *Organizational Risks*: These risks pertain to policies, procedures, work practices, culture of an organization, or implementing change within an organization. Such risks include careless management and staff attitudes toward workplace violence prevention.[44]
- *Stakeholder/Stakeholder Risks*: These risks relate to possible stakeholder changes or needs from stakeholders that may change over time. For example, when Randy Mott—a former HP executive—joined GM as their Chief Information Officer, he made a decision to insource work done by HP just two years after HP won a supplier of the year award, resulting in a significant loss of business to HP.[45]
- *Transition Risks*: These risks relate to unknowns associated with ramping up the supplier, such as shifting work from an incumbent supplier to a new supplier. For example, KFC's transition from a long-term supply to UPS resulted in the chain running out of chicken for almost two weeks, forcing the chain to close restaurants throughout the United Kingdom.[46]

---

42. *6 Discontinued Software to Stop Using Immediately*, Bright Flow (Aug. 29, 2022), https://www.brightflow.net/6-discontinued-software-to-stop-using-immediately/.

43. *Top 5 ERP Implementation Failures: Costs, Causes, and How to Prevent*, Spinnaker Support (Dec. 13, 2023), https://www.spinnakersupport.com/blog/2023/12/13/erp-implementation-failure/.

44. *Organizational Risk Factors*, CDC (May 16, 2024), https://wwwn.cdc.gov/WPVHC/Nurses/Course/Slide/Unit3_9.

45. *GM to shift 3,000 Hewlett jobs to its payroll*, Reuters (Oct. 18, 2012), https://www.reuters.com/article/business/gm-to-shift-3-000-hewlett-jobs-to-its-payroll-idUSBRE89H17A/.

46. Kate Vitasek, *KFC Chicken Crisis: A Royal Foul-Up In Britain*, Forbes (Feb. 22, 2018), https://www.forbes.com/sites/katevitasek/2018/02/22/kfc-chicken-crisis-a-royal-foul-up-in-britain/.

- *Extraordinary Risks*: These risks are your worst-case scenarios. Although they have little likelihood of occurring, when they do occur, they can result in financial ruin or worse, loss of life.

Step 2: Analyze, Prioritize, and Estimate the Cost of Risks

Step 2 is to prioritize the risks associated with your agreement and, if appropriate, estimate costs for each risk. The University of California shares an easy-to-follow process for assessing risks.[47]

The first step in analyzing and prioritizing risks is to determine the probability a risk will occur and assign a probability code (Figure 17).

Probability of Occurrence (%)	What is the probability the risk event will occur?	Code
91–100	Certain	C
61–90	Highly Likely	HL
41–60	Likely	L
11–40	Unlikely	U
0–10	Remote	R

Figure 17: Determining the Probability of a Risk

Next, determine the potential impact of each risk, as shown in figure 18. Again, this can be done by using the combined knowledge of the team as well as considering historical data and trends.

Impact	Description	Code
Negligible	An event which, if it occurred, would have no effect on the program	N
Minor	An event which, if it occurred, would cause only a small increase in program cost and/or schedule. Requirements would still be achieved.	MI
Moderate	An event which, if it occurred, would cause moderate cost/schedule increases, but the requirements would still be achieved.	MO
Serious	An event which, if it occurred, would cause serious cost/schedule increases. Secondary requirements may not be achieved.	S
Critical	An event which, if it occurred, would cause program failure (inability to achieve minimum acceptable requirements).	C

Figure 18: Determining the Potential Impact of a Risk

47. *How to Assess Risk*, UCLA, https://www.finance.ucla.edu/corporate-accounting/controls-and-accountability/control-practices/how-to-assess-risk.

Lastly, you can analyze risk using a simple matrix, as shown in figure 19. This is done by cross-referencing the probability of an event with its impact to assign the risk priority.

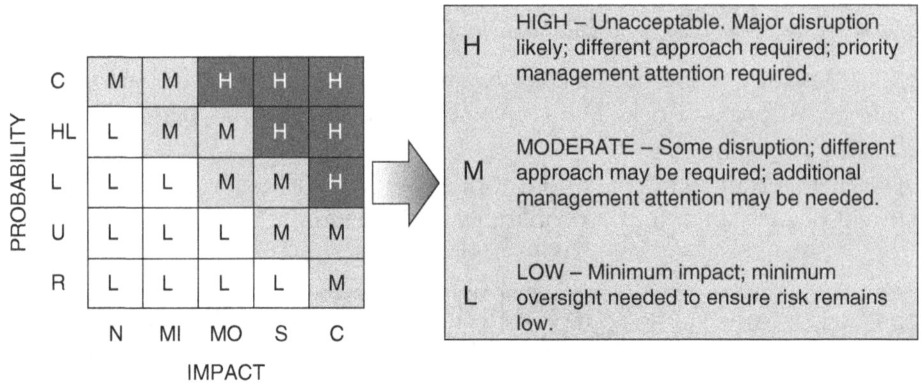

Figure 19: Determining the Risk Priority

Step 3: Fairly Allocate Risk

Step 3 is to fairly allocate the risk. The basic principles of realistic risk allocation are:

- *Balance*: Risk should be allocated reasonably, considering the interests of each party. A general rule of thumb is:
  - Every risk has an associated cost, which must be assumed somewhere in the process; the parties should collaboratively and transparently identify as many risks as possible with the goal of jointly determining the best approach for mitigating, managing, and allocating the risks.
  - The ideal—or most cost-effective—contract is one where risks are allocated to the party who can best evaluate, control, manage, and minimize the risk given the unique circumstances of the relationship to reduce the total cost of risk.
- *Ownership*: Every risk should clearly define—"Who is the owner?"—even if the ownership is shared.
- *Insurance*: Insurance must be used to cover risks that are difficult to allocate or cannot be mitigated.
- *Risk Sharing*: It must be recognized that some risks cannot be fairly given or are best managed collaboratively. This is especially true for uncontrollable risks that cannot be insured against.

Often, it will be obvious that certain risks should be assigned to a particular party. However, in other cases, either party can handle risks equally well, or some risks might not be effectively handled or insured against by either party. In those cases, the assignment of those risks must be dealt with through bargaining, likely reflected in the economic terms of the deal.

A good example of realistic risk allocation stems from a trend in supply agreements to shift payment terms—often to as long as 120 days. Below are three examples of how buyers and suppliers have addressed realistic risk allocation through collaborative and transparent discussions.

In the first example, the supplier shared they would need to work with a bank to secure working capital to fund the inventory needed to procure raw materials. As part of the discussion, both parties shared their cost of capital. The procurement lead's "ah-ha" was that the buyer's cost of capital was far lower than the supplier's. The parties ultimately decided to have a seven-day payment term for the raw materials while keeping a sixty-day payment term associated with the supplier's services.

In a second example, the buying organization had a corporate mandate from the Chief Financial Officer to have a 120-day payment term. It was important to the buying company that they did not have a "waiver" in any supply agreements. The parties uncovered a unique twist for managing the protracted payment terms; the supplier would invoice the buyer quarterly in advance. The net result was keeping the 120-payment term but tactically achieving a 30-day payment term for the supplier.

In a third example, the buyer and supplier openly discussed the cost of capital the supplier would bear with long payment terms. In this case, the parties agreed the supplier would invoice for their monthly price and include a "cost of capital" charge in line with current interest rates.

Step 4: Joint Planning and Mitigation

Step 4 is joint planning and mitigation. The most progressive organizations are moving beyond simple realistic risk allocation and adopting risk management and mitigation techniques in their formal governance structure (see chapter 5). This includes using a Joint Risk Register and other governance mechanisms to enable the development of proper strategies to manage and mitigate risks as part of your governance mechanism. The result is cost avoidance and/or real cost reductions associated with reduced risk.

Case Study

The case study of BuyCo—a health care provider—offers a good example of how to use realistic risk allocation when outsourcing. BuyCo outsourced the management of its environmental services operations. BuyCo had multiple locations, which the winning supplier would need to service. As part of the bidding process, potential suppliers had an opportunity to go on-site and see firsthand the work they would do. However, from a cost and time perspective, not all suppliers could visit every location.

BuyCo had used a "scope sweep" clause in previous outsourcing contracts. Sweep clauses—used in outsourcing agreements—supplement statements of work by obligating the supplier to perform functions that may not be described in the Statement of Work description but are an inherent part of the services provided. For example, if a service provider takes over a company's in-house work, the scope sweep clause assumes if the work was being done in-house before outsourcing, the scope would appear in the contract even if the Statement of Work was silent on the task.

On the surface, using a scope sweep clause was brilliant because it shifted risk to the service provider for failing to price the scope of service in question accurately. Unfortunately, the clause created significant friction and seemed to end in a never-ending "scope creep" battle, with the service provider constantly arguing for contract changes and increased prices.

The procurement and operations leaders involved in the outsourcing effort discussed the risk of unknowns with their legal department and agreed to replace the scope sweep clause—as well as many other clauses—with more fair and balanced contracting clauses that would better balance the risk to both parties.

As part of the contracting process, the parties completed a joint risk assessment, which included prioritizing the risk and estimating costs for each risk where appropriate. The parties then added a clause into their agreement pointing to the joint risk assessment and how they would deal with risks. The clause read:

> As part of the Pricing Model, the parties identified the risks related to the delivery of the Environmental Services under the Agreement and allocated the identified risks to the party in the best position to manage each risk. These risks are set out in the Risk Assessment Worksheet in Schedule C Risk Assessment Worksheet. The Contract Price includes a risk premium for the risks allocated to the Service Provider, subject to the terms set out in the table below.

Figure 20 below is an excerpt from the contract showing the parties' risk allocation for the transition of the work.

As you can see from figure 20, the parties identified each risk by category (columns 1 and 2). They then analyzed the risks to determine the potential impact (columns 3–5). A key part of the joint risk assessment was to allocate who would own each risk—the service provider, BuyCo, or shared (column 7). The team also developed a mitigation plan used in their ongoing governance meetings and factored it in the cost of the risk if it resulted in a financial impact on the pricing model. For example, for "delayed implementation," the pricing model factored in the costs of delayed implementation (column 6).

Using realistic risk allocation helped BuyCo and the service provider prevent disputes and guided them on how best to manage risk.

ID Date	Risk Description/Reason	Probability of Occurrence	Impact on Project	Category: High, Medium Low	Mitigation Plan	Responsible Party
Transition	Lack of buy-in from stakeholders, low priority placed on governance	L	H	M	Change management planning and resources	**Shared**
	Hiring of existing staff	L	H	M	Addressed by Service Provider labor strategy	**Service Provider**
	Call Centre transition issues	H	H	H	Should be addressed in transition planning, including engagement of all critical stakeholders, resource scheduling, and contingency plans	**Shared**
	IT interface issues	H	L	M	IT group should be involved early in transition process to allow time to identify and resolve issues	**Shared**
	Delayed implementation	H	M	H	Addressed in transition planning. Pricing model to address cost of delayed implementation	**Shared**
	Public relations risk	L	M	M	Addressed by joint communications strategy	**Shared**
	BuyCo resource availability and timing	L	H	M	Engagement of critical stakeholders and resource availability should be factored into transition scheduling	**BuyCo**
	Temporary decline in quality	L	H	M	Performance monitoring systems and governance model to identify and address quality gaps	**Shared**
	Limited or blocked access to facilities	L	H	M	Should be factored into transition planning with contingency plans for unexpected barriers to access	**Shared**

Figure 20: Example Risk Assessment Worksheet

Incentives

Incentives encourage cooperation and can be a valuable tool to align interests and encourage superior performance—both of which can prevent disputes. When used effectively, incentives can align behaviors toward a common goal even when one or more parties might otherwise seek to achieve short-term interests that benefit their own organization.

Using incentives in contracts is not new. For example, the U.S. Army wrote performance metrics into the Wright brothers' contract.[48] The three-page contract

48. *Defense Acquisition University Catalog*, Continuous Learning Ctr., Online Module CLL011, 1–156 (2005) (Wright brothers' contract with U.S. Army).

had a target price of $25,000 and required a minimum speed capability of 36 mph and a target speed of 40 mph. The army included an incentive where the Wright brothers would receive an additional $2,500 for every mph over the 40-mph target. In addition, the contract had a penalty of $2,500 for not meeting the minimum 36 mph requirement. The final delivered speed was 42 mph, and the Wright brothers earned a $5,000 incentive bonus.

There are many types of incentives, with the most common being:

- Shared savings (for reducing costs)
- Value share (for increasing value beyond cost—such as having an impact on the total cost of ownership)
- Performance incentives (for achieving certain target levels—such as the Wright brothers' incentive to build a faster plane)
- Award fee (for success of a deliverable/requirement)
- Award term (for contract extensions)

Although coupling incentives to business agreements is not new, it is not common and is easier said than done.

Why

Traditional contracts rely on a transactional economic model (e.g., a supplier is compensated per unit, per hour, per mile, per shipment, per call, etc.). This creates an Interest Conflict (see chapter 1) where a supplier may have an inherent perverse incentive to perform the contracted task rather than activities that may generate more value. Take a construction contract as an example. The architect creates a design, and the builder leads the construction efforts. Each organization has a price for its work. If the builder finds an issue in the design, they will face added time and work to resolve any problems—which often will reduce the margins it would otherwise realize from the work. Depending on how the contract allocates risk, the builder may not want to spend the needed time to remedy design flaws (e.g., fixed fee contract), or they could be careless with controlling costs (e.g., a cost-plus contract where the builder charges by the hour to work with the architect).

And when there is an issue, it often turns into a debate of "not my fault," which creates conflicts and disputes.

Incentives seek to align the interests of contracting parties and promote collaboration on mutually defined desired outcomes. A shared incentive pool on a construction project should encourage, in the above example, the builder to work with the architect to create the best product measured by some metric at an overall targeted cost—with incentives for doing so. This promotes a "what's best for the project" behavior by linking rewards to achieving project goals.

How It Works

It is important to establish incentives that are not too cumbersome to track and monitor. The simpler the incentives are, the better. Administrative costs should not, under any circumstances, exceed the expected benefits, and the incentives must be easily measurable. We recommend creating an incentive framework, which is a mechanism that the parties use to measure performance and trigger incentive awards or payments. Typically, the value of the incentive is determined using a mathematical formula.

Agreements should also provide for evaluation at stated intervals to keep the parties informed of performance quality and the areas of expected improvement. Partial payment fees should correspond to the evaluation periods. This partial payment approach will induce the service provider to improve poor performance or to continue with good performance.

University of Tennessee researchers developed an open-source Requirements Roadmap toolkit to help organizations jointly define contracting objectives and align incentives with the parties' agreed objectives. Figure 21 provides an example of how this works using an outsourced logistics contract.

Performance			Annual Incentive	Inspection			
Objective	Standard	Tolerance/ AQL		Who	Data Source	Calculation	How Often Collected
Create Quality for our customers that exceeds their expectations	Reduce Damage	Baseline Starting Point	Monetary Incentive	Facility Designee	Whse Facilities Report + Trans. Damage Report + Mfg Damage Report	Total Whse Damage (cases received + Cases shipped/2) + damage in other SC nodes	Monthly
	Food Quality - DNV Audit score	Goal: 95% - "Approved-plus" Minimum: 85% - Approved	Announcement/ press release	DNV Auditor	Invoicing system	Score provided by DNV	Annual

Figure 21: Requirements Roadmap for Linking Incentives to Buyer Objectives

Let's examine how the Requirement Roadmap works in practice. First, contracting parties agree on objectives. In this case, one of the objectives was high quality (Objective column). The parties then identified two metrics (noted in the Standard column). Here, the parties agreed on two metrics—reducing damage and food quality as measured by a government-defined audit. Once the Standard was defined, the parties agreed on the performance target (noted in the

Tolerance/Acceptable Quality Level [AQL] column). For example, the supplier would be expected to have a minimum audit score of 85 percent with a stretch goal of a 95 percent score.

The fourth column in the Requirements Roadmap is the Incentive column. Here, the parties determined if the buyer would award an incentive. In this case, the buyer would actively promote the supplier in terms of publicity for achieving the stretch goal.

The final four columns outline how the parties validate performance and include who is responsible for tracking each metric, the required data sources, the calculation for each metric, and how often the parties report performance.

Case Study

In chapter 3, we briefly shared how the Minnesota Department of Transportation (MnDOT) used best value assessment when picking a supplier to rebuild the I-35 bridge. In addition, they used incentives as a way to create an alignment of interests with MnDOT's goal to replace the bridge quickly while maintaining high quality.

Recall when the I-35 bridge unexpectedly collapsed on August 1, 2007, the Minnesota Department of Transportation (MnDOT) found itself in an urgent situation to replace the state's major interstate connecting Minneapolis and St. Paul. Minnesota Governor Tim Pawlenty challenged MnDOT to complete a replacement bridge within eighteen months. Considering that it typically takes that long (or longer) just to identify the scope of a major project, MnDOT approached the rebuild in a radically different way. In addition to using a best value supplier selection, MnDOT added time, quality, and safety incentives into the contract.

Early Completion Incentive

MnDOT knew that every day the bridge was not open would cost both the economy and the public crucial time and hard expense. The Minneapolis Regional Chamber of Commerce estimated the daily cost to businesses exceeded half a million dollars. The State Department of Economic Development Impact Analysis believed the average net economic impact was an additional $113,000 daily reduction in the state's economic output. MnDOT's Office of Investment Management's own estimate pegged the daily cost to motorists at $400,000.

MnDOT used incentives as a key contracting tactic to reward the supplier—Flatiron Manson—for opening the bridge on time or early. Per the contract, Flatiron Manson had 437 days from the date of contract signing to open the new bridge to the public. MnDOT used a clause to establish the project completion date of December 24, 2008. Flatiron Manson was in line to receive a $7 million no-questions-asked-incentive if they completed the project on time and agreed to waive all claims. The clause also specified a $200,000 per day incentive for early completion and, conversely, a $200,000 per day penalty for completion post-target date. In total, MnDOT set aside $27 million in incentives if Flatiron Manson finished early. Flatiron Manson opened the project ninety days early and earned $25 million—92 percent of the incentive pool.

Safety, Quality, and Public Relations Incentives

MnDOT also established a separate sum over and above the contract price, which formed a second incentive bonus that applied only if certain standards were exceeded. Three areas—safety, quality, and public relations—were eligible for the additional bonus. It was another way for MnDOT to ensure focus on their priority areas and for the contractor to reap a financial reward.

However, the speed with which the organizations developed the contract prohibited MnDOT and Flatiron Manson from ever fleshing out the second incentive bonus measures. Public relations was the only area sufficiently defined to receive an additional $100,000. Even though the project exceeded safety and quality specifications, the second incentive was not awarded because of a lack of definition about incentive payments. This point brings home a valuable lesson when using incentives: how important it is to develop clearly defined and measurable incentives.

Peter Sanderson, Flatiron Manson's Project Manager, holds a philosophical view about losing the second incentive, "We never managed to negotiate a measure … but we were very glad to have the same goal in mind, particularly about quality and safety."

The $234 million I-35W bridge was completed in record time—just thirteen months after the bridge's collapse—something many thought impossible. In addition, the project won almost two dozen prestigious awards, including the Federal Highway Administration's *Award of Excellence* and the Associated General Contractors of America/Aon's *Grand Award*. This efficiency and delivery could not have happened if, instead of aligning interests, the parties had been engaged in endless disputes, which marks so many other construction projects. Incentives can help drive dispute avoidance.

CONTRACTUAL CLAUSES

At the outset of this chapter, we discussed the value good contract design can bring in helping the parties avoid disputes. In addition to the design, the actual contractual provisions—defining the parties' rights and obligations—play a critical role in avoiding disputes. We want to end this chapter by highlighting four contractual clauses designed to support dispute prevention: covenants of good faith and fair dealing clauses, contract change clauses, notice and cure agreement clauses, and dispute management clauses.

Why

At the beginning of contracting, the parties should identify mechanisms for addressing the inevitable frictions and problems that will arise in the course of their relationship. In doing so, it is advisable to consider including clauses to promote good faith and fair dealings between the parties, to allow for necessary changes in contract language, to encourage remedying problems, and to guide the parties in managing conflicts as they occur. That is the impetus behind the clauses we discuss below.

How It Works

Covenants of good faith and fair dealing obligate contracting parties to deal with each other honestly, fairly, and in good faith with the intent not to destroy the right of the other party or parties to receive the benefits of the contract. The laws of many jurisdictions impose an implied duty of good faith and fair dealing in every contract. However, parties can explicitly include a formal covenant of good faith and fair dealing clause. Formal good faith and fair dealing clauses often include contractual language steering the parties toward constructive behavior if a conflict or controversy emerges. While skeptical lawyers often wonder what value such clauses bring, the act of negotiating such a clause can itself increase the parties' awareness of the need to make fair decisions and work swiftly to de-escalate tensions. Explicitly including formal good faith and fair dealing clauses are important anchors in long-term business relationships where the contract, as stated, may not be in step with the changing business conditions, and the parties can use the clause to foster good faith discussions.

Contract change clauses enable contracting parties to make changes to a contract. A good contract change clause seeks to keep the parties in alignment—allowing flexibility while also recognizing that a need for a contract change should not adversely affect the other party. Staying aligned ultimately helps the parties prevent disputes. A good contract change clause formally outlines how the parties should address changes to the contract. For example, in a construction contract, the contract change clause typically gives the owner the right to change the contract while recognizing the contractor's right to payment for the reasonable costs engendered by the changes.

Dispute management clauses guide how the parties should handle problems, conflicts, and disputes in their business relationship. Contracting parties often use provisions such as a notice and cure provision in conjunction with a dispute management clause. In drafting dispute provisions, parties can choose the best process to meet their underlying goals.

For example, the parties might choose an escalation management process committing the parties to step negotiations. Step negotiations encourage organizations to engage in commercially rational processes, such as good faith notice and negotiation as a pre-condition to initiating arbitration or litigation. Some clauses require the participation of indemnitors at an early stage. Some negotiation "steps" are further divided to contemplate the involvement of senior managers only if junior managers cannot resolve the problem (thus rewarding junior managerial negotiation skills but allowing recognition of the potential need to remove the individual whose conduct is at issue from the negotiation process). Mediation is often utilized either prior to initiation of a formal claim or at a designated point in the pursuit of such a claim. Some multi-step clauses also set forth a schedule for the exchange of certain information so that mediation can take place in an informed manner early in the process. In the event of failure to resolve the dispute using these methods, the clauses call for arbitration or litigation, usually also addressing the parties' selection of venue, choice of law, waiver of jury, and other issues.

The International Institute for Conflict Prevention and Resolution (CPR) prepared a model set of dispute prevention provisions, which parties can incorporate into their contracts. These provisions aim to enable the parties to create a framework to identify potential conflicts early and to introduce a standing neutral (see chapter 5) into the process to help avoid the conflict from turning into a dispute.[49]

Notice and cure agreement clauses in a contract signal a warning when there is a serious issue between contracting parties—typically a potential breach of contract. The logic behind this clause is to allow the parties to send a warning signal before issuing a termination. This lets the offending party respond by explaining how they will address any issues to get back into compliance with the contract.

Case Study

DefenseCo is a leader in providing defense services to the U.S. government. Strategic supplier agreements are a cornerstone of their success. DefenseCo has been an early adopter of formal relational contracting, which seeks to embed relational constructs into its contract. In this case study, we share how DefenseCo changed the lens of five contract clauses from more traditional power-based wording to one that promoted a bilateral commitment focusing on dispute prevention and management. The wording in the clauses below is an excerpt from their actual contract. However, the names of the companies were changed to DefenseCo and Supplier.

Covenants of Good Faith and Fair Dealing Clause

DefenseCo and Supplier expanded the traditional covenants of good faith and fair dealing due to the strategic nature of their relationship and the decision to create a formal relational contract.

49. *Model Dispute Prevention and Resolution Provisions,* CPR Inst., https://drs.cpradr.org/images/Introductory-Memo-to-Term-Sheet-and-Sample-Provisions-11.2022.pdf.

For this Agreement, the Parties have committed to a "Vested" relationship. As part of that goal, DefenseCo and Supplier have mutually established the following One Team Shared Vision and the following high-level Desired Outcomes.

Shared Vision: *OneTeam to provide innovative solutions addressing dynamic challenges of today's workplace. Our drive for operational excellence ensures we consistently deliver exceptional value, enabling our businesses to grow and thrive in a competitive landscape.*
Cost Control: Be outstanding fiscal stewards of all resources.
Performance & Teaming: Sustain a high-performing, fully integrated team, and a winning culture.
Workplace Experience: Provide an optimal and sustainable workplace environment enabling OneTeam employees to achieve enterprise objectives and mission success.
Growing Together: Committed partners recognizing and executing on opportunities to advance our mutual growth goals.

To achieve their mutual Shared Vision and their high-level Desired Outcomes, the Parties agree to a highly collaborative relational contract founded on the following **Guiding Principles**. These Guiding Principles are the shared set of critical social norms and values that will guide the Parties in all dealings during the Term of the Agreement.

- *Reciprocity*: Each organization will make fair and balanced exchanges that are mutually beneficial. We will place no expectation upon the other that we are not willing to bear.
- *Autonomy*: Each organization is empowered and expected to make objective business decisions toward our Shared Vision.
- *Honesty*: Each organization will act in a sincere, forthcoming and truthful manner.
- *Loyalty*: Each organization is committed to this partnership, regardless of other business interests.
- *Equity*: Each organization will act equitably to fairly balance risk and reward.
- *Integrity*: Each organization will act transparently and ethically.

In addition to their strong commitment to promoting and striving to achieve the Guiding Principles of their Vested relationship set forth above, the Parties understand and agree that they will each be legally bound by the covenant of good faith and fair dealing implied in contracts governed by Virginia law.

Contract Change Clause/Process

The following wording appears in the Master Services Agreement which references a more detailed schedule (Contractual Change Management Procedure):

> *Flexible Contract Framework*: This Agreement is designed as a flexible contracting framework in order to embrace the dynamic nature of the business relationship between the Parties. Accordingly, the Parties agree to use the Change Process set forth in Schedule XX (Contractual Change Management Procedure) as frequently as necessary to adapt to changing business needs.
>
> *Potential Changes to Services*: Either Party may request changes or modifications to the scope or specifications for the Services or to this Agreement (including any Schedule or Appendix hereto) in accordance with the change management procedures set forth in Schedule XX (the "Change Process").

As you can see, the Master Services Agreement points to a much more detailed schedule, which is five-pages long. Due to its length, we are highlighting only some of the elements.

> *Introduction to Contractual Change Control Procedure*
>
> The Parties agree that changes to the Agreement reflect a healthy, timely and disciplined practice to ensure continual alignment. The Parties further agree to use a formal Contractual Change Management Procedure which:
>
> - ensures alignment to the Shared Vision/Desired Outcomes and Guiding Principles when executing Changes;
> - records and tracks Change requests; and
> - ensures the timely implementation of any agreed Changes.
>
> Any change in business practice that varies from the Agreement will trigger the Change Control Procedure. Changes may reflect additions, deletions, modifications, adjustments and updates to the terms and provisions of the Agreement and/or any Schedules or Appendices to manage, improve or optimize the relationship between the Parties.
>
> Changes may be operational or strategic in nature and generally cover:
>
> - an activity or event that changes or modifies the scope or specifications of the Services or the Agreement (e.g., a New Service request);
> - any action taken by or on behalf of Supplier or a Subcontractor on its own initiative (i.e., not at the request of DefenseCo) that will or can reasonably be expected to impact costs or performance; and
> - an activity requested by DefenseCo that would constitute or result in a change to the scope or nature of, or the specifications or performance schedule for, the existing Services.

Changes often derive from:

- Periodic reviews of Desired Outcomes, Strategic Objectives and Portfolio Management Strategies including changes resulting from DefenseCo corporate activity (e.g., mergers, acquisitions and divestitures);
- Revisions to policies and procedures to comply with statutory or regulatory changes;
- Changes to scope including New Services or updates to the Requirements Roadmap, Taxonomy or Workload Allocations;
- Revisions to the Pricing Model (Schedule ABC);
- Updates or modifications to performance standards, metrics, key performance indicators and service level agreements;
- Revisions to resource and infrastructure requirements; and
- Changes to Key Personnel as people leave Supplier and DefenseCo or change roles within either organization.

Administration of Change Control Procedure

The Parties' respective Commercial Managers have the primary responsibility for jointly managing the Change Control Procedure. Upon receipt of required approvals to proceed with the Change, Commercial Managers will log the approved Change. Signed Changed Orders will be memorialized by amendment to the Agreement periodically as needed, but no less than on a quarterly basis. The Parties agree that, for ease of use by the reader, the MSA, Schedules and Appendices will not be amended in a piecemeal fashion. Instead, any change to the MSA, a Schedule or an Appendix will result in a fully amended and restated version of that document.

The Commercial Managers will maintain a SharePoint site (or other platform accessible by all One Team members) to physically update the Agreement, assigning a revision number and date to each revised Schedule or Appendix, so that the current version of the Agreement and each of the Schedules and Appendices thereto are available 24/7 for quick access by the One Team. Commercial Managers will also be responsible for including a copy of the original Agreement and all previous versions/revisions in the Change Control Log.

In addition, the Contract Change Management Procedure Schedule includes a step-by-step process (including a flow chart to help easily show the stepped escalation process) and the inclusion of a standing neutral (see chapter 5).

Dispute Management Clause

DefenseCo and their Supplier's dispute management clause has the following six sub sections:

1. *Governing Law*: This Agreement and performance under it will be governed by the laws of the Named State without giving effect to conflicts of laws.
2. *Jurisdiction*: Each Party agrees that any lawsuit or proceeding brought by it relating to this Agreement must be brought exclusively in any federal or state court in the Named State. Each Party submits to the exclusive jurisdiction of the courts in Named State with respect to any action, suit or proceeding brought by it or against it by the other Party.
3. *Jury Waiver*: DefenseCo and Supplier acknowledge that the right to trial by jury is a constitutional one, but that it may be waived. Each Party, after consulting with counsel of their choice, knowingly and voluntarily waives any right to trial by jury in the event of litigation relating to this agreement.
4. *Obligation to Proceed*: Pending resolution of any dispute or controversy relating to this Agreement, the Parties agree to proceed diligently with the performance of this Agreement. Supplier acknowledges and agrees that any interruption to the Services could cause irreparable harm to DefenseCo, in which case an adequate remedy at law may not be available. Supplier agrees that, pending resolution of any dispute or controversy, it will not deny, withdraw, or restrict Supplier's provision of the Services to DefenseCo under this Agreement.
5. *Dispute Prevention and Resolution*: The Parties agree to follow a defined structure for the management of the relationship as set forth on Schedule XX (Relationship Management Framework).
6. *Dispute Resolution*: Any dispute or controversy between the Parties concerning the interpretation, performance, breach, threatened breach or termination of this Agreement will be resolved as provided on Schedule XX-YY (Issues Resolution Process).

In addition, DefenseCo and Supplier outlined a detailed issue resolution process as part of a Relationship Management Schedule. The issue resolution was three full pages and included ten key points. Due to the length, we are highlighting only some of the elements.

1. *Issue Escalation Procedures*: From time to time, issues will arise that cannot be resolved at the various levels of management within the DefenseCo and Supplier teams, and the Parties may wish to resolve such issues through the alternative procedures set forth in this Schedule XX-YY. These issues may involve obligations of a Party, performance, commercial issues, business impacts, personnel and others. It is the intent of DefenseCo and Supplier to resolve issues in a constructive way that reflects the concerns and commercial interests of each Party. Both Parties' primary objective and intent is to have issues resolved by the appropriate levels of authority without the need for

escalation. With this in mind, the following steps are to be followed by the Parties:

1.1 *Empowerment*: Both parties agree that issues are to be resolved at the lowest level possible in keeping with the intent of the Agreement.
1.2 *Documentation*: Both Parties will jointly develop a short briefing document that describes the concern, relevant impact and positions of both Parties. All briefing documents will be stored in a central location that's accessible by both Parties.
1.3 *Request for Assistance*: A meeting will be scheduled with appropriate individuals as described below (phone or videoconference in most cases). The briefing document will be sent in advance to the participants.
1.4 *Escalation*: It is the intention of DefenseCo and Supplier that concerns will be escalated for review and resolution to the next management level as shown on the following chart. Additionally, a flowchart is provided to further illustrate the issue resolution process.

A key part of the issue resolution process was the inclusion of a standing neutral (see chapter 5).

Notice and Cure Agreements

DefenseCo and their Supplier's Notice and Cure Agreement was a sub-section of a much broader termination clause. It reads:

If either Party

(a) commits a material breach of this Agreement, which breach is not cured within thirty (30) days after notice of the breach;
(b) commits a material breach of this Agreement which is not capable of being cured within thirty (30) days; or
(c) commits numerous breaches of its duties or obligations which collectively constitute a material breach of this Agreement and fails (i) to cure such breaches within thirty (30) days after receiving notice of such breaches and (ii) to give the other Party adequate assurances that the cause of such breaches has been corrected and will not recur again;

then either Party may terminate the Term with respect to all or any part of the Services, in whole or in part, as of a date specified in the Notice of termination. If DefenseCo chooses to terminate this Agreement in part under Section XYZ the amounts payable under this Agreement will be adjusted to reflect such partial termination.

The Master Agreement also included a formal notice clause with guidance on how the parties should use notices.

> *Notice*: All notices, waivers, approvals, consents, demands, requests or other communications required or permitted under this Agreement will, unless otherwise expressly provided, be in writing and be deemed to have been properly given, served and received (i) if delivered by messenger, when personally delivered, (ii) if mailed, on the second business day after deposit in the United States Mail, certified or registered, postage prepaid, return receipt requested, or (iii) if delivered by reputable overnight express courier, freight prepaid, the next business day after delivery to such courier; in every case addressed to the Party to be notified as follows: (*the clause went on to list who and how it is appropriate to send notices):*

A LOOK AHEAD

In this chapter, we showed how embedding preventive mechanisms in a party's formal contract can help prevent disputes through six preventive mechanisms. We provided an example of how contract architecture can prevent disputes by making contracts easier to understand with good contract design and easier to execute with smart contracts. We shared how formal relational contracts create a flexible contract framework and embed relational contract constructs to help parties stay in continual alignment when business needs change. We then provided an example of how risk/reward alignment can create fair and balanced contracts that motivate good performance. Last, we shared how contract clauses can provide guidance on how the parties should respond to unanticipated events and manage problems with the goal of preventing disputes.

In the next chapter, we shift further along the Dispute Management Continuum and share how to deploy dispute prevention after signing a contract. We profile five mechanisms that fall into two categories: relationship management and using third-party neutrals to help the parties solve problems before they turn into disputes.

Chapter 5

Managing the Relationship

Business is dynamic, and it is easy for contracting parties to fall into misalignment. Problems—either caused by the fault of one party or simply by changing business conditions—can easily cause friction in a business relationship. Typically, problems start small and only become disputes if they are not properly addressed.

We have already discussed dispute prevention mechanisms that parties can use when entering into and forming a relationship. In this chapter, we delve into mechanisms parties can deploy *after* signing a contract. We profile five mechanisms that fall into two categories: relationship management and using third-party neutrals to help the parties solve problems before they become disputes (Figure 22).

Managing the Business Relationship

Relationship Management

Partnering

Relationship Governance

Relational Negotiations

Third Party Neutral

Traditional Standing Neutral (e.g., Dispute Review Board)

Modern Standing Neutral

Figure 22: Prevention Mechanisms for Formalizing the Relationship

RELATIONSHIP MANAGEMENT

The concept of relationship management is a relatively new discipline. Much of the original work around relationship management stems from managing complex outsourcing and construction contracts, as well as strategic alliances. Three key dispute prevention mechanisms can help in managing the ongoing business relationship: partnering, relationship governance, and relational negotiations.

Partnering

Partnering is a process designed to create a positive and cooperative relationship at the outset of a business-to-business (B2B) relationship. The goal of partnering is to encourage parties to adopt a cooperative environment that promotes teamwork, addresses potential problems promptly, and focuses on attaining common goals.

The early concepts of partnering were formalized when the Construction Industry Institute (CII) formed a task force in 1987 consisting of twenty academic, construction-company, and federal government representatives to explore a process to achieve the goals of total quality management and to reverse the trend of litigation rapidly rising in the construction industry. The CII 1991 report, *In Search of Partnering Excellence*, referred to long-range strategic partnering as a "long-term commitment between two or more organizations to achieve specific business objectives by maximizing the effectiveness of each participant's resources." The report stated that the relationship between contracting parties should be "based upon trust, dedication to common goals, and an understanding of each other's expectations and values." It described the potential benefits of partnering as "improved efficiency and cost-effectiveness, increased opportunity for innovation, and the continuous improvement of quality products and services."[1]

Traditionally, "project-specific" partnering is considered a post-contract signing dispute prevention mechanism. However, partnering concepts can also apply before signing a contract when using collaborative bidding and deal facilitation (see chapter 3).

The Army Corps of Engineers (ACE) was the first to pioneer project-specific partnering in its construction and operations contracts. ACE defines partnering as "a voluntary organized process by which multiple stakeholders having shared interests perform as a team to achieve mutually beneficial goals. It is based on establishing these goals early in the project lifecycle, building trusting relationships, and engaging in collaborative problem-solving."[2]

Why

Multiple studies show that partnering has the power to prevent disputes. The partnering process requires partners to begin communicating candidly and at the very inception of their post-contract business relationship about their organizational strengths, challenges, culture, methods of operation, internal and external communication, and decision-making style. This helps identify the potential conflicts that might arise in their relationship (see chapter 1). By focusing on potential areas of conflict, contracting parties can better respond in mutually supportive ways should those conflicts materialize. Consequently, deal partners come to know and trust one another as collaborators in uniquely unifying ways that help when conflicts inevitably emerge down the road.

---

1. *SP17-1—In Search of Partnering Excellence*, UNIV. TEX.–AUSTIN: CONSTR. INDUS. INST. (1991) (description and benefits of partnering).

2. *Partnering: A Tool for USACE, Engineering, Construction, and Operations*, U.S. ARMY CORPS ENG., Pamphlet #4, 1–53 (1991) (description and benefits of partnering).

Research shows that partnering can have remarkable results for dispute prevention. In one study on construction claims, researchers found organizations participating in partnering reported that claims arise between them only 29 percent of the time versus 100 percent for those that do not use partnering.[3]

Data from the Maryland's State Highway Authority (SHA) study of the effect of partnering on claims reduction between 1991 and 2011 further validates the success of partnering. For example, while Maryland SHA increased average construction expenditures by 138 percent since 1999, partnering helped them reduce the size of claims made against them by 48 percent and reduced settlements by 37 percent with average savings of over $600,000 with the trend continuing toward zero.[4]

In yet another study conducted by the University of California, Davis on the Caltrans partnering program, researchers found the average total claims value in partnered projects for the six-year study totaled $780,000, while non-partnered projects amassed claims averaging $1.03 million. The study concluded that partnering drove cost savings by diminishing the expense and burdens of post-contract arbitration.[5]

However, the benefits of partnering go beyond dispute prevention. The Caltrans study not only reported an 80 percent reduction in the number of claims but also cited additional benefits like:[6]

- 10 percent reduction in total project cost
- 20 percent reduction in project duration
- 83 percent reduction in lost-time accidents
- 50 percent reduction in rework
- 30 percent improvement in job satisfaction
- $60 saved per $1 spent on partnering

Currently, the highway departments of forty-six of the fifty states use partnering.[7] Although partnering has predominantly been used in the construction industry, it can easily be applied to any B2B relationship.

---

3. Veronica Voyton & Khalid Siddiqui, *Partnering: Tool for Construction Claims Reduction*, 10 J. Archit. Eng. 2–4 (2004) (claims in partnered construction projects).

4. *Partnering Delivers … Results*, Int'l Partnering Inst. & Md. Stat. Highway Admin., 1 (stats on partnering).

5. *Partnering Program Yields Big Benefits*, MileMarker, https://dot.ca.gov/-/media/dot-media/programs/risk-strategic-management/documents/mile-marker/mm-2017-q2-partnering-program-a11y.pdf.

6. *Partnering with Us*, U.S. Army Corps Eng., https://www.usace.army.mil/Business-With-Us/Partnering/mod/129895/details/443/.

7. Frank Carr & Brian Polkinghorn, *A Best Practices Manual for Partnering*, SHA 1–41 (2007) (Maryland SHA's partnering program).

How It Works

There is no "standard" way to conduct partnering. Various organizations promote different best practices and processes.[8] One of the best resources is the Caltrans *Field Guide to Partnering*, which was revised and published in June 2022 to include lessons learned from almost three decades of partnering experience.[9]

Recently, the International Institute for Conflict Prevention and Resolution (CPR), working with its stakeholders in a dispute prevention task force, focused on how partnering can generate a deal overview among the parties in a business relationship to "prevent or mitigate future disputes while enhancing the value of the relationship amongst the parties." The deal overview seeks to have the parties align around the purpose of the deal, its objectives, risks, and potential conflicts. The task force also emphasized the importance of relationship-building exercises to build a bond between the parties.[10]

Typical Steps in Partnering

A benefit of partnering is its flexibility with the unique partnering process defined by the contracting parties. Below, we share steps commonly found in partnering programs.

Commitment During Contracting: The partnering process typically begins when two or more organizations contract to work together and agree to use partnering. Some organizations, like CalTrans, require partnering on all construction projects over $10 million and one hundred or more working days, and it is encouraged for projects over $1 million.[11]

Post-Contract Planning: Stakeholders from each organization select a third-party neutral facilitator. They also identify the necessary stakeholders for the project and determine the agenda and time for the initial partnering meeting, often referred to as the kickoff workshop. The duration of the kickoff workshop typically ranges between half a day and two days, but it can be longer based on the scope and complexity.

Kickoff Workshop: The facilitator helps participants from each organization establish their partnering commitments and begin to build a cohesive team culture. During the kickoff workshop, the contracting parties establish a formal charter and identify key issues and risk management strategies. A key goal of the

8. *Field Guide to Partnering*, CalTrans Partnering 1–59 (2022) (partnering best practices and processes); *Partnering supra* note 2; *Construction Partnering: Informal Partnering Toolkit*, NAVFAC, 1–137 (partnering best practices and processes).

9. *Field Guide to Partnering supra* note 8 (decades of partnering experiences).

10. 13 *Joint Best Practice Approaches to Dispute Prevention in Business Arrangements*, CPR, https://assets-002.noviams.com/novi-file-uploads/cpr/pdfs-and-documents/Joint-Best-Practices-Outline-for-Dispute-Prevention.pdf.

11. *Field Guide to Partnering supra* note 8.

kickoff workshop is to develop a dispute management plan and process. This includes creating a dispute management "ladder" and a defined process for escalating unresolved conflict to a formal dispute resolution process(es).

Periodic Partnering Meetings: Successful partnering uses monthly or quarterly "refresher" meetings to review issue status, revisit and modify resolution ladder steps, if necessary, and evaluate and measure the meeting of tangible and intangible objectives to allow for adjustments.

Close-Out Workshop: Final evaluations are completed with any lessons learned to improve processes in the future, and individual partnering contributions are recognized.

Typical Roles in Partnering

There are three key roles in partnering.[12] These include:

Relationship Managers: This includes a senior-level individual from each organization responsible for leading the partnering effort. In a construction engineering project, this may also include the project manager(s) or resident engineers accountable for the day-to-day operations of the project.

Facilitator: A partnering facilitator is a third-party neutral who assists the relationship managers in developing and maintaining the partnering program. The facilitator is not the leader of the partnership effort but rather works with the parties to ensure the success of their relationships.

Participants: Participants include key stakeholders involved with the relationship. This can also include critical third-party stakeholders who could potentially delay or pose a risk to the relationship (e.g., in a construction project, such third-party stakeholders might include utilities, railroads, or government agencies).

Costs of Partnering

The costs of partnering are generally low when compared to the overall cost of the contract. Typically, the largest cost is the facilitator. Other costs include meeting facilities, food and beverages for the participants, and workshop materials. When the kickoff workshop spans more than a day and is held at a distance from the stakeholders' offices, there are additional expenses for lodging and transportation.

Case Study

The Broad Run Water Reclamation Facility (BRWRF) project of the Loudoun County Sanitation Authority (LCSA) in Virginia is an example of a successful

12. Frank Carr, *Partnering: Aligning Interests, Collaboration, and Achieving Common Goals*, CPR Dispute Prevention Briefing: Construction 1–19 (2010) (roles in partnering).

partnering program.[13] The case study shares how partnering encourages collaboration, accountability, and consistency, leading to the project having only three issues escalated to senior project leadership and no disputes.

The $180 million project included the following key components:

- *Contract 1 ($86 million)*: Site, yard work, and liquid treatment facilities
- *Contract 2 ($43 million)*: Secondary treatment/membrane treatment facility
- *Contract 3 ($27 million)*: Digesters and solids treatment facility
- *Contract 4 ($14 million)*: Operations complex
- *Contract 5 ($10 million)*: Influent sewage pumping station

The series of contracts included the following key stakeholders:

- *LCSA*: Owner and operator
- *CH2M Hill*: Design engineer and construction services manager for contracts 1, 2, 3, and 4
- *Black and Veatch*: Design engineer and construction services manager for contract 5
- *Hill International*: Owner consultant
- *Pizzagalli*: General contractor for contracts 2, 3, and 5
- *Fru-Con*: General contractor for contracts 1 and 4

During program planning, LCSA decided to use a formal partnering process and engaged Bill Spragins, an experienced management consultant in the construction industry. The partnering process was designed to encourage collaboration, accountability, and consistency among the stakeholders and focused on timely problem-solving at the lowest levels.

Initial Partnering Sessions

Executive-Level Kickoff Session: Participants for this session included senior-level personnel from each of the general contractors. A key purpose was to build relationships at the senior level and agree on overall project values and goals. The executive group also established a high-level escalation process and communication protocols the parties would rely on to work through potential problems. Building foundational relationships at the senior level was important, and executives would continue to meet in impromptu lunches and phone conversations during the project.

13. *Partnering Project Success Case Study*, For Construction Pros (July 13, 2009), https://www.forconstructionpros.com/business/article/10292311/partnering-project-success-case-study

Project-Level Kickoff Session: In subsequent sessions, the team convened from each general contractor expanded to include all on-site supervisory personnel and project engineers. During the project-level kickoff session, the broader team developed a formal team charter and detailed the issue escalation process. The issue escalation process included a five-tiered structure of collaborative teams composed of representatives from each business organization at each organizational level. The intent was to level the playing field and ensure issues were addressed at the project level. If team members could not address an issue, the issue would escalate equitably upward to the next level of management.

Ongoing Partnering Activities

The partnering program included ongoing activities, which involved thirty-one sessions and twenty-four team evaluation conference calls over 3.5 years.

Quarterly Executive Sessions: At these sessions, project managers for the key organizations for each contract provided a joint project update. The group then assessed team performance against the goals developed in the project charter and developed action items for any key issues. Thirteen of these sessions were held for each general contractor during the project.

Team Evaluation Process (Internal Customer Satisfaction Survey): The parties used a team evaluation rating tool administered by the partnering facilitator every quarter for each of the five contracts. Participants reviewed the results and comments generated by the surveys at the quarterly executive-level session.

Early Commissioning and Start-Up Session: Approximately one year after the initial partnering sessions and once the contracts were up and running, the team held an "all projects, all hands" session attended by supervisory personnel from each project. The session aimed to generate collective input from the considerable expertise in the room on everything needed to properly commission and start up the plant across the five separate contracts. The result of this session was the initiation of a commissioning and start-up team comprised of representatives from all business organizations. The team took the input from the session and developed an initial strategy. The team then met regularly for the duration of the project.

Project Success

The BRWRF project of the LCSA was completed on time in just under four years. Project change orders were kept to less than 3 percent, which is less than 50 percent of the industry average. Project quality and safety exceeded expectations as well, with the program having less than 2.0 Occupational Safety and Health Administration (OSHA) recordable incidents per 200,000 person-hours compared to the industry benchmark of 6.9.

Partnering helped the stakeholders engage in effective communication and problem-solving, which prevented disputes. In total, only three issues escalated to the executive level (the fifth level), resulting in effective dispute prevention.

Bill Spragins, the partnering facilitator, observed that parties could prevent disputes by centering decision-making at the lowest project management levels. Rather than encourage escalating the conflict to higher management, supervisors and superintendents were empowered to resolve issues at their level of engagement. This emphasis created pride in the work effort and strong ownership of the outcome of the product. According to Rick Thoesen, Deputy General Manager for LCSA, "Leadership was expected from everyone, not just management, and a project culture was established where face-to-face dialog or phone calls for the purpose of resolving issues was emphasized. Emails to resolve issues were discouraged. This resulted in the avoidance of 'claim missiles' and helped to provide empathy and resolution for all parties."[14]

Relationship Governance

Oliver Williamson (2009 Nobel Laureate in Economic Sciences) wrote that governance is the "framework within which the integrity of a transaction is decided."[15] Formal relationship governance includes a variety of tools and tactics contracting parties use to collectively manage their relationship post-contract signing. This includes managing the ongoing operations and relationships between the parties. For purposes of this book, we use the term relationship governance to refer to both contract and relationship governance.

Relationship governance began to get traction with the rise of outsourcing agreements when many organizations began to make a connection between a lack of governance and failures associated with poor contract and relationship management. The early concept of relationship governance centered on contract management and compliance.[16] As the need for relationship governance evolved, the concept of supplier relationship management (SRM) emerged, which expanded on "contract management" to include how to best manage the relationships with suppliers.

Over the years, the concept of relationship governance has further evolved, and today it includes a robust view of how to manage the contract and the relationship between contracting parties.[17] In addition, consulting firms, industry associations, government organizations, and universities have researched and developed training, tools, and guidance around what good relationship governance means.

---

14. *Id.*

15. Oliver E. Williamson, *Transaction-Cost Economics: The Governance of Contractual Relations*, 22 J.L. & Econ 233–61 (1979) (relationship governance).

16. Tim Cummins, *The Role of a Contract Manager: 2014 Update*, Commitment Matters (Jan. 28, 2014), https://commitmentmatters.com/2014/01/28/the-role-of-a-contract-manager-2014-update/.

17. Arne Keller et al., *Alliance Governance Mechanisms in the Face of Disruption*, 32 Org. Sci. 1542–70 (2021) (evolution of relationship governance).

Why

Assuming that complicated B2B relationships will take care of themselves is a flawed premise, to say the least. Like any relationship, let alone those as complicated as business relationships, constant maintenance is necessary. Nowhere is this better illustrated than in outsourcing arrangements where teams from varying backgrounds and roles are quilted together to accomplish difficult tasks. The Sourcing Industry Group explains the need for governance on their website[18]:

> Transferring responsibilities to an outside source can lower capital expenses and overhead, free employees' time to work on other tasks, increase efficiency for time-consuming functions and improve the quality of specialized work. But how do companies manage teams that are hundreds or even thousands of miles away, to ensure the best quality of work, and the greatest return on investment? Outsourcing governance, or the process of managing outsourcing engagements has become a hot-button issue. In order to manage risks effectively and get the most value, a strong outsourcing governance strategy is critical. Unfortunately, many companies lack such a strategy—which may be why so many outsourcing arrangements fail.

The below studies highlight the conflicts, value leakage and failed business relationships that can arise from a lack of proper governance:

- The Outsourcing Center reports that poor governance plays a role in outsourcing failures as much as 62 percent of the time.[19]
- The London consultancy Hudson & Yorke cites governance as "one of the main reasons why managed service or outsource agreements succeed or suffer."[20]
- The Corporate Executive Board found that in a typical outsourced deal, the outsourcing company can erode up to 90 percent of anticipated value due to poor governance of the relationship.[21]
- World Commerce and Contracting reports typical organizations lose up to 9.2 percent of their revenue due to poor contract management.[22]

---

18. *Creating a Better Outsourcing Governance Model*, SIG-ORG, https://www.sig.org/src-documents/creating-better-outsourcing-governance-model-0/.

19. *Id.*

20. Mark Gibbons, *Telecommunications and Network Services: Ten Steps to Successful Contract Governance*, Hudson & Yorke Ltd., (White Paper Executive Summary, 2009) (governance and outsourcing outcomes).

21. *3PL Management: New Tips and Tools,* Corp. Exec. Bd.: Operations Leadership Exch., (2009).

22. Tim Cummins *supra* note 16.

- A Queensland government auditor general report cites poor contract management as a major contributor to cost overruns and timing delays on projects, noting the state lost approximately 12 percent in contract value (127 million Australian dollars on a base of A$1.5 billion) and had delays on average of four months.[23]

How It Works

Interestingly, when considering relationship governance, there is no standardized approach companies can follow. Why? Because contracts are varied and complex. Consequently, experts suggest organizations should design their governance structures to address the unique needs of their relationships.[24]

The University of Tennessee (UT) has studied relationship governance since 2003. As part of their work, UT researchers teamed to develop a framework—published in the book *Strategic Sourcing in the New Economy*—for managing different contracts ranging from basic transactional contracts to a highly collaborative Vested sourcing business model with strategic suppliers.[25] The UT research suggests good relationship governance includes four elements: relationship management, transformation management, exit management, and compliance with external regulations and internal requirements.[26]

By implementing each of these elements, the resilience of the relationship is strengthened and inevitable conflicts can be better managed. Relationship management can include dispute prevention and resolution mechanisms. Transformation management often involves procedures for accommodating changes to the contractual relationship to minimize resulting disruption and conflict and instead refocusing the parties on value creation. Effective exit management perhaps best illustrates how thoughtful relationship governance can avoid disputes. As supplier relationships become more dependent, exiting a relationship becomes harder and costlier. Exit management outlines how contracting parties will manage either a full or partial agreement termination. Exit management practices can vary significantly, ranging from a simple termination for convenience to a comprehensive exit management strategy, which guides how the parties will unwind during an exit.

---

23. Australian Associated Press, *Cost blowouts for Queensland Projects Caused Partly by 'Poor Contract Management'*, The Guardian (May 17, 2022), https://www.theguardian.com/australia-news/2022/may/17/cost-blowouts-for-queensland-projects-caused-partly-by-poor-contract-management.

24. Oliver E. Williamson *supra* note 15.

25. Bonnie Keith et al., Strategic Sourcing in the New Economy: Harnessing the Potential of Sourcing Business Models in Modern Procurement (2016).

26. Kate Vitasek et al., *Unpacking Outsourcing Governance*, Univ. Tenn., 1–45 (2023) (elements of good relationship governance).

For example, performance-based agreements, by design, are typically longer-term with suppliers making asset-specific investments and taking on risk to achieve performance improvement and/or guaranteed cost savings. In addition, performance-based agreements often involve system integration and processes that enable suppliers to drive efficiencies. The added codependency and asset-specific investment from suppliers require that contracting parties look beyond simple termination clauses. As such, the "rule" for a good exit management plan for a performance-based agreement is to use a more fair and balanced exit for both parties. For example, the buying organization may have clear termination rights based on performance levels, and the supplier may include safeguards to recoup unamortized investments if the buyer terminates early. This approach helps reduce the prospects for disputes that might otherwise arise from the termination of a long-term relationship.

Case Study

Microsoft embarked on a complete reengineering of its global finance processes and operations in 2006.[27] Called the OneFinance initiative, the effort outsourced back-office finance operations spread across ninety-five countries to Accenture. In February 2007, Microsoft signed an outsourcing agreement with Accenture, with an original contract term of seven years at a value of $185 million. The contract spanned their entire back-office finance processes, including accounts payable (expense reports and invoices), requisition to purchase order process, and general accounting services.

In March 2010, the Shared Services Outsourcing Network honored the Microsoft–Accenture outsourcing relationship as the Best Mature Outsourced Service Delivery Operation. A key success factor was their robust governance structure. The parties used a Vested sourcing business relationship model (refer to chapter 3), which included contract schedules dedicated to each of the key functional governance areas:

- Relationship management
- Transformation management
- Exit management
- Compliance

In this case study, we highlight some of the relationship management governance practices designed to create and sustain a healthy working relationship.

27. Kate Vitasek et al., *How Microsoft and Accenture Transformed Global Finance Operations*, UNIV. TENN., 1–49 (2020) (case study on Microsoft and Accenture).

Core Governance Roles

Microsoft and Accenture wanted to develop a working relationship that would not only streamline communications but would also help promote and drive their transformational and compliance efforts. As part of the relationship, Microsoft and Accenture embedded four separate and core roles that make up the governance structure. Individuals filling the roles were named key personnel (someone deemed critical to the success of the relationships) in the contract. The key personnel roles were noted in the contract to ensure both parties properly invested the appropriate resources into the overall governance of the contract and the relationship. The four core governance roles are:

Service Delivery and Management

This includes regional service delivery managers for the five geographic regions—Europe, Latin America, North America, Asia, the Middle East, and Africa. These individuals monitor end-to-end delivery and performance levels for all in-scope services and processes for both Microsoft and Accenture in their respective regions.

Process Championship and Transformation

This includes dedicated resources accountable for the end-to-end process area solution design and policy. In the early phase of the relationship, the Global Process Owners provided guidance and support during the original ramp-up of the relationship. After the initial transition phase, the job of the Global Process Owners changed to focus on driving what Microsoft coined "Transformation Projects," which included both continuous improvement projects and larger innovation initiatives.

Commercial and Relationship Management

This includes dedicated resources to manage the commercial and contractual aspects of the relationship as well as facilitating overall relationship health across the various stakeholders in the two organizations. For example, key functional responsibilities included managing the pricing model, facilitating key governance meetings such as Quarterly Business Reviews, and coordinating contract changes.

Controls and Compliance

This includes individuals responsible for developing a robust world-class controls and compliance environment. For example, these individuals work together to ensure that performance standards are met and the parties remain in compliance with external regulations.

Peer-to-Peer Communications

To ensure alignment, the parties created peer-to-peer "two-in-a-box" teams where team members from both Microsoft and Accenture align for each of the core governance functions. Using a two-in-a-box approach streamlines communication and promotes timely problem-solving at the lowest possible levels before escalating to higher levels. If two-in-a-box teammates cannot solve a problem, it escalates to the next governance tier. If, after going through the issue resolution process, differences remain, either party can flag a problem as a dispute.

Tiered Management Structure

In addition to the functional governance roles, Microsoft and Accenture rely on a three-tier governance structure. The three tiers given below enable smooth escalations and decision-making at the appropriate level:

A Joint Steering Group

The group provides overall sponsorship, program direction, and governance oversight to assess progress, review overall performance, set strategic direction, and make decisions related to escalated issues and contract change requests, if any. This group and senior executives from both Microsoft and Accenture meet semi-annually.

A Joint Operations Group

The group provides management oversight of global service delivery and monitors the progress of OneFinance. This group is responsible for service quality across process areas, regions, and Accenture delivery locations and sets continuous improvement and implementation priorities. The Joint Operations Group meets regularly (e.g., Quarterly Business Reviews).

A Regional Management Group

The group oversees day-to-day operations in each geographic region.

Recall that if a two-in-a-box team cannot resolve a problem, they can escalate it to the next governance tier. Microsoft and Accenture outlined a formal dispute management process in their agreement, defining a "dispute" as any question or difference that arises concerning the construction or meaning of, or affecting, the agreement. Microsoft and Accenture use the following procedure for handling disputes:

- The first instance of a dispute should be settled by the Microsoft Global Head of BPO (business process outsourcing) Management, Finance Operations and the Accenture Program Director with a resolution target of fourteen (14) days after the question or difference is brought to their attention.
- If not resolved, the dispute will be referred to the Joint Steering Group, which must meet within fourteen (14) days (or such other period as the Parties may agree) of the reference to attempt to resolve the dispute.

- If the dispute is not resolved within this period, the escalation will continue with the same maximum time interval up to the Microsoft COO and the Accenture Outsourcing Executive.

Results

Microsoft and Accenture's outsourcing partnership has garnered over a dozen industry awards. Their relationship governance has helped them evolve from the early days and has been extended several times. In the last contract extension, Grace Lao, General Manager for Microsoft Finance Operations, recognized the importance of the partnership and what the parties had accomplished:[28]

> Our longstanding collaboration with Accenture has enabled us, through our OneFinance initiative, to standardize our finance and accounting processes across 120 countries, improving compliance and control across our operations and reducing related costs by 30 percent. Building on the past nine years, we look forward to continuing to innovate and drive new transformation projects together with Accenture designed to reinvent Microsoft's productivity and business processes.

Relational Negotiations

Negotiation is any method of direct or indirect communication where parties with opposing interests work together to resolve a problem, conflict, or dispute. Negotiation is a common mechanism contracting parties can use to prevent a problem from becoming a formal dispute.

There are hundreds of books on negotiating.[29] Negotiation strategies range from adversarial to win-win, with book titles sharing how to *Start with No*, *Getting to Yes*, and *Getting to We*. We advocate the use of a relationship-preserving negotiations approach.

Many negotiation experts distinguish between competitive/positional and cooperative/interest-based approaches designed to preserve a relationship.

---

28. *Microsoft Awards Accenture Seven-Year Contract Extension for Finance, Accounting and Procurement Business Process Services*, Accenture (Dec. 12, 2016), https://newsroom.accenture.com/news/2016/microsoft-awards-accenture-seven-year-contract-extension-for-finance-accounting-and-procurement-business-process-services.

29. Scholarly inquiry into negotiation is vast, spawning a rich and varied literature. Discussions of cultural or gender-based variations in negotiation style alone could fill several book-cases. Because this book's focus is on dispute prevention, we only skim the surface of this complex topic. For a sampling of additional reading on negotiation *see* Andrea Kupfer Schneider & Christopher Honeyman, The Negotiator's Fieldbook: The Desk Reference for the Experienced Negotiator (2006); and works by Eko Yi Liao on Style and Culture, Charles B. Craver on Distributive Negotiation, and Rishi Batra on Integrative and Distributive Negotiation.

Positions are what a party demands. Interests are a deeper expression of what a person or organization cares about, such as needs, concerns, and priorities.[30] In a competitive approach, the parties try to maximize their returns at the other party's expense. In contrast, a cooperative approach focuses on identifying common interests, building on common ground, and creatively brainstorming options to meet each side's interests to the greatest degree possible.

Interest in collaborative approaches rose after Roger Fisher, William Ury, and Bruce Patton launched the Harvard Negotiations Project. Their concepts got a boost in 1981 with the publication of *Getting to YES: Negotiating Agreement Without Giving In*, which became one of the world's bestselling negotiation books.[31]

Why

There are several benefits to using negotiation to solve problems before they become disputes needing formal resolution.

Voluntary/Maintain Control

Contracting parties are not forced to participate in a negotiation. If they opt for negotiation as a pre-dispute resolution mechanism, they can opt to negotiate directly or utilize a representative, such as a lawyer. In addition, the parties are free to accept or reject the outcome of negotiations and can withdraw at any point during the process.

Non-adjudicative: Negotiation involves only the parties—meaning they are not using a third party to decide on behalf of the parties. However, negotiating parties may request a third party to help facilitate their negotiation process (see also "Third-Party Standing Neutrals" later in this chapter).

Flexible: The parties can tailor the negotiation process to fit their needs. For example, they can agree on the timing and location of negotiations, the number of negotiating sessions the parties commit to, and the information they share. In addition, they can decide on the negotiation rules they will use (e.g., an interest-based approach).

Bilateral/Multilateral: A negotiation process can involve as few as two parties (e.g., a single buyer and supplier) or multiple parties (e.g., a construction project owner, the architect, and the builder).

Confidential: The parties may negotiate publicly or privately. Usually, organizations—especially in the private sector—opt to have confidential negotiations.

Cost-Effective: Negotiating is typically less expensive because there are no court, mediation, or arbitration fees and often does not include lawyers.

30. Lisa Blomgren Amsler et al., Dispute System Design (2020).

31. *History of the Harvard Negotiation Project*, Harv. L. Sch., https://www.pon.harvard.edu/history-of-the-harvard-negotiation-project/.

There is significant research into the benefit of collaborative negotiating approaches. Research in collaborative approaches grew when John Nash, John C. Harsanyi, and Reinhard Selten's research won a Nobel Prize in Economics in 1994.[32] Their work inspired academics around the world to delve deeper into what's known as game theory.[33] Game theory is the study of the outcome of strategic interactions among decision-makers. By using rigorous statistical methods, researchers can model what happens when people choose to cooperate or choose to take an aggressive, power-based approach to negotiation.

The University of Michigan's Robert Axelrod—a mathematician turned game theorist—used statistics in a famous game theory study to show that when individuals cooperate, they reach more advantageous outcomes than when they don't. He published his research and conclusions in the book *The Evolution of Cooperation*; which is widely taught around the world.[34]

Sadly, many business leaders are taught strategies focusing on using their power and playing to win at the other party's expense.[35] This is an easy trap to fall into when negotiating with books such as *Start With No*, *Get More*, and *The Negotiating Game*, all teaching how to win at the negotiating table. Nobel Laureate Oliver Williamson advises against this—stating, "Muscular buyers not only use their suppliers, but they often 'use up' their suppliers and discard them." As we noted earlier, Williamson calls a power-based muscular approach "*myopic and inefficient*."[36]

How It Works

Research supports using cooperative strategies to create value for all parties.[37]

---

32. *The Sveriges Riksbank Prize in Economic Sciences in Memory of Alfred Nobel 1994*, The Nobel Prize, https://www.nobelprize.org/prizes/economic-sciences/1994/summary/.

33. *Game Theory*, Stanford Encyclopedia of Philosophy, https://plato.stanford.edu/entries/game-theory/.

34. Robert Axelrod, The Evolution of Cooperation (Revised ed. 2006).

35. Kate Gibson, *4 Strategies for Shifting the Power Balance in Your Business*, Harv. Bus. Sch. (Aug. 9, 2022), https://online.hbs.edu/blog/post/shift-of-power-balance-in-business.

36. Oliver E. Williamson *supra* note 15.

37. Roger Fisher et al., Getting to Yes: Negotiating Agreement Without Giving in Paperback (3d ed. 2011). Of course, support for uniform application of a cooperative approach is not unanimous. *See* Harold Abramson, *Fashioning an Effective Negotiation Style: Choosing Among Good Practices, Tactics and Tricks*, *in* The Negotiator's Desk Reference (Honeyman and Schneider, eds., vol. 1, 2017) (noting that negotiators' style often includes "good practices," tactics, and tricks, and that understanding a counterpart's negotiation choices, especially the use of tactics and tricks, is important when fashioning one's own negotiating style); *see also* Charles Craver, *Distributive Negotiation Techniques*, *in* The Negotiator's Desk Reference 75–89 (Honyman & Schneider, eds., vol. 1, 2017) (discussing the reality of "hard bargaining" and how to engage and defend oneself against these techniques).

We suggest using the three relationship-preserving negotiation tactics given below to resolve problems and conflicts before they become formal disputes.

Use an Interest-Based Negotiation Approach

Negotiating has been studied for decades with dozens—if not hundreds—of organizations offering professional negotiation training. The best-selling book *Getting to Yes* began promoting a more collaborative interest-based negotiation approach in 1981.[38] Today, negotiation experts teaching collaborative/interest-based approaches generally agree on the following best practices:

- Concentrate on interests, not positions.
- Separate the people from the problem. This entails not blaming the other side for the problem(s) one has encountered and discussing the perceptions held by each side. It also requires a commitment to ensure effective communication between all parties.
- Listen carefully and actively to what the other side is saying and acknowledge what is being said. This can be done by asking questions and by making frequent summaries.
- Make the negotiations a "win-win" outcome by creating options for mutual benefit.
- Use objective standards. Ideally, the standards are agreed to before starting the negotiation sessions.
- Evaluate proposals and solutions in light of the BATNA, or "best alternative to a negotiated agreement."

Focus on Getting to We

The book *Getting to We* goes beyond interest-based negotiation and suggests the following three relationship-preserving tactics:[39]

Adopt Guiding Principles: Guiding Principles—used in relational contracting (refer to chapter 4)—are a powerful tool that can be applied to any negotiation. Even if the parties have not adopted the Guiding Principles as part of a formal relational contract, they can still agree on the Guiding Principles for their unique negotiation.

Agree on Allowable/Not Allowable Tactics: Many negotiation books teach tactics that promote adversarial behaviors. An effective approach for preserving the health of a business relationship is to go through a list of known negotiating tactics and define if each tactic is allowed or not allowed in the actual negotiations. A good rule of thumb is for the parties to not allow tactics that erode trust, such as bluffing, good cop-bad cop, and stalling.

---

38. *Id.*

39. JEANETTE NYDENET AL., GETTING TO WE: NEGOTIATING AGREEMENTS FOR HIGHLY COLLABORATIVE BUSINESS AGREEMENTS (2013).

Agree on the Level of Transparency the Parties Use: The premise is that, if information is power, information shared is exponentially powerful in helping parties work through solutions. When the goal is problem-solving (versus dispute resolution), being as transparent as possible will help the contracting parties solve their problem with a broader lens.

Incorporate Step Negotiation

Step negotiation encourages individuals at the lowest level in each organization to solve potential problems promptly when they arise. If these individuals cannot resolve a potential problem, they escalate the item to the next higher management level in each organization. A best practice is to encourage step-negotiation in your dispute management clause (refer to chapter 4), which outlines pre-agreed processes and timeframes to prevent problems from festering.

A step negotiation process provides an inherent incentive for resolving problems while they are small. How? When individuals from each organization have autonomy to work through potential problems when they are small, they can demonstrate to colleagues and supervisors their ability to solve problems; individuals are thus incentivized to promote their problem-solving prowess. The happy side-effect is a reduction in conflict that escalates into dispute. The defined step negotiation process also helps provide structure so potential problems do not fester. Lastly, this approach spares "upper management" from having to get involved, preserving their time and attention for more vital tasks.

Case Study

The below case study illustrates a step negotiation process in a construction project. OwnerCo is a typical organization funding a construction project. In this case, OwnerCo was the designer/architect/funder of the construction project. OwnerCo contracted with BuildCo as the general contractor who would perform much of the work, including overseeing subcontractors. The parties agreed to a five-step dispute prevention ladder to help them prevent disputes (Figure 23).

Level	OwnerCo	BuildCo	Defined Focus	Escalation Trigger
1	Inspector	Foreman/ Superintendent	Issues	Issues managed on a Project Risk Register
2	Resident Engineer	Project Manager	Potential Problems	Email or memo
3	Construction Engineer	Area Manager	Defined Problems	Problem Resolution Form
4	Division Chief	Operations Manager	Conflict (Claim)	Claim Form
5	Board	President/ Owner	Dispute	Notice and cure provision guidelines in contract

Figure 23: Five-Step Dispute Prevention Ladder

The process starts when either party has identified an issue that will require the parties to work together. The goal for the parties is to work through issues at the lowest level before they turn into problems, conflicts, and disputes. The process starts at the lowest level possible (inspector/foreman) and proceeds through both organizations' hierarchies. Unresolved issues at the lowest level are flagged to the next level in the escalation ladder. As issues escalate, the focus shifts from a simple issue to a potential problem, a defined problem, a conflict, and a formal dispute. An escalation to the next level is a formal signal to everyone involved that there is a heightened need for collaboration to work through the escalated item.

A Risk Register tracks issues to manage risks and prevent issues from becoming a problem. If appropriate, the parties can skip levels in the dispute prevention ladder. For example, if something urgent happens and needs immediate attention, an item can start at a higher level (e.g., a defined problem). However, the goal is identifying and managing risks before they become problems.

Escalating an item to the next level occurs in writing (an email or simple memo), which signals the lower-level participants are requesting help from the next level. A key part of the process is that at each step in the dispute prevention ladder, the individuals at the lower level must identify their points of disagreement and suggest what they might need for resolution. When an escalated item moves to a defined problem, the parties complete a form to help them document and articulate their misalignment to the next level. When an escalated item gets to the last level (a dispute), the parties trigger a formal Notice and Cure Agreement.

Once an issue escalates to the next level, it is incumbent on those personnel to meet as soon as possible to try to resolve the issue. However, once an item escalates to a potential problem, the individuals at the next level hold an ad hoc meeting to address the problems. As time is money in construction projects, the individuals in levels 2 and 3 of the dispute ladder have set aside pre-defined times on their calendars to work on potential problems and defend against increased discord. If there are no problems, the parties can simply cancel the meeting.

While this example comes from the construction industry, the concept can apply in any industry. For example, recall from the Microsoft case study cited previously how the parties embedded a simple step negotiation process into their tiered governance structure.

THIRD-PARTY STANDING NEUTRALS

Typically, third-party neutrals are associated with dispute resolution through mediation or arbitration. However, in the 1970s, organizations in the construction industry began using a panel of third-party neutrals (referred to as a Dispute Review Board, or DRB) in a more proactive manner where the neutral is embedded into the contracting parties' ongoing governance. Thus, the neutral is called a "standing" neutral.

By 1991, DRBs were used successfully on over one-hundred projects, and the concept was recognized as a superior process for keeping the peace on a construction project. The first use of the term "standing neutral" to characterize a DRB appears in a CPR 1991 publication titled *Preventing and Resolving Construction Disputes*.[40]

Today, a standing neutral is one of the most innovative and promising developments in preventing disputes. It is an excellent option for any long-term relationship (such as a joint venture, longer-term outsourcing and franchise agreements, and complex construction projects). The concept has evolved over the years. Standing neutrals are now often a single independent person whose role is more focused on prevention than a DRB that focuses more on early dispute resolution. Standing neutrals are often referenced as a "coach" and "mutual friend" who help contracting parties in various capacities. When organizations have difficulty resolving a problem or conflict, they can tap into their standing neutral to help them facilitate their negotiations and prevent it from becoming a formal dispute.[41] Indeed, depending on how the parties choose to deploy the standing neutral, the neutral can themselves identify potential areas of conflict and address them proactively.

In this chapter, we profile two types of third-party neutrals: traditional standing neutrals and modern standing neutrals. The primary difference between a traditional standing neutral and a modern standing neutral is how they work with contracting parties. A traditional standing neutral is typically limited to helping the contracting parties work through problems and conflicts before they become a dispute. A modern standing neutral typically provides more proactive support services that help keep the party's interests aligned well before problems or misalignments occur. The various roles of standing neutral are explained in more detail in the "How it Works" section of this chapter.

Why

Standing neutrals have had a remarkable record of success. The Dispute Review Board Foundation (DRBF) found in most cases the mere availability of the DRB results in the parties minimizing their conflicts and never needing to look to the

40. CPR Legal Program Construction Disputes Committee, Preventing and Resolving Construction Disputes (James Groton ed. 1991).

41. Kate Vitasek et al., *Unpacking the Standing Neutral: A Cost Effective and Common-Sense Approach for Preventing Conflict*, UNI Scholarworks 1–70 (2019) (the Dispute Management Continuum).

standing neutral to make any recommendations or decisions. In the small minority of cases where the standing neutral makes a recommendation, the parties accept 95 percent of the recommendations without resorting to mediation, arbitration, or litigation.[42]

Why does the presence of a standing neutral have such a powerful impact? The nature of the standing neutral provides a helpful dose of reality to the parties and encourages them to be more objective in their dealings with each other. When differences of opinion arise, the parties' continuous access to the standing neutral lets them quickly use the standing neutral as an objective sounding board, obtaining a recommended course of action minimally disruptive to the business relationship.

How It Works

The basic concept of a standing neutral works the same whether using a traditional or modern version. When designing a standing neutral process, it is important to understand three critical success factors.

Critical Success Factors

Early Mutual Selection

The parties jointly select the standing neutral early in the relationship. This allows the standing neutral to be embedded in the continuing governance mechanisms. The parties mutually agree and designate a single neutral or a board of three neutrals. The parties jointly select their standing neutral, where each has high confidence in the neutral's integrity and expertise. A standing neutral is typically an expert in the industry in which the parties are involved (e.g., construction, facilities management, or IT services).

Continuous Involvement

Following the standing neutral's selection, the parties brief the standing neutral on the relationship and provide them with the necessary documents. The standing neutral is then formally embedded into the parties' ongoing governance (e.g., attending Monthly Operation Reviews and/or more strategic Quarterly Business Reviews). In some cases, they may choose to limit the role of the standing neutral to only being involved on an ad hoc basis. In this case, the standing neutral acts more like a "standby" neutral.

42. *Dispute Board Manual*, DRBF, https://www.drb.org/dispute-board-manual.

Prompt Action

A key objective of a standing neutral process is to preserve cooperative relationships between the contracting parties. While the role of modern and traditional standing neutrals vary—both aim to "keep the peace." A good standing neutral process emphasizes "real-time" involvement—especially if there is a potential problem or conflict brewing. If the contracting parties are using a standby neutral, they are expected to be available on relatively short notice to consult with the parties and discuss issues while misalignment and problems are still new and where the parties' positions have likely not hardened.

Process of Selecting and Ramping Up a Standing Neutral

Selecting the Neutral

At the outset of their relationship, parties select one or three persons with whom they have trust and confidence to serve as their facilitator (the standing neutral) throughout their relationship. A single standing neutral should always be entirely independent. In cases where there is a multi-member standing neutral panel, there are several ways to choose the panel; often, each party nominates one member, and the two nominated neutrals select a third member. In such cases, it is typically required that every panel member be acceptable to both parties and that all panel members be independent and impartial, with no special allegiance to the nominating party.

Defining the Role of the Standing Neutral

As part of the selection process, the parties formalize an agreement with the standing neutral, including determining the standing neutral's responsibilities and authority. As shown in figure 24, there are nine design principles contracting parties should use when designing their standing neutral program.

Briefing

After selecting the standing neutral, the parties brief the standing neutral regarding the nature, scope, and purpose of the relationship. As part of the briefing, the standing neutral is usually equipped with a basic set of contract materials and supporting documents to get ramped up and help them properly serve the parties throughout their relationships.

Costs

The parties equally absorb the cost and expenses of the standing neutral.

Below, we share how both a traditional standing neutral and a modern standing neutral work and provide a case study of organizations that use each in practice.

<table>
<tr><th>Design Principles</th><th colspan="7">Options for Your Standing Neutral Program</th></tr>
<tr><td>Timing of Involvement</td><td colspan="4">Pre-Contract Signing (e.g., Deal Architect)</td><td colspan="3">Post-Contract Signing</td></tr>
<tr><td>Number of Neutrals</td><td colspan="4">One</td><td colspan="3">Three</td></tr>
<tr><td>Skills Required</td><td colspan="2">Deep Subject Matter Expert / Industry Experience</td><td colspan="2">Facilitation/Soft Skills</td><td colspan="2">Project Management</td><td>Legal/Lawyer</td></tr>
<tr><td>Level of Involvement</td><td colspan="4">Continuous—Standing Neutral (embedded as part of ongoing governance)</td><td colspan="3">Ad hoc—Standby Neutral (only when called upon)</td></tr>
<tr><td>Depth of Engagement</td><td colspan="3">All levels of governance</td><td colspan="2">Mid-levels of governance</td><td colspan="2">Only the highest levels of governance</td></tr>
<tr><td>Role/Authority</td><td>Advice only</td><td colspan="3">Makes formal recommendation (non-binding)</td><td colspan="2">Facilitates resolution by the parties</td><td>Offers binding decision</td></tr>
<tr><td>Fact-Finding Latitude</td><td colspan="3">May only receive information and evidence provided</td><td colspan="2">May investigate personally</td><td colspan="2">Ability to hire outside experts</td></tr>
<tr><td>Types of Support</td><td colspan="7">Pre-Contract Support:
*Deal Facilitator
Post-Contract Support:
*Transition Support
*Performance Metrics/Performance Management Alignment
*Project Management Support
*Strategic Reviews
*Risk Management
*Onboarding Support/Training
*Relationship Health Monitoring
Dispute Management:
*Issue Resolution
*Offer Binding Decisions
*Facilitate Resolution</td></tr>
<tr><td>Reference in Contract</td><td colspan="4">Formal: Reference in contract (may be an appendix or schedule)</td><td colspan="3">Informal: Not referenced in contract</td></tr>
</table>

Figure 24: Nine Design Principles and Options of a Standing Neutral Program

How a Traditional Standing Neutral Works

The traditional standing neutral concept was first used in the construction industry in 1975 when contracting parties to a difficult tunneling project conceived the idea of enlisting the help of three impartial geological engineers to help them solve difficult rock and soil technical and pricing problems.[43] The vision was

43. A. A. Mathews et al., Construction Dispute Review Board Manual 10 (1996).

that a trusted three-party panel of independent expert advisors (DRB) would be immediately available to help resolve disputes arising between them during their contractual relationship.

By far the most common form of a traditional standing neutral is a DRB, which has most often been used in the construction industry. CPR defines a DRB as a party-appointed panel chaired by a trained neutral, which is generally formed at the start of a project and which meets regularly to follow work progress and provide guidance to the parties.[44]

DRBs both provide guidance to the parties and help them avoid problems and also offer early and effective dispute resolution. Early dispute resolution focuses on maintaining a constructive process between the parties so they continue their working relationship even while trying to reach an agreement on divergent positions.

This focus is accomplished by emphasizing the preservation of trust throughout the dispute-handling process. When the parties have a claim, a DRB hearing is often more informal and less adversarial than an arbitration hearing or litigation, with openness and candor encouraged.

Typically, the parties submit short, concise position papers and relevant documents. No discovery is permitted, although the DRB members have the right to request information necessary to resolve the dispute. The businesspersons involved make presentations and, typically, lawyers do not play a role apart from addressing legal issues. In addition, cross-examination is not allowed. Unlike arbitration or litigation, a DRB does not issue a decision, verdict, or award. Instead, the DRB provides written findings and non-binding recommendations that include an analysis to support its conclusions. The parties typically use these recommendations to negotiate a final resolution of the dispute. In some cases, the parties agree that recommendations become final and binding if not rejected promptly. In addition, DRB findings and recommendations are generally admissible in a subsequent court or arbitration proceeding.[45]

Thus, while offering a form of dispute resolution, as noted above, the DRB is also woven into the governance structure of the business relationship, routinely involved in regular (e.g., monthly) review meetings, and asked for advice on problems or conflicts as they arise. Today, the DRBF outlines three types of standing neutrals that act in the capacity of a Dispute Board (DB):[46]

---

44. Dispute Resolution Board, Int'l. Inst. Conflict Prevention & Resol., https://www.cpradr.org/adr-primer.

45. Sarah B. Biser et al., *Duels, Litigation, Arbitration, or Dispute Review Boards: The Better Choice in Complex Construction Projects*, ABA: Bus. L. Today (Mar. 2016), https://web.archive.org/web/20161103064851/http://www.americanbar.org/publications/blt/2016/03/03_biser.html.

46. *Dispute Board Manual supra* note 42.

1. *Dispute Board Panels*: For large and complex construction projects with multiple contracts or alternative delivery methods, the most cost-effective means of dispute avoidance and resolution may be to establish a DB panel. The panel should include experienced DB practitioners, from which individual DB members can be selected to work on specific contracts within the overall project. A DB panel member may act as a facilitator, mediator, or adjudicator, as appropriate, when a dispute arises.
2. *One-Person Dispute Board*: A one-person DB is particularly suitable for smaller projects where the cost of a three-person DB cannot be justified. However, a one-person DB is only fully effective when an independent person with all the desired qualifications and experience is available. In practice, the primary benefit of a one-person DB versus a three-person DB is cost savings.
3. *Dispute Resolution Advisor*: A DRA is similar to a one-person, standing DB set up at the commencement of the project. However, instead of the DRA having the power to provide a decision or recommendation on the merit of a dispute, the DRA's role is primarily that of an independent and experienced consultant, identifying potential areas of dispute and ensuring issues are addressed by the parties as soon as possible. The DRA member's other primary role is to assist the parties in informally resolving any dispute. The DRA assists the parties by acting as a facilitator to achieve an amicable dispute settlement or structure a suitable formal dispute resolution mechanism.

Case Study—Traditional Standing Neutral

The Olympics represent a good example of using DRBs.[47] DRBs helped the 2012 London Olympics be delivered on specification, ahead of time, and within budget. Only two disputes required adjudication, and no court actions commenced.

In 2016, the Rio Olympics (Rio 2016) took the lessons learned and implemented DRBs for dispute avoidance and resolution across thirty-five contracts. The Brazilian government was responsible for the delivery of city bid commitments, which included the main venues and infrastructure. Rio 2016 was responsible for the actual delivery of the games, including the "overlay" contracts.

As experience with DRBs was limited in Brazil at the time, Rio 2016 worked with the DRBF to develop a strategy for how they would use DRBs. The DRBF created two DB panels. The first DB panel had members from which each party

47. Andrew Stephenson, *Dispute boards and the Olympic Games: A Tried and Tested Method of Dispute Avoidance*, Corrs Chambers Westgarth (Mar. 2, 2023), https://www.corrs.com.au/insights/dispute-boards-and-the-olympic-games-a-tried-and-tested-method-of-dispute-avoidance#_ftn19.

could select one member, with the DB members selecting the DB chair. The DB chair was to be selected from the second DB panel.

The parties drafted bespoke DB rules based on agreed-upon principles and were consistent with local laws. These bespoke rules formed part of the contract between Rio 2016 and the individual contractors. Key features of the DB panels were:

- A separate DB was established for each contract, which could be permanent or ad hoc with one or three members. The preference was a permanent or standing DB with three members.
- Party-selected DB members were chosen from a list of trained and certified local members. The DB members were required to have undergone training under the Rio 2016 DRB Training Program (run by the DRBF), be properly certified, and be fluent in Portuguese or Spanish. Either party had the right to reject a party selected member, although grounds for rejection were limited in scope.
- DB chairs were also to be selected from the DB members list based on their familiarity with local law, geographic proximity to the Rio Olympics, previous DB experience and fluency in Portuguese or Spanish and English.
- Short timetables were in place to ensure that construction timelines were met. These timetables included appointing the DBs at the outset of the contract, setting frequent DB site visits, and requiring rapid delivery of the DBs' opinions and decisions.
- The DBs had the power to provide written advisory opinions when jointly requested. A formal referral of a dispute could be made to the DBs to obtain a binding decision. DB decisions were binding unless and until overturned by arbitration.
- A DB Program Manager provided operational assistance to help the parties in the initial establishment of the DBs and in the procedural operation of the DBs. This was important given the short timetables and to provide consistency across the thirty-five DBs.
- Remuneration rates for the DBs were fixed as a daily rate and monthly retainer. The parties split DB fees equally and included administration charges and the DB Program Manager fee.

The use of DBs in the Rio Olympics was regarded as successful, with the DBs rarely used. Experts suggest the sheer existence of the DBs motivated the parties to resolve their issues as they arose, which upheld the concept that DBs contribute to dispute prevention simply by being present. The use of DBs in the Rio Olympics also had a positive side benefit because it raised the profile of DBs in Brazil and fueled a spike in DBs used in more public works contracts in Brazil.

How a Modern Standing Neutral Works

Over the years, the role of standing neutrals has evolved. A modern standing neutral differs from a traditional standing neutral in that its role is typically more expansive and preventive.

The table below (Figure 25) highlights the key differences between a modern standing neutral and a traditional standing neutral as found with a construction industry DRB.

Design Principles	Modern Standing Neutral	Traditional Standing Neutral
Timing of Involvement	Involvement can be pre- or post-contract signing, when precontract signing serve as a deal facilitator	Almost always involved after contract is signed
Number of Neutrals	Typically One	Typically a "Board" of Three
Depth of Engagement	Typically mid and highest level of governance	Typically only the highest levels of governance
Role/Authority	Typically a coach or an expert evaluator	Typically an expert evaluator with the goal to make a recommendation on a dispute. Recommendations may become binding if not rejected.
Fact Finding Latitude	Typically may receive information and personally investigate. May be able to hire outside experts.	Typically only receive information
Types of Support	**Pre-Contract Support:** *Deal Facilitator **Post-Contract Support:** *Transition Support *Risk Management *Performance Metrics/Performance Management Alignment *Project Management Support *Onboarding Support/Training *Strategic Reviews *Relationship Health Monitoring **Dispute Management:** *Issue Resolution (rarely mediates or arbitrates disputes)	**Dispute Management:** Focus is on early real-time dispute resolution. May be given the authority for binding arbitration. May also be engaged to help prevent disputes.

Figure 25: Differences Between a Modern and a Traditional Standing Neutral

While there are several differences between modern standing neutrals and traditional standing neutrals, the biggest difference is that the modern standing neutrals play a more comprehensive role of providing post-contract signing support as illustrated in figure 25.

Case Study—Modern Standing Neutral

When Ernst & Young (EY) set out to rethink its strategy for outsourcing workplace services (e.g., food service, cleaning services, and maintenance of its facilities), it incorporated a modern standing neutral from the outset. Figure 26 shows how the parties incorporated a modern standing neutral with the design principles shown with highlighting.

<table>
<tr><th>Factors to Consider</th><th colspan="12">Typical Post-Contract Standing Neutral Options</th></tr>
<tr><td>Number of Neutrals</td><td colspan="6">One</td><td colspan="6">Three</td></tr>
<tr><td>Timing of Involvement</td><td colspan="6">Pre-Contract Signing
(e.g., Deal Facilitator)</td><td colspan="6">Post-Contract Signing</td></tr>
<tr><td>Skills Required</td><td colspan="3">Deep SME/Industry Experience</td><td colspan="3">Facilitation/Soft Skills</td><td colspan="3">Project Management</td><td colspan="3">Legal/Lawyer</td></tr>
<tr><td>Depth of Engagement</td><td colspan="4">All levels of governance</td><td colspan="4">Mid-levels of governance</td><td colspan="4">Only the highest levels of governance</td></tr>
<tr><td>Level of Involvement</td><td colspan="6">Continuous involvement (embedded as part of ongoing governance)</td><td colspan="6">Ad hoc
(only when called upon)</td></tr>
<tr><td>Authority</td><td colspan="3">Advice only</td><td colspan="3">Makes formal recommendation (non-binding)</td><td colspan="3">Non-binding decision</td><td colspan="3">Binding decisions</td></tr>
<tr><td>Fact-Finding Latitude</td><td colspan="4">May only receive information and evidence provided</td><td colspan="4">May investigate personally</td><td colspan="4">Ability to hire outside experts</td></tr>
<tr><td>Common Types of Support</td><td colspan="12">The team used the types of support noted in bold italics
Pre-Contract Support:
*Deal Facilitator
Post-Contract Support:
*Transition Support
*Risk Management
*Performance Metrics/Performance Management Alignment
*Project Management Support
*Onboarding Support/Training
*Strategic Reviews
*Relationship Health Monitoring
Dispute Resolution:
*Issue Resolution
*Mediation
*Arbitration</td></tr>
<tr><td>Reference in Contract</td><td colspan="6">Formal: Referenced incontract
(may be an appendix orschedule)</td><td colspan="6">Informal: Not referenced in contract</td></tr>
</table>

Figure 26: Modern Standing Neutral Responsibilities (EY Case Study)

EY and Integrated Service Solutions (ISS) first incorporated a standing neutral to support the parties in developing a formal relational contract. The parties selected one standing neutral to support the parties—Erik Linnarsson, a lawyer from Cirio Law Firm—as a deal facilitator. Linnarsson was trained as a Certified Deal Architect (CDA) to craft complex outsourcing agreements.

At first, some EYers didn't understand why they should use a neutral coach. For EY's Becky Burningham (EY's Procurement Lead) having a neutral coach "felt odd." But after being on the team, the value of the coach became apparent. Burningham shared that the standing neutral played a critical role in "helping challenge traditional power-based approaches and getting both parties to a true win-win agreement."

Post-contract signing, the parties continued to use a standing neutral. The parties designed the standing neutral role to embed the standing neutral as part of the party's ongoing governance, with Linnarsson supporting both mid- and higher-level governance forums. Linnarsson would act as both an expert coach and evaluator for issue resolution, providing advice as problems arose. However, if needed, Linnarsson had the authority to make formal, non-binding recommendations.

The parties also tapped into their standing neutral for additional post-support services that are preventive in nature. This included ongoing performance management alignment, facilitating strategic reviews, and performance relationship health monitoring. For example, one role of the standing neutral was conducting an annual health check using a Compatibility and Trust (CaT) assessment. Isabella Liljeström is the contract owner from ISS. She found great value in doing the yearly CaT assessment, stating, "Each year, Erik administers the CaT assessment, which concludes with a formal workshop of team members learning how healthy their relationship is. The workshop helps guide us on what is important and helps us think through how to close gaps in compatibility and trust."

The standing neutral also supports strategic reviews, including reviewing their contract for any misalignments. An excellent example was the metrics around sustainability. When the parties initially created the agreement, it had a sustainability metric. However, since signing the agreement, regulatory requirements around sustainability have become stricter. In addition, EY wanted to be a global leader in sustainability. As part of the proactive review and with the help of the standing neutral, the parties worked together to revamp their sustainability metrics.

Jens Holmberg, ISS Legal Director for Sweden, liked incorporating a standing neutral: "A standing neutral is a very proactive dispute prevention mechanism. Simply having a trusting and credible standing neutral post-contract signing gives team members a sounding board that helps people make better decisions. Using a standing neutral is truly a powerful tool to keep contracting parties' interests aligned."

A LOOK AHEAD

In part II, we provided an overview of eighteen dispute prevention mechanisms, explaining what each mechanism is, why it helps prevent disputes, and how it works. We also shared a case study for each mechanism. In part III, we show how to put dispute prevention into practice. We kick off part III by sharing how to design a Dispute Management System. We then provide research and data that provide a compelling business case for making the shift to dispute prevention.

Part III

Putting Prevention into Practice

Chapter 6

Putting Dispute Prevention into Practice

In chapter 2 of this book, we introduced the concept of a Dispute Management Continuum. Our goal up until this point has been to provide insight and inspiration regarding eighteen dispute prevention mechanisms. In this chapter, we turn our focus to the practical question of how to introduce these concepts into your company so they may be available in future business relationships.

We recommend you design a *Dispute Management System (DMS)* within your company that incorporates the various mechanisms. Recall from the Introduction we defined a DMS as a purposefully designed program that organizations put into place incorporating various dispute prevention and resolution mechanisms. We use the term "system" to encourage your company to consider holistically which mechanisms to include in its DMS and how they will work together to reduce friction and transaction costs in relationships with contracting parties. The ultimate goal of a DMS is to optimize working relations between business partners, effectively and efficiently preventing disputes where possible, and resolving those disputes that cannot be prevented.

Think of a DMS as your company's toolkit, with each mechanism offering a unique way to prevent and resolve disputes. As you enter, formalize, and manage business relationships, you can use the tools in your toolkit best suited for the circumstances and requirements of that particular relationship. This chapter will help you build your toolkit. In the following pages, we provide steps and tips for helping you prepare your company to create your toolkit—your DMS. We start by explaining the basic characteristics of a good DMS. We then share four steps for turning the concepts we teach in this book into a reality for your business relationships.

Over the years, we have heard many reasons why individuals and organizations don't want to change their focus to dispute prevention. We are almost certain you will also hear some of these objections from within your company or from prospective partners. For this reason, we conclude this chapter with a list of common obstacles and how to overcome them.

CHARACTERISTICS OF A GOOD DMS

Since each company's approach to identifying conflict and working with other businesses is different, there is no one-size-fits-all DMS. Rather, it is worth keeping in mind three foundational design principles in any DMS you develop:

- Include both dispute prevention and resolution mechanisms.
- Ensure flexibility and adaptability to the myriad problems, conflicts, and potential disputes that may arise.
- Deploy your chosen mechanisms at the earliest possible time in the relationship.

Include Both Dispute Prevention and Resolution Mechanisms

A good DMS seeks to go beyond simply resolving disputes and includes mechanisms to address misalignment efficiently and in the most cost-effective manner. A great DMS goes even further upstream and includes mechanisms to prevent misalignment while the parties are entering into and formalizing their relationships. Moving further upstream helps business partners mitigate or even avoid unproductive conflict altogether.

With this in mind, the best practice is to establish a mindset that prevention is better than the cure and incorporate as many dispute prevention mechanisms as appropriate. Ideally, your DMS should:

- Promote cooperative behaviors over adversarial behaviors.
- Adopt prevention mechanisms that span the life cycle of a business relationship, including mechanisms for entering, forming, and managing the relationship.

When problems arise, your DMS should:

- Incorporate real-time techniques (or near-real-time when appropriate) designed to help the parties work through problems, conflicts, and disputes promptly.
- Include a backstop should prevention fail, incorporating methods for final and binding resolution if necessary.

Be Flexible and Easily Adapted

The second feature of a good DMS is flexibility, letting you easily adapt your system across a wide range of business relationships. A key goal when designing a DMS is to create a diverse suite of mechanisms (i.e., your toolkit) that your organization can choose from for any relationship. As you consider which of the thirty-three mechanisms to put into your toolkit, recall the discussion in chapter 1 about the kinds of conflicts that often lead to disputes: interest conflicts, relationship conflicts, structural conflicts, data/information conflicts, and value conflicts. It is easy to see the array of preventive upstream mechanisms that may be called for in responding to such a diversity of types of conflict.

Let's take a look at Procter & Gamble (P&G). P&G has 80,000 supplier relationships.[1] In addition, P&G does business with thousands of customers and has hundreds of other business arrangements, such as the creative win-win licensing agreement with the Japanese brand Unicharm, a competitor for the Swiffer billion-dollar brand.[2] Simply put, not all of these relationships have the same risk factors; therefore, they do not all need to use the same set of dispute prevention and resolution mechanisms. Some of these relationships are low-risk, low-value, and short-term in nature. For these relationships, the best-fit mechanisms may be dispute management clauses embedded into contracts with directions to use a step negotiation approach followed by mediation and then arbitration. However, for a large and complex outsourcing relationship, it will be more appropriate to adopt a full complement of dispute prevention and resolution mechanisms where it is important to tightly align interests during the early phases of supplier selection and contract development.

Implemented at the Onset of a Business Relationship

Last, a good DMS should encourage your company to deploy dispute prevention mechanisms as early as possible in relationships with other parties. While it is possible to introduce the tools in your DMS to existing relationships, we find it much more powerful to introduce the concepts at the onset of a business relationship.

One of the more effective ways to ensure alignment is for the parties to establish a Steering Committee at the outset of the relationship. The Committee convenes at the earliest stage of the relationship and takes on the role of anticipating and identifying the kinds of potential problems that might arise. In so doing, the parties can decide which mechanisms are best suited for their particular situation. For example, should they lean on a deal facilitator? Or would a formal relational contract be beneficial when thinking about the long-term nature of their business relationship?

1. *Procter & Gamble Recognizes Its Top Global Suppliers*, Reliable Plant, https://www.reliableplant.com/Read/26927/Procter-Gamble-top-suppliers.

2. Harry West, *A Chain of Innovation: The Creation of Swiffer*, 57 R.T.M. 1–5 (2014) (P&G's win-win partnership with Unicharm).

DESIGNING YOUR DMS

Many organizations are new to designing and implementing a DMS. We suggest starting by stepping back and approaching the task of designing a DMS strategically. The good news is we need not look far for guidance as legal scholars are elaborating on the concept and offering the following definition: Dispute system design is the art and science of designing the means to prevent, manage, and resolve conflict and disputes efficiently and effectively.[3]

We suggest a four-step process that starts by *diagnosing* your current practices. The second step is *designing* your system, followed by the third step, *implementing your system*. The final step is *evaluating* the effectiveness of your program. We share insights and tips for each step and have returned to the SemiCo case study from chapter 1 to provide examples of each step.

Step 1: Diagnose Your Current Practices

The first step is to diagnose how your organization currently deals with problems, conflicts, and disputes in its existing business relationships.

While a holistic review of your organization's business relationships would be ideal, many organizations may find that daunting because they are not currently collecting data on problems, conflicts, and/or disputes. If you feel overwhelmed or resource-constrained, consider starting with a pilot to create a DMS for one area of your business.

SemiCo was able to find success with a pilot. Olivia Operations was the Vice President in charge of managing SemiCo's construction contracts—a part of the business that was historically fraught with claims and disputes. While we like the idea of SemiCo designing a DMS for all their business relationships, Olivia Operations started with a more manageable project: piloting a DMS for construction relationships only. And within that, Danny Dispute Manager selected one relationship for a micro-pilot to test core concepts before rolling it out to other regions and suppliers.

What if you don't have a good pilot in mind, or, more broadly, you are not even sure where to start? We recommend creating a cross-functional task force and challenging team members to answer the following what, who, and how questions.

What

- Are there any business focus areas or relationships currently causing you issues?
  For SemiCo—the focus area was construction contracts.

3. Lisa Blomgren Amsler et al., Dispute System Design (2020).

- For those focus areas, do you have any data on what you are doing today?
  For SemiCo, the data supported the need for change. Even the best subcontractors and suppliers seemed to have claims stemming from unexpected changes in the project. For example, one construction project valued at $220 million had $30 million in claims, and another $1.3 billion project had $50 million in claims.
- What training (if any) are you currently doing (e.g., negotiation skills, collaborative contracting, etc.)?
  SemiCo had done extensive negotiation training, but most of the training focused on how SemiCo could "win" when negotiating. SemiCo team members had never been trained in dispute prevention.

Who

- For the focus areas you pick, who is most affected when potential problems escalate?
  Construction claims often would escalate within SemiCo to the procurement manager and then to the worldwide procurement manager. Claims would get stuck, and most of the time, the businesspeople involved had no understanding of what the law might actually say. The claim would then be escalated to the lawyers. So, for SemiCo, the individuals most affected were the field-based project managers, SemiCo's procurement manager (Billy Buyer), and the contractor's account managers (e.g., Simon Supplier). For claims going on to mediation and arbitration, both companies involved their lawyers.
- Is there anyone currently tasked with managing problems if they remain unresolved?
  While there was a clear escalation path for problems, SemiCo and their suppliers did not have anyone to support managing the problems through to resolution. The general sentiment was a "kick the can down the road" with the hope the problem (and associated claim or dispute) would go away if ignored.
- Is there anyone who will volunteer to champion designing a program?
  For SemiCo, this was Olivia Operations and Billy Buyer. Danny Dispute Manager reflects on the *importance of having champions: "Having senior management support meant I could point to project management saying this is the way they want a project to run."*
- Who will take on the responsibility of ongoing program management, including training and ongoing management?
  Recall that SemiCo first engaged Danny Dispute Manager as a consultant to brainstorm ideas. However, due to the size and scale of their construction contracts (SemiCo had five primary contractors with over $20 billion in spend), they decided to invest in having an in-house resource devoted to helping them design and maintain their program. SemiCo hired Danny as an employee to work on Billy Buyer's team. Danny's role would be to

lead the design of the program and ultimately roll out and maintain the program.

How

- What mechanisms are stakeholders currently using for problems, conflicts, or disputes that arise in these relationships? Which are working well, and which are not working well? Why?
  SemiCo's diagnosis revealed that SemiCo—like most companies—used dispute prevention mechanisms on only a very limited basis. The only formal dispute prevention mechanism SemiCo had adopted was a good faith and fair dealings clause in their contract. Informally, SemiCo used step negotiations.
- How are business problems handled as they expand when they are not resolved?
  When step negotiations failed and a claim turned into a formal dispute, the path to resolution was limited to classic arbitration and litigation.

Tip!

Use the Dispute Management Continuum as a checklist to identify which mechanisms you are using in your existing relationships and how they are being applied. For example, you may discover your current DMS only uses the items highlighted in gray boxes as illustrated in figure 27.

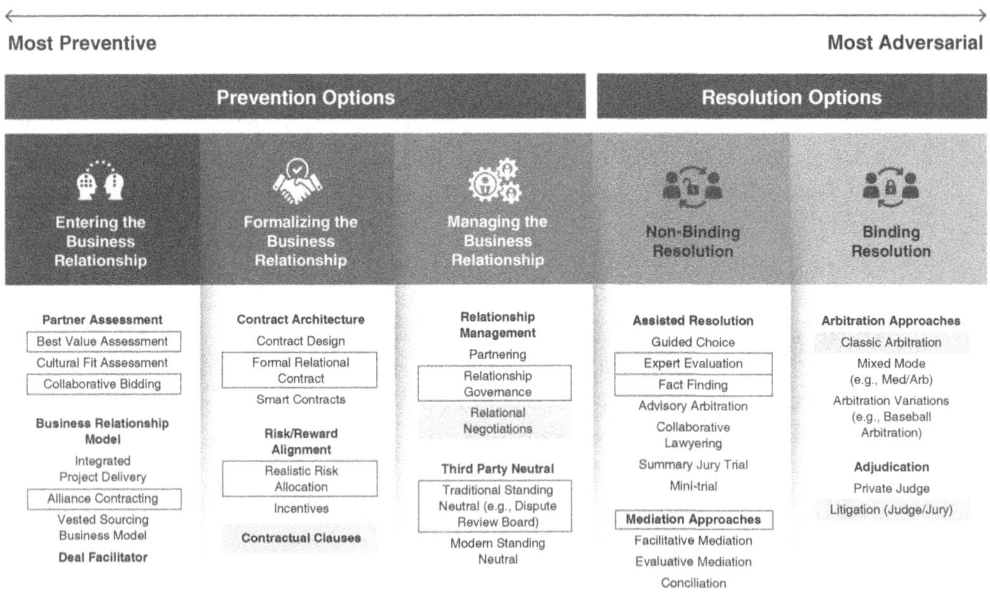

*Mechanisms highlighted in gray boxes represent current practices

Figure 27: Map of Existing Mechanisms Being Used on Pilot Contract

Step 2: Design Your New System

Once you have completed your diagnosis, it is time to begin the design phase. This includes determining which dispute prevention and resolution mechanisms to include in your toolkit and doing the appropriate work to close the gaps.

The individuals chartered with designing your DMS need to determine which dispute prevention and resolution mechanisms to include in the toolkit. Here it is important to keep the goal front and center: selecting the most appropriate mix of dispute management mechanisms that optimize for the time, cost, and outcome in addressing problems, conflicts and disputes, despite type or severity. We suggest creating a menu of all the mechanisms your organization is comfortable adopting.

Let's say your organization is new to dispute prevention and you want to start with a relatively small DMS with only the top ten most promising mechanisms. One idea would be to convene a cross-functional group to participate in an educational workshop to learn about the suite of potential dispute prevention and resolution mechanisms. Using the Dispute Management Continuum, at the end of the workshop, the group votes on the top ten mechanisms they feel would create the most value. Figure 28 illustrates the DMS your organization might go on to adopt, with a box indicating the new mechanisms.

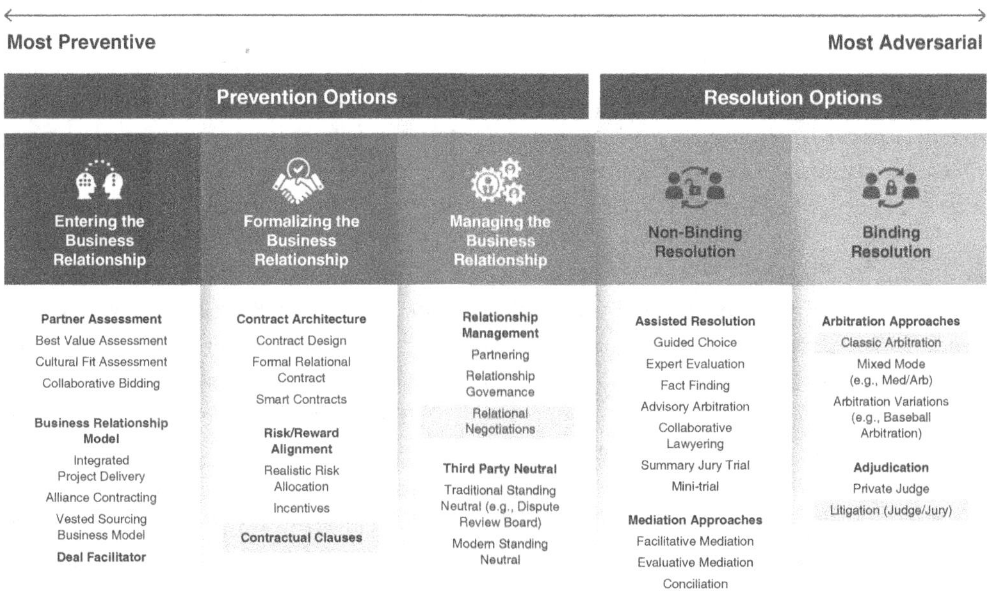

*Items outlined with a box represent the mechanisms you might want to begin using with a specific relationship

Figure 28: Example of a Potential Dispute Management System

Tip!

- Don't design a system that will encourage, accelerate, or prematurely escalate grievances and claims.
- Ensure user's flexibility in deciding which mechanisms to use for their situation.

Step 3: Ramp Up and Roll Out

Once you have designed your DMS, it is time to implement it. You will need to consider how to educate team members, how you close any gaps in processes, tools, or resources you use, and how you will roll out the program with a specific business partner. Sometimes, the rollout may include internal work to close gaps between what you are doing now and how the new mechanisms work.

Education: Ramping Up Team Members for What Is "New" and "Different"

A good DMS includes a training component. One aspect of training is general education about the program itself: what it is, why you are doing it, and team members' roles in using new dispute prevention and resolution mechanisms. This education often helps to get buy-in for what you are doing.

The bp case study from chapter 3 provides a good example of how Wendy Cuthbert—bp's Global Head of Workplace Solutions—leveraged training to get buy-in. Recall from chapter 3 how bp decided to shift from a transactional contract to a strategic Vested relationship model with Jones Lang Lasalle (JLL). Well before bp engaged in discussions with JLL, they set out to conduct internal training for key stakeholders to help get buy-in on why and how these employees would make the shift.

Wendy engaged the University of Tennessee and Ernst & Young (EY) to host three regional workshops where key bp real estate and facilities management team members could do a deeper dive into the Vested model. As part of the training, team members diagnosed their existing relationship, which revealed how making the shift to a Vested model would solve many of their problems.

Wendy believed those early workshops were key to getting buy-in for the need to change: "The workshops helped team members take the Vested theory and see how it could work with what bp wanted to do. I remember the team had to complete some self-assessments. We scored ourselves against the '12 ailments of outsourcing' as well as how well our contracts followed the Vested Five Rules. The team would see the gaps and use the workshop time to understand how the Vested methodology could help bp close the gaps."[4]

4. See pages 47–53 for a discussion of performance-based agreements, including Vested/Vested Outsourcing Agreements. For a detailed discussion of Vested, the Five

Wendy added, "Don't get me wrong, there were skeptics. But once team members did the first wave of training, we started to see more and more stakeholders begin to realize just how old-school we were in our outsourcing efforts. As a team, we ultimately decided we would go down the Vested path."

Closing Gaps

In many cases, you will need to do some work to close the gaps between what you are doing today and what you want to do. Here you will need to do the work necessary to execute each mechanism. For example, recall the General Electric Company (GE) case study from chapter 4. Let's say you have a goal like GE's Shaun Burton, general counsel of GE Aviation's Business & General Aviation and Integrated Systems businesses, who wanted to adopt better contract design practices by using plain-language contracts.

As a first step, GE's legal team organized a multiday off-site with the newly formed plain-language team—a group that included people from sales, engineering, and product support as well as the legal department. A goal of the off-site was to help legal team members gain insight into the offerings and the associated operational risks. Next, GE set aside time for team members to rethink the contract clauses they used in their contracts. The team drew up contract clauses from scratch—consciously leaving behind existing contract templates and "sample" clauses. Their goal? Develop contract clauses that would pass a simple litmus test: Can a high schooler understand this?[5]

Rolling Out the Program

The last element relates to integrating your DMS into your business relationship(s). After all, the mechanisms are of no value if they simply remain in the toolkit. The key is to use them most appropriately in the context of particular business relationships. At times, there will undoubtedly be skepticism and concerns over adopting new and different mechanisms for parties' business arrangements. We discuss some of those concerns and how to overcome them later in this chapter. But, first, let's turn to examples of how parties have worked together to adopt mechanisms from the toolkit.

Let's first explore how bp's DMS evolved as the parties shifted from entering their relationship to forming the relationship to finally managing the relationship.

Once internal stakeholders at bp were onboard in understanding and supporting the Vested relationship model, it was time for bp to take a big step and introduce the concepts to their potential partners. In the case of bp, they had

---

Rules, and the ailments, *see* Kate Vitasek et al., Vested Outsourcing: Five Rules That will Transform Outsourcing (2d ed. 2013).

5. Shawn Burton, *The Case for Plain-Language Contracts*, Harv. Bus. Rev., Jan.–Feb. 2018, at 134.

introduced the concept of using a Vested relationship model during their competitive bidding process. A key strategy of the final phase of the bidding process was to deploy collaborative bidding and partner assessment mechanisms (both covered in chapter 3). During the collaborative dialogue sessions, bp and each of the potential partners openly discussed the benefits of moving to a Vested relationship model.

JLL was ultimately selected as the partner of choice. Dominic Soocoormanee, JLL's Sales and Solutions Development Director, was excited about bp's direction: "bp had been on track to buy the same services in exactly the same way using the same type of contractual relationships. bp's reimagine mandate—combined with the Vested relationship model—created the perfect storm for driving real change in how bp delivered workplace solutions. As a global leader in real estate and facilities management services, this was very exciting to JLL."

Both bp and JLL knew shifting to a Vested model would be a change from the status quo. The parties ultimately engaged EY to provide a Certified Deal Architect coach as a neutral deal facilitator (see chapter 3) to guide them through creating their Vested agreement.

Soocoormanee remembers challenging the decision to use a neutral coach: "As a business development person, I had done many contracts. So, I remember pushing back and saying, 'So what's EY going to do for us? Surely, we're grown-ups and we can do the training and talk to each other about the process. But it wasn't until I started the journey that I realized the value of having a neutral coach. There are so many times when we went two steps forward and one step back. It even felt like three steps back sometimes. The value Alex (the deal facilitator) brought was a calm hand to bring us in alignment. Sometimes he would allow people to explore their own feelings and behaviors and almost at times show them a mirror so they could see how they were behaving. Other times Alex would remind us about real-life examples we'd learned in the coursework and share additional examples from his own experience doing other Vested deals. When I look back, what EY did was phenomenal in helping us take the Vested theory and operationalize it into practice."

A key role of the deal facilitator was to help the deal architect team design their ongoing governance structure and practices (refer to chapter 5) and to develop an onboarding program where the parties would roll out the fundamentals to team members who worked in the relationship. This also included helping team members understand how the parties would address potential problems through their formal governance structure.

While it is ideal to get out of the gate using dispute prevention practices at the onset of a business relationship like bp did, it is also possible to integrate dispute prevention practices into existing relationships. For example, consider SemiCo. When SemiCo first developed its DMS, it kicked off implementation with just one supplier relationship to pilot the concepts.

Danny Dispute Manager took the learnings from the initial rollout and worked with other project teams to modify the toolkit for different suppliers in other regions. For example, SemiCo's program was modified to factor in the scale of a trading partner relationship and adjusted based on operational processes used in specific relationships. A good example is in one region where SemiCo had a multi-billion-dollar contract, the parties invested in a dedicated standing neutral. However, in another region, the project teams leveraged the same standing neutral across multiple suppliers because the scale and scope of each relationship were much smaller. In addition, the program was also adapted to be fit for purpose for both design-build and design-bid-build construction projects.

Step 4: Measure and Evaluate

The fourth step is to put processes and tools in place to measure and improve the effectiveness of your DMS.

Your DMS can be measured and evaluated both at the broader company level and/or at the individual business relationship. One way to facilitate this is to allocate charges for disputes to the budget that generated the dispute. Organizations do this to help educate the organization and key staff in departments where conflict escalates into a dispute about the true costs of such disputes.

Next, it is also useful to consider not only the direct costs associated with resolving the disputes but also the indirect costs, including time spent by employees, the impact on the business relationships, and other reputational repercussions of such disputes and conflicts before they become disputes.

The SemiCo case study provides an example of measuring the costs of disputes. SemiCo's program has been in place for over six years, with only one incident using the predescribed arbitration process and outside counsel. For comparison, before the program, two of SemiCo's larger construction contracts suffered from a stifling stack of claims. One project had $30 million in claims on a $220 million project, and another had $50 million in claims on a $1.3 billion project. Some claims took over five years to settle, with one particularly pesky claim going to a six-week trial. While the case settled outside of court in three weeks, SemiCo spent over $15 million in outside legal fees, expert opinions, and discovery costs. And that $15 million did not include the internal cost or the employee's time redirected to support the litigation.

After measuring the costs of disputes as a baseline, it is useful to track the deployment of dispute prevention mechanisms and the outcomes experienced in the relationships for which they were deployed. The company might develop a questionnaire and database asking colleagues: (1) to identify dispute prevention mechanisms deployed in a particular business relationship, (2) to identify any mechanisms considered by the parties but not deployed and the reasons why not, (3) to describe the utilization of the mechanisms deployed and the experience using them, and (4) to describe the outcome of using the mechanisms—did they work or not and some explanation.

It is then useful for the team overseeing the deployment of the company's DMS to analyze these responses and integrate learnings from them into future trainings and discussions of the DMS.

OVERCOMING COMMON OBSTACLES

Change is hard. For many organizations, the concept of dispute prevention may be new. Even if the concept is not new to your organization, you may have learned some new mechanisms in this book that can make your program more robust.

SemiCo's Danny Dispute Manager knows firsthand how hard change can be. Even though Danny had top-down support from Oliva Operations and Billy Buyer, he knew he would also need to get the buy-in of the team members working in the project teams—from both SemiCo and the contractors. This meant engaging the project teams working in the trenches on-site on individual construction projects.

Danny found that some stakeholders responded critically to the program's rollout. He comments on the initial challenge he had in getting buy-in at the local project level, saying "Change, even for the better, often feels like pushing a boulder uphill. For example, bringing a standing neutral (see chapter 5) into the room in a mega construction project where it has never been done in a preventive way has the potential to flare egos, particularly with construction managers who are accustomed to being fairly autonomous."

In many cases, people felt they were losing control if they incorporated a standing neutral into the governance structure. Using a standing neutral was especially hard for those who had grown to like the "kick the can down the road" culture. Danny Dispute Manger found the people at the project level who most eagerly accepted using a standing neutral had firsthand experience from adversarial negotiations or, even worse, from arbitration or litigation. In most contracts—even the good ones—there was at least some history of claims resolution that had soured team members. Danny shared, "People who had spent three days in lawyers' offices preparing for a deposition and then another two days in a deposition never wanted to go there again."

Over time, the success of the program won people over. People began to realize that smart dispute prevention mechanisms create efficiencies and reduce the pain associated with the traditional claims process.

Throughout our journey of helping organizations understand the benefits of dispute prevention and implement best practices, we often hear objections. In the below pages, we share common obstacles and how to overcome them. Your internal stakeholders are bound to raise these concerns, as well as external stakeholders, to whom you will want to propose such mechanisms. In addition to describing the obstacles, we also offer tips to consider for helping you overcome each of the obstacles.

Resistance to Change

One lawyer nicely summed up the reason his company has yet to adopt dispute prevention practices: "People get set in their ways. Teaching an old dog new tricks is very tough. Change is upsetting the apple cart and people don't want to hear it." So, while including dispute prevention may seem logical at first blush, proponents often face significant barriers that make it challenging to adopt and sustain this innovation.

Common reasons cited for not wanting to change include:

- Inside counsel and middle-level employees feel they handle disputes effectively and resent efforts to reduce their autonomy.
- Outside counsel worry about interference with their professional responsibility to produce the best legal results.
- A company culture of fighting the good battle to prove they are right.
- It will likely take more time to embed dispute prevention mechanisms, and the business does not want to face delays when they are eager to enter into a relationship.
- Doing something different seems risky and brings criticism if the new idea does not work well.
- There is a concern, often on the supplier side, that the standing neutral may get "in-between" or block them from building a deep connection with their client.

Overcoming this Barrier

The good news is that the success of both traditional alternative dispute resolution (ADR) and the newer prevention mechanisms, such as standing neutrals, has become better known, and resistance is diminishing. The best way to diminish resistance is through education on the why, what, and how of using dispute prevention mechanisms. Sharing lessons from this book and case studies is a significant first step as well as suggesting skeptics talk to someone who is an expert in using dispute prevention mechanisms.

In addition, people rarely change unless the pain to change is less than their current pain. In this case, try piloting the concept on the rebound of a strained business relationship. For example, let's say you have a bad supplier relationship and you are planning to do a competitive bid to find a new supplier. Use this opportunity to "pilot" concepts such as partner assessments and collaborative bidding (both covered in chapter 3).

Other good ways to get buy-in are putting in preventive techniques such as measuring dispute prevention versus disputes and charging the cost of disputes to the department(s) involved. This fact-based data will open the eyes of individuals to the hidden cost of traditional approaches.

Some Outside Counsel Do Not Support Prevention

It is natural to be skeptical of something new. For example, some cynical lawyers criticized the ADR movement in the late 1980s and early 1990s, saying that the initials "ADR" stood for "Alarming Drop in Revenues." Richard Susskind's book *The End of Lawyers?* uses the metaphor of a lawyer watching their client walking precariously along the edge of a cliff. The lawyer, instead of erecting a barricade or warning lights at the top of the cliff, simply parks an ambulance at the bottom of the cliff.[6]

The perception of outside lawyer antagonism to the prevention objectives of ADR was illustrated by the voting at the Global Pound Conference series (GPC). In response to the question, "Which stakeholders are likely to be the most resistant to change in commercial dispute resolution practice? The overwhelming verdict among the GPC delegates (including the lawyer delegates) was "external lawyers."[7] The good news is that, since the GPC, many outside lawyers have stepped up to lead dispute prevention efforts at organizations like CPR and elsewhere.

Overcoming this Barrier

There are two ways to overcome this barrier. First and foremost, continuing resistance reflects the transformative nature a focus on dispute prevention presents and underscores the opportunity for leadership at the Bar. In that sense, don't run from the barrier; instead, embrace it as a challenge to be overcome.

Second, it is important to make sure you are working with an outside lawyer that is open to—and preferably already practicing—dispute prevention. If you find your existing outside counsel is resisting your desire to apply the various dispute prevention mechanisms profiled in this book, consider educating the lawyer about prevention mechanisms or asking the lawyer's firm to assign someone else in their firm to work with you who may be more open to exploring these mechanisms. Alternatively, if your existing outside counsel is not open to working with you in your desired approach, consider finding a different firm.

The Hope There Won't Be Problems

It is human nature to ignore issues and hope they go away. Organizations and individuals often believe they will find ways to work through friction with strong personal relationships. Sometimes this strategy can work, but often it does not. Rather, research shows it is easy to fall into a negative tit-for-tat trap that leads from a win-win discussion to win-lose and ultimately a lose-lose mindset and behaviors which can easily lead to the concept of shading which we explored previously.[8]

---

6. Richard Susskind, The End of Lawyers? 224 (Revised ed. 2010).

7. *Global Data Trends and Regional Differences*, Global Pound Conference Series 1–36 (2018) (outside lawyer antagonism).

8. Friedrich Glasl, Konfliktmanagement: Ein Handbuch für Führungskräfte, Beraterinnen und Berater (10th ed. 2011); Oliver Hart & John Moore, *Contracts as Reference Points*, 123 Q.J.E. 1, 3–4 (2008) (definition of "shading")

Indeed, some fear that addressing the subject of dispute prevention is akin to suggesting to a happily engaged couple they should sign a prenuptial agreement. Just acknowledging the possibility of future disharmony might lead to resentment or even conflict.

But even the most trusting relationships can falter over time and benefit from having dispute prevention mechanisms in their toolkit. Take, for example, Huy Fong Foods, the maker of the popular "Rooster" Sriracha sauce. Huy Fong Foods' founder and CEO had a "close and friendly" relationship with the owner of Underwood Ranches for over twenty-five years. Underwood Ranches had an exclusive relationship with Huy Fong to provide peppers. The more Rooster sauce Huy Fong sold, the more peppers they would buy from Underwood Ranches. Together the parties collaborated to dominate the Sriracha sauce market.

That was until Huy Fong tried to hire a key employee from Underwood Ranches and slowly began to take actions to develop other pepper supply sources. Huy Fong's actions strained the relationship. But because the parties didn't have dispute prevention mechanisms such as a standing neutral or relational negotiations, the parties let their tension grow. The once trusting relationship grew apart until the relationship reached a breaking point ending up in a lawsuit with Underwood Ranches winning a $23 million settlement for breach of contract.[9] Huy Fong has faced numerous supply-chain problems and production gaps in working with other suppliers while Underwood Ranches launched a hot sauce brand of its own.

Overcoming this Barrier

Have team members complete a "what if" exercise: "What if a new sheriff comes in and demands the supplier to cut cost by 20%?" or "What if XX happens, how will you deal with it fairly?" Augment this exercise by having team members share real stories of what has happened in other business relationships. Then, look at the existing processes for managing disputes. What would happen if one of these "what ifs" or war stories arose in your relationship, and all you had was your existing dispute management process versus embedded practices for more collaborative and early resolution?

A Perception that Adding Dispute Prevention Slows Down the Process

Some people may feel that adopting dispute prevention and resolution mechanisms add unneeded costs and time. For example, partnering (refer to chapter 5) may create a distraction from getting real work done. Or the parties will need to cover the cost of a standing neutral (also in chapter 5) when it might never be used.

9. *Huy Fong Foods, Inc. v. Underwood Ranches*, LP, 66 Cal.App.5th 1112 (2021).

Overcoming this Barrier

The Association of Corporate Counsel reports problems that evolve into disputes are expensive and take valuable time to resolve.[10] According to the report, companies with revenue of more than $1 billion spend on average more than $200,000 per litigation. However, smaller companies also suffer. In addition, the survey reports that 71 percent of disputes related to breach of contract last longer than one year, with 22 percent taking more than two years.

As part of your diagnosis step, one approach you can take is to analyze recent disputes to understand how key data, such as how long disputes take to resolve and how much they cost (factoring in direct and indirect costs), affect your organization. Mapping out one or two disputes should be eye-opening for revealing why it would be better to embed a dispute prevention mechanism that can help business partners solve problems while they are still relatively small and the parties are still in a win-win mindset.

The Perception that a Powerful Party Will Benefit from an Inefficient Method of Resolving Disputes

Sadly, organizations with power often use (and abuse) it. For example, a powerful party draws out a dispute with a weaker party, hoping the weaker party will give in as the transaction costs associated with the dispute become too much to bear. Using power to influence an outcome typically stems from the buy-side in a buyer–supplier relationship, but not always. For example, Mondelez International issued a letter to all suppliers that (despite their contract) they would be moving to a 120-day payment term.[11] Most suppliers—especially small and midsize companies—simply can't fight back. When a buying company knowingly (or unknowingly) is using their power negatively, it will probably lead to negative tit-for-tat behavior from the supplier—most often in passive-aggressive behaviors. This dynamic is particularly destructive when initiated after a contract is signed—especially for large or complex contracts such as outsourcing agreements that are hard and costly to unwind.

Overcoming this Barrier

This barrier is the hardest to overcome. Organizations and individuals who maintain that power-based approaches are preferable are unlikely to change. Our

---

10. *The State of Corporate Litigation Today Survey Report*, Assoc. Corp. Couns., https://www.acc.com/resource-library/state-corporate-litigation-today-survey-report.

11. Stephanie Strom, *Big Companies Pay Later, Squeezing Their Suppliers*, N.Y. Times (Apr. 6, 2015), https://www.nytimes.com/2015/04/07/business/big-companies-pay-later-squeezing-their-suppliers.html.

view? If you cannot persuade your business partner of the logic of embedding even the simplest of mechanisms into your arrangements, question the path forward for the relationship and/or factor in the risk so you will be compensated for their bad behavior and the hassles you will have. For example, one supplier shared that when they find themselves working with an unreasonable customer, they invoke the PITA (pain in the ass) price factor as a markup to compensate for the risk premium they will have to bear for working with this particular client.

The Difficulty of Measuring the Value of Disputes Prevented

In a business world that relies on statistics, managers look for data to support their decisions. When considering whether to adopt a dispute prevention strategy, they are likely to ask the question: "Show me the proof that dispute prevention works."

In almost every area of human endeavor, success can be recorded and measured. Paradoxically, due to its unique nature, every time dispute prevention meets its intended goal, there is no "happening" or "event" to record or measure. A prevented dispute has become a "non-event."

The "non-event" paradox is one of the biggest obstacles to gaining acceptance of dispute prevention in a fact-based, statistics-driven business world. Richard Susskind addressed this phenomenon in his book *The End of Lawyers?*:

> [I]t is hard to make a business case for spending money on legal problems that have not yet arisen ... [I]t is hard to quantify the benefits of disasters averted. And so, irrational though it may appear, it is much harder to sell legal risk management services than legal services. When a dispute arises, the budgets often seem to be without limit. A tiny fraction of that budget is rarely released to avoid litigation in the first place.[12]

Overcoming this Barrier

First, when educating someone about dispute prevention, candidly note the "non-event" paradox to explain the lack of statistical proof.

Second, and most importantly, call attention to the multiple documented case histories of successfully prevented disputes. These are the highest and best proofs of the value of dispute prevention. (Some of these proofs appear in case studies throughout this book.) And, as noted above, begin collecting your own experiences to demonstrate both your openness to data-driven methods and to better identify what is occurring within the company.

---

12. Richard Susskind *supra* note 6 at 227.

Tip!
This book provides excellent examples of case studies.

A Lack of Trust in Trying New Approaches

Many times, you will find yourself entering a new relationship with a party. It is already complicated and taxing enough to put in place the framework for a new transaction. You now begin to suggest innovative ideas for deploying dispute prevention mechanisms. Your counterparty is skeptical about trusting you to go in these new directions. How to respond?

Overcoming this Barrier

Return to the purpose of the mechanisms you are proposing and align around some of the following basic principles:

- Both contracting parties should view their relationship as one of mutual trust working together to advance the business enterprise or transaction.
- Both contracting parties should strive to understand and respect the forces driving their counterparty.
- Neither party should seek an unfair advantage or "something for nothing."
- Both parties should recognize the reality that problems and unexpected events will occur during the course of their relationship.
- Both parties should recognize the expense and waste inherent in an extended and escalating dispute resolution process.

These principles are designed to help you and your counterparty realize the full value of the work and effort you are putting into building this framework. Disputes will dissipate that effort. Instead, the mechanisms described in this book are meant to better align you and your business partner to make sure that the inevitable conflict that arises will not become toxic or disruptive. Use this book to describe the mechanisms and the case studies demonstrating their effectiveness to convince your business partner and stakeholders that they will serve everyone better.

A LOOK AHEAD

In this chapter, we provided four steps to help you take the concept of dispute prevention and put it into practice in your company. We also shared ideas for overcoming common objections. In the next chapter—the final chapter of this book—we provide a compelling business case for expanding the focus from dispute resolution to dispute prevention.

Chapter 7

The Business Case for Dispute Prevention

It usually costs less to avoid getting into trouble than to pay for getting out of trouble.[1]

Louis M. Brown—Father of Preventive Law

There is good news and bad news when it comes to disputes. The good news is that it's rare for disputes to actually go to trial.[2]

Now for the bad news. Even though you might never end up in court, managing disputes is costly and time-consuming. Our experience working with companies has taught us that individuals and organizations often get sucked into a negative tit-for-tat cycle of conflict escalation taking a toll on all involved. Costs include lost profits and other damages, third-party costs for lawyers, accountants, and claims consultants, and losses in stock price or other valuations.

In addition to the direct costs are the indirect costs relating to damage to relationships, the diversion of company resources, and potential damage to reputation. Not surprisingly, disputes also take a toll on the individuals involved in the form of added stress, reduced morale, and diminished trust.

A PREDICTABLE PATTERN

The lessons of Austrian-born Dr. Friedrich Glasl provide insight into how organizations can understand the evolution of conflict. Glasl, an international authority on conflict escalation, combined a unique background of political science, psychology, economics, and management theory to create a model for analyzing

1. Louis M. Brown, Manual of Preventive Law (1950).

2. Iva Bozovic & Gillian Hadfield, *Scaffolding: Using Formal Contracts to Build Informal Relations in Support of Innovation*, USC CLASS 1–63 (Research Paper No. C12-3, 2015) (disputes seldom reaching trial).

conflict. Glasl divides conflict escalation into nine stages spanning three phases: a win-win phase, a win-lose phase, and a lose-lose phase (Figure 29).

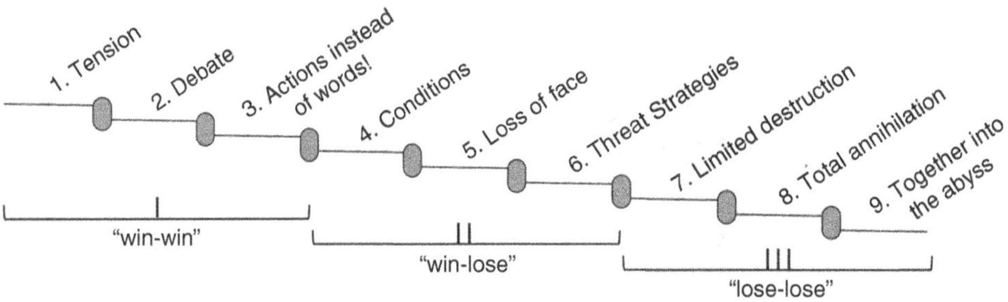

Figure 29: Friedrich Glasl's Three-Phase Conflict Escalation Model[3]

Within the first phase, each party can still construct a resolution that advantages both sides. But, as the conflict intensifies and the parties begin to view one another with distrust and hostility, the possibility for mutually advantageous outcomes dims. Finally, in the third stage, the parties shift to a lose-lose mindset, which results in unremitting strife, waste, and cost.[4]

Glasl's model illustrates how easy it is for individuals and organizations to fall into a negative cycle of tit-for-tat behavior when working through conflict.[5]

Let's explore how Glasl's model works in practice through the lens of a relationship between Suburbia Town, United States (Suburbia) and their Firefighters. As part of the analysis, we also provide tips on how Suburbia and the Firefighters could have used dispute prevention mechanisms for more efficient and effective management of potential problems and disputes.

The city of Suburbia developed as a quaint suburb in the shadows of a much larger city. Suburbia had grown over the years from a sleepy suburb to an affluent and hip alternative to the nearby city. Suburbia's fire department has grown alongside Suburbia and includes over 120 staff working at six fire stations. The city and its Firefighters would go through a consistent cycle of renewing their contract every three years—something that neither party looked forward to.

3. There are several graphical versions of Glasl's model. We have chosen to include an image from the Creative Commons as found in Wikipedia, *The nine stages of conflict escalation*, https://en.wikipedia.org/wiki/Friedrich_Glasl%27s_model_of_conflict_escalation#/media/File:Glasl's_Model_of_Conflict_Escalation.svg.

4. Chris Wheeler, *Conflict Escalation by Complainants*, 2 Perspektive Mediation 118–24 (2015) (lose-lose mindset).

5. Friedrich Glasl, Konfliktmanagement: Ein Handbuch für Führungskräfte, Beraterinnen und Berater (10th ed. 2011); Thomas Jordan, *Glasl's Nine-Stage Model of Conflict Escalation*, Mediate (Oct. 10, 2000), https://mediate.com/glasls-nine-stage-model-of-conflict-escalation/.

When Big Chief took over as Suburbia's Fire Chief in 1997, he committed to building solid working relationships between the city and the Firefighters. Under Big Chief's leadership, the relationship between Suburbia and the Firefighters went from good to great, with Firefighters referring to Suburbia as "a great place to live and work."

Big Chief organized leadership retreats—often facilitated by a partnering expert. Together, leaders from the city and the Firefighters would periodically review the plans for Suburbia and collaborate on how to staff and manage fire services for the city. Big Chief also introduced the concept of interest-based bargaining for contract renewals, which took place every three years. While neither party looked forward to contract negotiations, the city and the Firefighters found using interest-based negotiations to be a much more effective way to negotiate.

Things started to change for the city in 2009. First, the financial crisis meant tightening budgets. In addition, Big Chief retired; the new fire chief came from out of state and did not have relationships with either Suburbia's leaders or the Firefighters. And in 2010, Suburbia hired a new City Manager who seemed to be more concerned with the business and politics of the city than with building and maintaining relationships with the Firefighters.

For example, the City Manager stopped the practice of leadership retreats due to budget cuts. In addition, the typically amicable contract renewal process took on a more adversarial tone. To make matters worse, the good working relationship between the city and the Firefighters became fractured when the Firefighters issued a vote of no-confidence in the fire chief, who ultimately resigned.

By 2014, Firefighters and city leaders referred to the relationship as "unstable" and "complex." The relationship began to take a turn for the worse as the parties began to work through a problem that later resulted in a formal dispute. What was once a good relationship fell into Glasl's predictable pattern of conflict escalation.

Below we diagnose the relationship between Suburbia and the Firefighters through the lens of Glasl's conflict escalation model and share tips on how the parties could have deployed dispute prevention mechanisms.

1st Level (Win-Win)

The first stage of Glasl's model is where parties seek a win-win solution. This was the intent of Suburbia and the Firefighters, as the parties had used interest-based negotiations over the years to reach amicable solutions. In April 2014, the Firefighters raised an issue with Suburbia about a potential problem by putting the item on the agenda for discussion during the parties' monthly management-labor staff meeting.

Between April 2014 and October 2014, the sides continued to discuss the problem at the monthly meetings. At this point, the parties entered stage 2 of Glasl's model—debate. According to Glasl, when parties first enter a debate, they often do not perceive they are entering into conflict because they feel they are still actively trying to work through a solution.

After six months of discussions, team members from Suburbia and the Firefighters felt this problem should be escalated. The contract between Suburbia and the Firefighters was coming up for renewal and the parties agreed to address the problem through a formal bargaining process as part of the broader contract renewal. Both sides were optimistic because the parties had a positive history of using interest-based bargaining and had always worked through to a successful resolution.

In November 2014, Suburbia's and the Firefighter's negotiation teams took on the task of negotiating a solution to the problem in the broader contract renewal. However, unlike previous negotiations, the parties began to anchor on their positions. To make matters worse, the City Manager delegated the negotiating function to a team with instructions to abandon an interest-based approach. To the Firefighters, the city was playing a classic "good cop, bad cop" game indicative of classical (and not interest-based) negotiations. During this time, trust levels between the city and the Firefighters eroded. It was also during this time the parties transitioned into what Glasl defines as a win-lose stage.

2nd Level (Win-Lose)

Glasl's model indicates that as time passes without an amicable solution, parties shift from a win-win mindset to a win-lose mindset. Each party takes actions to try to "win" even if this means the other side may lose. During this time, parties seek sympathizers for their cause, which typically amplifies tension. Differences of opinion widen, conflict exacerbates, and relationships get damaged. Glasl's predictable pattern indeed happened between Suburbia and the Firefighters.

With slow to no progress, Suburbia's City Manager brought in a labor union expert as a consultant to facilitate discussions with the Firefighter's Union in July 2015. The Firefighters responded by hiring an expert advisor to help them develop a negotiation strategy. The idea to bring in outsiders was well-intentioned; however, instead of bringing the parties closer together, it further widened the trust gap between the city and the Firefighters. In October 2015, the City Manager dismissed the expert on their side since there was no progress. By November 2015, the Firefighters' expert adviser suggested mediation, citing the parties were too far apart.

Suburbia's city leaders and the Firefighters dreaded mediation but felt there was no way to avoid it. Both parties further amplified their positional thinking, with each party hiring an outside legal counsel to represent them in the mediation to help them win. The Firefighters could not afford to keep both their expert advisor and their lawyer on retainer, so they decided to retain the lawyer and dismiss the expert advisor in January 2016.

The formal mediation process began in February 2016. After nine long months, the mediator suggested both parties move to binding arbitration due to "irreconcilable differences." By this time, the Firefighters and city officials were exhausted from the distraction. In addition, the Firefighters had been working under an expired contract for almost two years and had gone without a cost of living increase due to the expired contract. Needless to say, morale was low and emotions were running high.

In January 2017, on the doorstep of an arbitration hearing and nearly four years since the problem escalated, the parties begrudgingly settled. It was here the parties felt they had "caved in" and entered into Glasl's lose-lose stage.

3rd Level (Lose-Lose)

The third level of Glasl's conflict escalation model is when the parties become so disillusioned and angry that they revert to tactics to severely damage their opponent. Lose-lose conflict is often depicted as the parties being "at war" and wanting to "win at all costs."

While at times this "war" may take the form of overt actions, at other times, retaliation may come as more subtle tactics, such as "shading."[6] Recall from chapter 4 that shading is retaliatory behavior in which a party stops cooperating, ceases to be proactive, or makes aggressive countermoves because of disappointment. Shading happens when a party doesn't get the expected outcome from the deal and feels the other party is to blame for failing to act reasonably to preserve value or mitigate losses.

Some Firefighters felt that since they had "lost" in the contract settlement, they could game the system and "win" in another area. For example, the city reported a record number of sick days, and there was an increase in firefighters filing for disability benefits prior to their retirement. In addition, to "keep the city fair," the Firefighters kept their lawyer on retainer to help manage grievances. Thus, what used to be potential problems the parties could easily work through became formal grievances, some going through mediation and others only settled by arbitration.

Over the years, Glasl's predictable pattern of increased adversarial actions continued. Recall that every three years, Suburbia and the Firefighters are back at the negotiation table for a contract renewal cycle. Adversarial actions amplify with each contract renewal cycle. For example, in 2021, the Firefighters replaced the union leadership with individuals more comfortable playing hardball with the city leaders. The parties' internal struggles went public when the Firefighters shared their plight with local news channels to garner public support, claiming "staffing levels are at crisis levels" and "public safety is at risk."

Once again, painful and protected negotiations took over two years and were only settled right before an arbitrator got involved. Sadly, neither party is trying to find a better way.

6. Oliver Hart & John Moore, *Contracts as Reference Points*, 123 Q.J.E. 1, 3–4 (2008) (shading).

Lessons Learned

The case study of Suburbia and Firefighters provides several lessons relevant to dispute prevention.

First, it illustrates how easy it is for parties in a contractual relationship to fall into the predictable pattern of escalating and adversarial actions Glasl outlined. Most organizations, like Suburbia and the Firefighters, start with good intentions. However, without using dispute prevention mechanisms, one or both parties often turn to a protectionist mindset when they feel frustrated or perceive they have been treated unfairly.

The second lesson is that conflict can be costly and time-consuming, turning easily-resolved problems into formal grievances which go through mediation and arbitration. The city and Firefighters incur hard costs associated with expert advisors (on each side) and an outside counsel (on each side). Besides the hard costs, the city and the Firefighters spend countless hours in contract negotiations and dispute resolution instead of performing their jobs. Suburbia taxpayers ultimately suffer because the city bears hard costs associated with paying overtime to backfill the off-duty Firefighters during contract negotiating days.

The third lesson? As parties move through Glasl's model, actions become more adversarial, which erodes trust. Once healthy relationships turn toxic, taking a toll on team members.

Sadly, neither Suburbia nor the Firefighters recognized that there are proven dispute prevention mechanisms they could consider. Even sadder is none of the outside advisors, lawyers, mediators, or arbitrators recommended that Suburbia or the Firefighters escape Glasl's predictable pattern of conflict escalation by using dispute prevention. Instead, all of these professionals personally profited from the increase in disputes.

Indeed, when the relationship began, Big Chief and Suburbia were deploying dispute prevention mechanisms. They had instituted partnering (see chapter 5) in the form of annual planning and relationship building, and relationship governance (also shared in chapter 5) in the form of smaller working teams working through issues before escalating. Unfortunately, the new leadership eliminated the dispute prevention mechanisms.

Suburbia and the Firefighters are not alone in not using or stopping to use tools in their toolbox that can help them prevent disputes. Too often, parties view the mechanisms they are engaging in as costs rather than investments in the relationship.

A HARD LOOK AT THE HARD FACTS ABOUT DISPUTES

The story of Suburbia and the Firefighters reflects what we all know intuitively: the longer a potential problem lingers, the more likely it is to turn into a conflict and even a dispute. And the more adversarial the parties become, the greater the potential for long-term negative impact.

But just how big a problem are disputes? Are we making a mountain out of a molehill? Let's consider some statistics to put the need for dispute prevention into perspective.

Disputes Are Costly

The Norton Rose Fulbright's "2024 Annual Litigation Trends Survey" reports that, on average, organizations spend $2.3 million on litigation for every $1 billion in revenue, with larger companies spending six times more than smaller companies.[7] A 2022 Association of Corporate Counsel (ACC) study adds further insight, stating, "By a long distance, the most common types of litigation are those related to employment and labor (70 percent) and breach of contract (58 percent).[8]

Many people associate dispute costs only with paying third-party fees (lawyers, paralegals, accountants, claims consultants, and other experts), but there are many other added costs. For example, the time to work through legal processes and costs associated with the "discovery" process (most commonly used in the United States) is also a significant burden. For example, Microsoft reported that for every page of evidence used in a discovery process, they produce 1,000 pages, manually review 4,500 pages, collect and process 90,000 pages, and preserve 340,000 pages.[9]

But direct costs—the third-party fees occasioned by formal dispute resolution processes—are only part of the costs associated with disputes. An International Institute for Conflict Prevention and Resolution (CPR) task force outlined seven cost categories for managing disputes[10] (Figure 30).

Only three categories constitute direct costs; the other four categories identify the indirect costs that afflict disputing parties. Indirect costs include failed goals and objectives, relationship damage, diversion of company resources, and damage to reputation and public scrutiny.

7. *2024 Annual Litigation Trends Survey*, Norton Rose Fulbright 1–40 (2024) (litigation spending).

8. *The State of Corporate Litigation Today Survey Report*, Assoc. Corp. Couns. (Oct. 10, 2022), https://www.acc.com/resource-library/state-corporate-litigation-today-survey-report.

9. Gillian K. Hadfield, Rules for a Flat World (2016).

10. *CPR's Dispute Prevention Pledge for Business Relationships*, CPR 1–15 (2023) (seven cost categories related to for managing disputes).

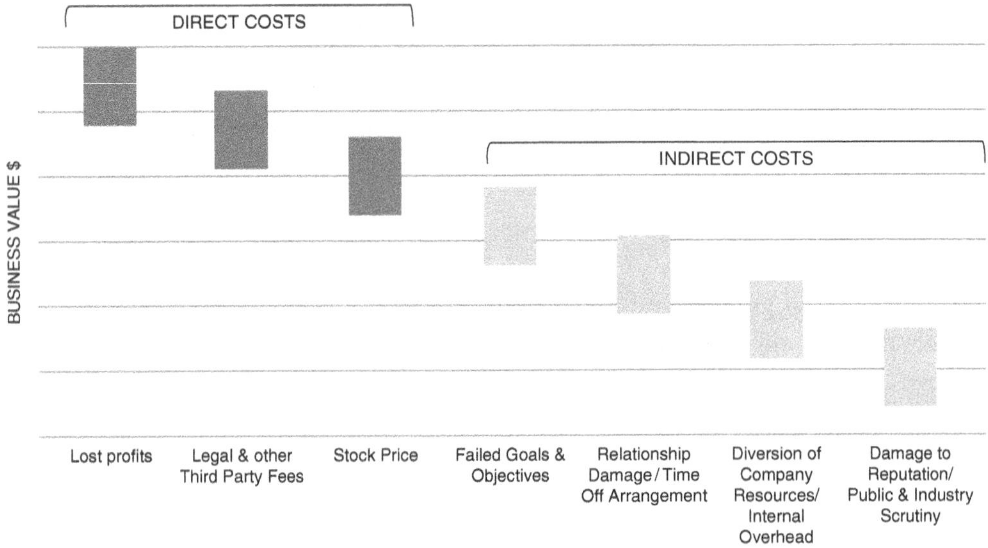

Figure 30: Costs Associated with Disputes

Reflect on the cost of relationship damage associated with Suburbia and the Firefighters. Employees cite the relationship as "zero trust." Stephen M.R. Covey's book *Speed of Trust* outlines seven "organizational taxes" that are directly related to low trust.[11] Each of Covey's "taxes" exemplifies increased transaction costs due to low trust.

1. *Redundancy* is unnecessary duplication. Redundancy stems from the mindset that people cannot be trusted unless they are closely watched.
2. *Bureaucracy* is when too many rules and regulations are in place, such as when too many people must "sign off" on something.
3. *Politics* is when people use strategy to gain power. Sadly, too much time is wasted interpreting other people's motives and trying to read hidden agendas.
4. *Disengagement* is when people are still getting paid even though they "clocked out." Simply put, team members put in the minimal effort required to get their paychecks.
5. *Turnover* results when an organization's best performers leave to pursue a job where they are seen as trusted and valued contributors.
6. *Churn* is the effort and costs associated with constantly finding new customers, suppliers, distributors, and investors because of a lack of loyalty.

11. Stephen M.R. Covey, The Speed of Trust: The One Thing That Changes Everything (Reprint ed. 2008).

7. *Fraud* is flat-out dishonesty. Fraud is a circular tax; when companies tighten the reigns to prevent fraud, they reduce their fraud-related losses, but they inevitably see an increase in the other six areas.

Disputes Are Time-Consuming

The previously cited ACC study notes that 46 percent of in-house counsel report the length of litigation is increasing (versus only 8 percent citing that it is declining). The study also provides insight into the time it takes to resolve a dispute. Seventy-two percent of employment and labor disputes last longer than one year, and 71 percent of breach of contract disputes last longer than one year (with 22 percent taking more than two years).[12]

Disputes Are Increasing

Despite the emphasis on ADR, litigation is on the rise. Between March 2023 to March 2024 there were 31,803 private contract cases filed in the U.S. District courts.[13] Data from the National Center for State Courts notes that contract case filings were up 19 percent from 2021 to 2022, with thirty-nine states reporting 3.6 million incoming cases.[14]

International investment disputes are also on the rise. The International Centre for Settlement of Investment Disputes (ICSID)—the world's leading institution devoted to international investment dispute settlement—reports dispute data every six months since 1972. In the last ten years, the number of ICSID cases has risen from 209 to 329 with a steady increase every year except 2020 where there was a slight decrease of only three cases that year.[15]

The Norton Rose Fulbright survey predicts litigation will continue to increase. In fact, 42 percent of in-house counsel report they expected the tide of litigation to continue to rise over the next twelve months (with only 14 percent expecting volume to go down).[16]

---

12. *The State of Corporate Litigation Today Survey Report supra* note 8.

13. *Table C—U.S. District Courts–Civil Cases Commenced, by Basis of Jurisdiction and Nature of Suit (March 31, 2024)*, United States Courts, https://www.uscourts.gov/statistics/table/c-2/federal-judicial-caseload-statistics/2024/03/31.

14. Morgan Moffett et al., *2022 Caseload Highlights*, CSP 1–5 (2024) (contract case filing statistics).

15. *The ICSID Caseload—Statistics*, ICSID 1–27 (2024) (ICSID case statistics).

16. *2024 Annual Litigation Trends Survey*, Norton Rose Fulbright 1–40 (2024) (litigation expected to continue).

A COMPELLING CASE FOR DISPUTE PREVENTION

Throughout chapters 3–5, we shared the quantitative and qualitative benefits of adopting dispute prevention mechanisms.

Let's return to the SemiCo case study in chapter 1 to highlight the benefits they have achieved from shifting upstream by adopting dispute prevention practices.

When Olivia Operations first challenged the conventional approach for managing construction disputes, she didn't have a quantifiable business case to support her hunch that shifting upstream to focus on dispute prevention would have a positive return on investment. But her intuition told her that every dollar SemiCo spent on dispute prevention would save money downstream. SemiCo hired Danny Dispute Manager to create SemiCo's first Dispute Management System.

The before-and-after descriptions of the relationship between SemiCo and contractors are nothing short of transformational, with people sharing adjectives to describe the relationship. Before the Dispute Management System, team members used words like hostile, protracted, and emotional to describe the dispute resolution process. Now, team members describe the Dispute Management System as collaborative, efficient, and preventive (see figure 31 for the adjective word cloud comparison).

Word Cloud Before **Word Cloud After**

Figure 31: Word Cloud Comparison of Before and After Adjectives

Recall the results we shared in chapter 1 from SemiCo's Dispute Management System. Before adopting its DMS, SemiCo's construction contracts faced multiple claims, generating huge losses and delays. One large construction project valued at $220 million had $30 million in claims, and another $1.3 billion project had $50 million in claims.

After six years, SemiCo's Dispute Management System grew to include five prime contractors spanning almost $20 billion in large and complex construction projects. Since the program started, there has been only one claim escalated to the traditional post-project formal arbitration process.

Team members all agree the program has taught them how to make the shift from resolving disputes to monitoring, managing, and mitigating risks that arise. Team members are glad to see the prevention focus and the processes that help them work through issues while they are small. The benefits fall into six primary categories. Figure 32 lists benefits and provides insight from team members that illustrate each benefit.

Benefit	Team Member Insight
Less Transactional and More Teaming	"Our Standing Neutral is involved from day one and is embedded into the ongoing project governance. This means the Standing Neutral is fully aware of the nuanced dynamic in motion and transforms discussions into a facilitated collaborative dialogue. In a conventional dispute resolution, there is a tendency to be positional, and then when a mediator gets involved, they 'enter in' the dispute blindly with each side putting time and effort into being positional."
Faster and More Efficient	"Let's say you've been dealing with an issue for some period of time, whether it's two months, six months, or a year. Now, you have to take all that data that you've gathered, all that information, all those conversations. And you've got to boil it down into a one-hour, a two-hour meeting with an attorney or even a mediator, whereas our Standing Neutral is sitting in those meetings, is gathering the same information, is exposed to the same thing that you are. With one particular big issue, a real benefit was our neutral had the history because he sat through all of the governance meetings. We didn't need to regurgitate data and facts. It was a lot more efficient for everyone."
Better than Just a Decision-Maker	"The process calls for the neutral to make recommendations and, if needed, make a formal decision on a claim. But the neutral is far more than a decision-maker. The real power is the ability of the neutral to harvest the ongoing wisdom of the project team. The risk workshops, for example, are priceless because they help us identify risks and hold us accountable for taking actionable steps to mitigate risks."
Saves Money	"The cost to have a Standing Neutral embedded in a project team varies based on the size and services the neutral provides to a project team. I once had someone question why we were spending $100,000 on a neutral for a project. I explained the $100,000 is a drop in the bucket compared to the $14 million we paid out to attorneys and experts in claims on a similar project."
More Versatile	"I really appreciate the flexibility of our neutral to take on tasks and work that benefit both parties. It's very efficient to have a neutral do tasks such as change order administration. But equally important is that having a neutral do the work builds trust that it is being done fairly."
Less Frustrating	"The traditional dispute resolution process is painful and protracted. The processes we have put in place are proactive and preventative. It's night and day in terms of stress on the people involved."
Better Advice	"The advice isn't a narrow band one might typically get from an attorney. Rather, our neutral's advice revolves around how to mitigate risks and resolve issues."

Figure 32: Summary of Benefits with Team Member Insights

Danny Dispute Manager reflects on success: "The program has taught SemiCo and our suppliers the power of a preventive approach. The typical dispute resolution process promotes a 'We want to be right. We want to win.' mindset. But this mindset promotes a zero-sum game when it doesn't have to be that way."

Olivia Operations is pleased with the shift that happened on her watch and summed up why organizations around the world should care: "The shift to a preventive focus is brilliant. Risks are identified upfront, and people openly talk about them. Transparency and collaboration completely change the dynamics of what is inherently a risky business. The shift is truly transformational."

THE BOTTOM LINE

In this chapter, we set out to make the business case for shifting to dispute prevention. The results? Making the shift to dispute prevention does not just make intuitive sense; there is a bottom-line business case for adopting upstream dispute prevention mechanisms. It brings more value to all parties involved.

After reading this chapter, we hope you can clearly see what Friedrich Glasl has pointed out in his research: it is easy to fall into a predictable pattern of conflict escalation. And when the negative cycle of tit-for-tat behavior kicks in, it increases costs and takes an emotional toll on team members, which can turn a healthy relationship into a toxic relationship.

We hope the compelling data we shared regarding disputes gives you the justification you need to invest in dispute prevention. And—most importantly—we hope the quantitative and qualitative results SemiCo had after implementing a Dispute Management System inspire you to implement your own program.

Conclusion

To raise new questions, new possibilities, to regard old problems from a new angle, requires creative imagination and marks real advance in science.
—Albert Einstein

The conclusion of this book doesn't represent an ending. Instead, it represents an opportunity for you to rethink and prevent future conflicts from becoming disputes. Our wish is that you will take Albert Einstein's advice and forever view dispute management from a new angle—one with a much more preventative lens.

You can reinforce and underline your commitment to the dispute prevention movement by taking the International Institute for Conflict Prevention and Resolution (CPR) Dispute Prevention Pledge for business relationships—a step that dozens of high-profile companies like Microsoft, Visa, and General Motors have already taken. The Pledge aims to influence behavior through public commitment to developing systemic, sustainable, and global cost-effective dispute resolution processes.

Sign the Pledge online at https://www.cpradr.org/dispute-prevention-pledge-for-business-relationships.

> CPR Dispute Prevention Pledge for Business Relationships©
>
> To preserve relationships in business arrangements, and subject to mutually agreed-upon terms, we will incorporate dispute prevention mechanisms into our arrangements where appropriate. The range of mechanisms may include, for example, reliance upon resources internal to the parties, such as implementation of contractual escalation clauses to defuse conflict within and between organizations, or third-party mechanisms, such as jointly engaging a dispute prevention neutral; all designed to enable early identification of conflict and preventing it from hardening into a dispute. This statement of policy does not commit us to any particular outcome, but only to the willingness jointly to deploy dispute prevention mechanisms to help us avoid disputes and maintain our business relationships and purpose.

Carlos Hernandez, now-retired Chief Executive Officer of Fluor Corporation, an engineering and construction firm, shares why he signed the Pledge for Fluor Corporation: "There are ADR mechanisms to avoid litigation and set up a dispute resolution process. These include arbitration and mediation. But we should begin the dispute prevention process before we get to those stages. The processes should focus from inception on the contractual relationship. We'll all benefit from putting in place means to solve disagreements before they become full-fledged disputes. So, I urge you to consider adopting the new CPR Dispute Prevention Pledge."[1]

Bayer US took the challenge and signed the Pledge in 2021. Scott Partridge, General Counsel of Bayer US at the time of signing, shared his logic for getting behind the dispute prevention movement. Partridge stated, "The best time to agree not to fight is when you're not fighting. So, you can go to your competitors, your major customers, before you have a dispute, and you can agree on a process that, in the event you do have a dispute, you have already agreed on how you are going to handle it. And you can do that from a position where you're not giving up anything at that stage, you're not being weak, you're actually being thoughtful."[2]

We hope this book has inspired you to add your organization's name to the growing list of organizations who have signed the Pledge. But equally important, we hope this book serves as a comprehensive guide and inspiration for how you can begin to *apply* the concepts in practice.

As you begin to challenge your organization to try some of the dispute prevention practices in this book, you will likely find skeptics along the way. Trust us—we have. We hope the case studies and the data for making the shift to dispute prevention give you that extra ammunition you need to garner support to pilot some (if not all!) of the dispute prevention mechanisms we have shared.

If you find yourself in a situation that prevents you from creating a comprehensive Dispute Management System as we outlined in chapter 6, don't throw the baby out with the bathwater. Rather, pick just one or two of the mechanisms and adopt them with one business partner. The good news is the numbers are on your side—you have eighteen dispute prevention mechanisms to pick from and likely hundreds, if not thousands, of partners. And for those already implementing some of the mechanisms, we encourage you to expand your toolkit and add new mechanisms you learned in this book.

As you join the dispute prevention movement, we hope our collective knowledge shared in this book will make your journey easier.

Good luck on your journey!

---

1. *Less Conflict. More Purpose.*, CPR, https://assets-002.noviams.com/novi-file-uploads/cpr/Dispute_Prevention_Pledge_Deck.pdf.

2. *Id.*

Index

Note: *Italic* page numbers refer to figures.

About the Authors

Kate Vitasek is an international authority for her award-winning research and Vested® business model for highly collaborative relationships. She is a Distinguished Fellow for the University of Tennessee's Global Supply Chain Institute where she leads UT's Certified Deal Architect program. Kate's research has led to eight books and she has been featured on CNN International, Bloomberg, NPR, Fox Business News, and Forbes for her practical and research-based advice for creating—and sustaining—strategic business relationships. Vitasek has been named to the Hall of Fame for both the Sourcing Industry Group and the International Association for Outsourcing Professionals and was honored as the 2023 recipient of CPR's Outstanding Leadership in Dispute Prevention award.

Jim Groton is a retired partner of Eversheds Sutherland, where he led the firm's Construction and Dispute Prevention and Resolution practices. He was a pioneer advocate of proactive pre-dispute mechanisms in the construction industry, and was the editor and co-author of the 1991 CPR book *Preventing and Resolving Construction Disputes*. He has received numerous accolades for his conflict management leadership, including the American Arbitration Association's highest award, the Whitney North Seymour Arbitration Medal; Engineering News-Record's Medal of Excellence; and three CPR awards, including CPR's Inaugural Award in 2022 for Outstanding Leadership in Dispute Prevention. He is also an Honorary Member of the American Institute of Architects and was elected to membership in the National Academy of Construction.

Ellen Waldman is a conflict resolution expert with deep practical and academic experience who currently serves as Vice President of Advocacy and Educational Outreach at the Institute for Conflict Prevention and Resolution (CPR). In her role at CPR, she serves on the organization's Dispute Prevention Committee and seeks to educate corporate executives and in-house counsel on dispute prevention concepts and mechanisms. Prior to joining CPR, she was a law professor and founder of her school's court-connected mediation clinic. In the area of dispute resolution, she writes, trains, consults, and mediates in a broad range of cases. Ellen is a former chair of the International Mediation Institute's ethics committee, and task-force member for the California Judicial Council's working-group on training requirements for court-connected mediators. She has published more than 25 articles on numerous dispute resolution topics and crafted the first book-length treatment of ethical dilemmas in mediation.

Allen Waxman, of counsel at DLA Piper, is the former general counsel and head of litigation at Pfizer as well as the general counsel and a business unit leader at other domestic and international life science companies. Allen was also previously a partner at two national law firms, and his practice has included trying civil and criminal cases, serving as national counsel in pharmaceutical product liability cases, acting as a resolution leader of mass tort and commercial cases, and most recently supporting efforts to deploy artificial intelligence to enhance the practice of law. Prior to joining DLA Piper, Allen was the CEO of the International Institute for Conflict Prevention and Resolution (CPR). Under his leadership at CPR, the organization launched a pledge for dispute prevention in business relationships and developed tools for more effective, efficient ways to both resolve disputes and prevent them where possible. Allen also developed and moderated a podcast, sponsored by the ABA, called "Avoiding the Dispute Before It Begins," where he interviewed leaders in the dispute prevention field on implementing dispute prevention mechanisms.